P9-AZU-304

SCHOOLING FOR "GOOD REBELS"

Schooling for "Good Rebels"

Socialist Education for Children
in the United States,
1900–1920

KENNETH TEITELBAUM

Temple University Press

PHILADELPHIA

Temple University Press, Philadelphia 19122
Copyright © 1993 by Temple University. All rights reserved
Published 1993
Printed in the United States of America

Library of Congress Cataloging-in-Publication Data

Teitelbaum, Kenneth, 1949–
    Schooling for "good rebels": socialist education for children in
the United States, 1900–1920 / Kenneth Teitelbaum.
        p. cm.
    Includes bibliographical references and index.
    ISBN 0-87722-980-5 (cloth : alk. paper)
    1. Socialism—Study and teaching—United States—History—20th
century.   2. Socialism—United States—History—20th
century.   3. Curriculum planning—United States—History—20th
century—Case studies.   4. Working class—Education—United States—
History—20th century.   5. Education—Political aspects—United
States—History—20th century.   I. Title.
HX19.2.U6T45   1992
335'.007'073—dc20   92-7539

Portions of the Introduction, Chapter Seven, and the Conclusion are reprinted from Kenneth Teitelbaum, "Contestation and Curriculum: The Efforts of American Socialists, 1900–1920," in *The Curriculum: Problems, Politics,
and Possibilities*, ed. Landon E. Beyer and Michael W. Apple (New York:
State University of New York Press, 1988), pp. 32–55; Kenneth Teitelbaum,
"'Critical Lessons' from Our Past: Curricula of Socialist Sunday Schools in
the United States," *Curriculum Inquiry* 20, no. 4 (Winter 1990): 407–36; and
Kenneth Teitelbaum, "Outside the Selective Tradition: Socialist Curriculum
for Children in the United States, 1900–1920," in *The Formation of School Subjects: The Struggle for Creating an American Institution*, ed. Thomas S. Popkewitz (New York: Falmer, 1987), pp. 238–67.

To my parents,
Maurice and Dorothea,
with love and appreciation

Contents

Acknowledgments

Particularly helpful to me during the years in which I was engaged in this research project were my continuing interest in the subject of this study and the many individuals who provided me with personal and professional support. My abiding interest in this project stemmed in large part from its integration of three areas of scholarship that have been the focus of much of my research, teaching, and learning during the more than two decades since I first attended college: United States social history, democratic socialist politics, and conceptions of critical or transformative pedagogy. Moreover, from the beginning to the completion of this study, I have been motivated by the desire to make the existence and nature of these heretofore neglected radical educational experiments more widely known among readers of United States social and educational history, and to make the "lessons" of these settings more accessible to others concerned with educational, and especially curricular, issues. In a sense, then, it has been easy for me to work with this material; my interest in it has never waned.

My task has been made easier as well by the many individuals from whom I have gained knowledge and personal sustenance, both in and out of educational settings. In particular, I would like to thank two University of Wisconsin at Madison professors whose scholarship and teaching have greatly influenced my own. From Michael Apple and Herbert Kliebard I have learned not only specific aspects of educational history and theory, but more generally the vital importance of going beyond an examination of institutional characteristics of past and current schooling to the basic questions of what (and whose) knowledge is taught and why. Herb's work on the history of American curriculum, especially his discussions of John Dewey and the social reconstructionists, has greatly enhanced my own awareness of and appreciation for the progressive traditions of American education. Mike's critical examinations of schooling as a fundamental aspect of culture, and more specifically the ways in which schooling does and does not promote the interests of social equality and justice, democracy, and community, have profoundly shaped the focus and content of much of my own work, including this study. I am very grateful not only for the contributions that Herb and Mike have made to my understanding of educational history and theory but also for having had the opportunity to know them personally.

Many others also helped me in different ways during the last decade. Bill Reese deserves special mention, as he first alerted me to the existence of Socialist Sunday schools at the turn of the century. He knew very little about them when we talked during a lunch together on the Memorial Union terrace, but he told me enough to arouse my curiosity, and the rest, as they say, is history. Fortunately for me, my association with Bill did not end there, and he has continued to provide me with close friendship and welcome advice. I have also benefitted from the support and advice of others during the many years that I was engaged in this project, in particular Lanny Beyer, Tim and Margie Chandler, Jeff Haydu, Barbara Holmes, Lois Korzendorfer and Mark Mattucci, Don Leu, Ronni Lipman, Mike Olneck, Tom Popkewitz, Don Richgels, Maxine and Keith Steinkraus, Joel Taxel, Ken Zeichner, and Joe DeVitis, Wendy Kohli, and other colleagues at the State University of New York at Binghamton. I have also been helped in many ways by Linda Biemer and Ted Rector, Dean and Associate Dean respectively in the School of Education and Human Development at Binghamton, as well as by Diane Hinckley and Julie Quinn, two excellent department secretaries. I also want to thank Kathy Mooney, not only for her friendship but also for providing expert editorial assistance during a crucial time in the preparation of the manuscript. I am grateful to Bruce Nelson for his very helpful review of my original manuscript, and to Penelope Myers for her work in the copy editing stage. In addition, I want to acknowledge the supportive relationship that I have enjoyed with the staff at Temple University Press, and with Micah Kleit and Joan Vidal in particular.

Two other groups of individuals also deserve to be acknowledged. One group includes the staff members of the many libraries and historical societies whose services I utilized in an attempt to locate information about socialist efforts to educate children. Their very gracious and earnest responses to my numerous inquiries were greatly appreciated. The staffs of those places that I visited deserve special mention: the State Historical Society of Wisconsin, the Memorial Library at the University of Wisconsin at Madison, the Milwaukee County Historical Society, the Milwaukee Public Library, the Tamiment Institute's Elmer Holmes Bobst Library at New York University, and the Rare Books Room of Rush Rhees Library at the University of Rochester.

The second group includes the many individuals I interviewed who attended the Socialist Sunday schools or who knew others who did. Most of the names of those I interviewed are included in the text and notes of this book. I will always be very grateful for their willingness to share their remembrances of long ago with me. I was especially privileged to share memorable moments with those whom I was able to interview in person, including Edward Friebert Jr., Joseph Friebert, Jennie Yavner Goldman, Othelia Hampel Haberkorn, Ida and Abe Kaufman, Fred Shulman, and Lloyd Somers. I will never forget listening to several of them sing songs and recite poems that had been a part of their socialist weekend education as children.

Although never interviewed, for he died several decades before I began this research project, a special acknowledgment is due to Kendrick Philander Shedd. Without his sense of history, and the hard work that he put into collecting materials and recording events and activities, it is doubtful that this study could have been done at all. In the beginning of his second Rochester Socialist Sunday School Scrapbook, Shedd referred to his completion of the scrapbooks and wrote: "It will be found intensely interesting, as well as instructive. Look it over, reader, and realize that behind everything PASTED OR WRITTEN between these lines there is much of life. The time will come when this record will be of great value, so keep it well preserved." It is doubtful that Shedd had in mind the value his scrapbooks would have seventy years later in the completion of a full-length study of the American Socialist Sunday School movement. He probably had something loftier in mind. Still, from this researcher go sincere thanks to Shedd for his efforts.

Finally, I want to thank my family. My daughters Rachael, Emily, and Sarah have taken me into their thoughts, their hearts, and their arms, and I have been nourished by the experience. I am very fortunate to be able to share my life with three such interesting and wonderful children. And last, I want to acknowledge my closest friend, my wife, Nancy Steinkraus, whose patience, kindness, generosity, and love sustained me often during the time that I was engaged in this study. I am aware that without her help and encouragement, provided in so many ways, this project would never have been completed. To her I owe the greatest expression of gratitude; to her I declare my most heartfelt love.

Three small research grants provided me with additional resources during various stages of this project. I am grateful for having received a Bernard C. Korn Foundation Grant from the Milwaukee County Historical Society, a University Senate Research Committee Grant from Syracuse University, and a New Faculty Development Award from the New York State/United University Professional Development and Quality of Working Life Committee.

SCHOOLING FOR "GOOD REBELS"

History, Politics, and Curriculum

The Example of Socialist Sunday Schools

To speak of "Socialist Sunday schools" is to conjure up an image of small children sitting in rows with hands folded and a stern bespectacled young man or woman leading the assemblage in a rather dreary catechistic exercise on Marxian principles. The intensely earnest teacher, who might actually be more advanced in years, asks the children, "Why are you a socialist?" and the children recite back in unison: "We are socialists because we believe that the state that is called socialism is the next step in human progress." The teacher continues, "But why are you not content with things as they are?" and the children loudly respond: "Because there is a great deal of poverty, sorrow, and pain in the world that need not be if people were wise enough to change the laws." The teacher leans forward and prods the children further, "What makes the needless poverty, sorrow, and pain?" and the children proudly provide the appropriate (and expected) answer: "The laws and customs of capitalism that make it possible for a few to own the things that all depend upon for life—the things that socialists want to make social property."

Such a portrayal is not entirely farfetched; the format above, adapted from a children's book written by a prominent Socialist Party member, John Spargo, was utilized in several Socialist Sunday schools.[1] But for the most part, the reader of this study may be surprised not just by the very existence of at least one hundred English-speaking[2] Socialist Sunday schools in the United States during the first two decades of the twentieth century but also by the variety of teaching methods and curriculum materials that radical educators used to teach "the socialist perspective" to five- to fourteen-year-old children. While some of the Sunday school lessons were as didactic as Spargo's socialist catechism, others adopted class discussions, stories, songs, and plays to present the messages of American socialism in a way that was more suited to "the child mind," as one participant, Kendrick Shedd, referred to it.

This book explores the reasons that American socialists initiated radical weekend schools for children; the organization of schools in many different locales, and in particular New York City, Rochester (New York), and Milwaukee; the most significant institutional characteristics of the Socialist Sunday schools; and examples of the curriculum materials that helped to guide the instruction that workers' children received in these alternative educational settings. The research for this study was informed by particular trends in historical and curriculum scholarship during the 1970s and 1980s. This introductory chapter is intended to outline briefly aspects of this scholarship and the ways in which a study of Socialist Sunday schools relates to it.

One of the salient characteristics of American public schooling is that it is marked by a dual tension that emanates from its being enmeshed in a capitalist democratic state. At the same time that it strives to serve industrial needs, it is also expected to promote democratic purposes. While the first imperative has dominated throughout the twentieth-century, at various historical moments one or the other may have held sway. In the 1960s, for example, social movements that promoted egalitarian principles and policies seemed to make headway over the forces that sought more direct connections between schools and the needs of capital production and accumulation. The 1980s and early 1990s have witnessed the ascendency of conservative, business-oriented interests in educational debates about organization, policy, and the curriculum.[3]

During the past century, this fundamental tension has caused public schooling to function, in effect, as a contested terrain. Conflicts over goals and practices have taken place not just within the corridors, meetings rooms, and classrooms of schools but outside them as well. The history of educational debates in the United States has included the direct involvement not only of federal and state education officials, community school board members, teacher educators, school administrators, teachers, and parents but also of political and business leaders, conservative and liberal social reformers, and working-class, racial, ethnic, and women's interest groups.[4] In varying ways, to differing extents, and with unequal results, all have sought to influence educational goals, school organization, and the content and form of instruction.

It is only since the 1980s that the contested nature of schooling has been adequately addressed by educational historians and other researchers. Earlier approaches that embraced functionalist explanations or radical reproduction theories tended to reduce the evolution of public schooling to a consensual process on the one hand and to an exclusive focus on the structures of domination on the other. The tensions, conflicts, and resistances that have occurred around issues of educational policy and practice were largely ignored and thus rendered invisible.

This study deals with events that occurred at the beginning of the twentieth century. Rapid and widespread changes were taking place throughout American life. These included changes in material conditions, ideologies, and culture, caused in large part by a marked intensification of industrialization, immigration, and urbanization. Such changes directly affected public schooling, which witnessed a significant expansion of enrollment, began evolving into the more professionalized and bureaucratized state-sponsored mass education system that is familiar in the 1990s, and attracted intense scrutiny from many segments of society. Indeed, with the closing of the frontier and the growth of the corporate sector, schooling began to play an increasingly key role in American life, with regard not only to individual success but also to the shape American society would take in the years ahead. Philosophers like John Dewey, sociologists like Edward Ross, and other scholars wrote about the diminishing influence of traditional social institutions (such as the family and the church) on the young and the need for the public school to fill the breach in some way.[5]

The specific role that schools could and should play in twentieth-century America was a matter of bitter dispute. For while elite groups, in the face of destabilizing social conditions and increased opportunities for capital expansion, sought to link public schooling more closely to an ideology based on social control and efficiency, others viewed it primarily as a viable, indeed crucial, vehicle for needed social and economic reform. Thus, some groups advocated learning experiences that would enhance social order in an unstable age, while others either encouraged greater opportunities for creativity in a world that seemed to be stifling individual self-expression or promoted the broad acceptance of more democratic principles in both the political and economic spheres. In the process, public schools became a battleground for competing social interests.

Among those involved in the debates over the education provided to the young were American socialists. During this heyday of American socialism, radical activists agitated for reforms that addressed not only the inadequate educational facilities and resources existent in working-class communities but also the content and form of instruction to which workers' children were being exposed daily. A small number of Socialist Party activists worked on another front as well. They did not abandon the idea of refashioning the public schools so that they would be more responsive to radical principles and working-class interests, but they sought a way to contest more directly the overly individualistic, competitive, nationalistic, militaristic, and anti-working-class themes prevalent in contemporary public schools and other social institutions. They sought to establish and maintain weekend schools so that children from working-class families could receive a more formal and systematic alternative education than was available elsewhere in radical circles. Although they had no religious character, these educational settings were generally referred to as "Socialist Sunday schools." Despite the limited nature of these efforts and all the problems that were encountered, local radical activists succeeded in establishing a tradition of socialist education for children in the United States that has barely been mentioned in our historical and educational literature. Relatively speaking this was not a very extensive nor ultimately successful alternative educational movement. Still, with at least one hundred schools established in sixty-four cities and towns in various parts of the country, and with probably more than ten thousand children attending between 1900 and 1920, these counterinstitutions deserve to be more widely known for the sake of historical accuracy alone.

    The activities of these radical educators may represent an obscure and perhaps even surprising chapter of American social and educational history. In part this is because until the 1980s much of the history of American education was primarily concerned with the role of prominent, usually male, educational leaders in the development of the institution of public schooling. It is only since the 1980s that grass-roots activists, especially those activists working outside the public school site, have commanded serious attention from historians for their efforts to contest the dominant perspective of ideas, people, and events. Similarly, historical research on American socialism has, until recently, typically dealt with the political machinations of prominent adult members of different radical political parties and movements. This study, instead, largely ignores renowned progressive educators like John Dewey, Ella Flagg Young, and Lucy Sprague Mitchell to concentrate on little-known educators like Kendrick Shedd, Bertha Mailly, and David Greenberg. It deals hardly at all with socialist leaders like Eugene Debs, Morris Hillquit, and Meta and Victor Berger and more with infrequently mentioned activists like Frances Gill, Frederick Krafft, and Bertha Fraser. It focuses on an aspect of American radical culture at the turn of the century that, while not central to the fortunes of the socialist movement, was a significant experience in the lives of thousands of working-class children, their parents, and local supporters.

While it is important not to exaggerate the theoretical sophistication and practical achievements of these radical educational endeavors, or the numbers of children involved and the importance of the Sunday schools within the larger socialist movement, the development of this alternative educational movement represents one component of the larger effort in our nation's history to contest the dominant messages of capitalist culture. The significance of the Socialist Sunday schools can be seen through a Gramscian lens that focuses in particular on issues of hegemony and counterhegemony. Of course, Socialist Sunday School participants and their supporters never articulated their concerns and activities in quite the same way as Antonio Gramsci. (After all, his major theoretical contributions were published a decade after most of the schools had closed, and his writings were not widely available to non-Italian readers until the 1960s.) Still, their efforts reflected very closely some of the political ideas and strategies about which Gramsci wrote.

Put briefly, Antonio Gramsci's concept of hegemony freed Marxism from the base/superstructure metaphor. It entailed "the predominance obtained by consent rather than force of one class or group over other classes; and it is attained through the myriad ways in which the institutions of civil society operate to shape, directly or indirectly, the cognitive and affective structures whereby men perceive and evaluate social reality."[6] In advanced capitalist nations, dominant groups have been able to maintain effective control over the production, distribution, and legitimation processes of the cultural and ideological relations of society as well as the material ones. Such control enables the dominant interests to reproduce the social inequalities of class, gender, and race that saturate our everyday lives with reciprocally confirming ideas and conditions in which, for example, domination-subordination appears to many as the "natural way of life," the common sense social reality. Hegemony thus involves "not only . . . political and economic activity, nor only . . . manifest social activity, but . . . the whole substance of lived identities and relationships, to such a depth that the pressures and limits of what can ultimately be seen as a specific economic, political, and cultural system seem to most of us the pressures and limits of simple experience and sense."[7] Mainstream intellectuals, social-psychological helpers, the mass media, the arts, schooling and so forth, in part help to legitimate the dominant practices, visions, categories, and hierarchical forms, as well as the existing inequalities of material conditions. The lack of American working-class consciousness, then, can be explained in part as a product of hegemonic institutional relations.

However, the maintenance of hegemonic meanings, practices, and conditions is not a simple or straightforward process, nor is it always successful, as the existence of the Socialist Sunday schools and scores of other examples in the past and present attest. Lived culture is relatively autonomous, in part because the social and psychological nature of human existence is too complex and cannot be totally enveloped within dominant social forms. Subjects interpret culture in multiple ways; hegemonic meanings are not necessarily passively soaked in like a sponge. Moreover, not only is there autonomy in our personal lives and in superstructural institutions like schools but contradictions in the logic of advanced capital (such as social production and individual appropriation, and state intrusion into personal concerns and emphasis on privatization) are played out in virtually every aspect of social life as well. The tensions that result from these contradictory conditions provide the opportunities for the germination of concrete alternatives to hegemonic forces. Although their sources are sometimes difficult to specify, forms of resistance develop within and outside the hegemonic process. Whether of a residual nature (that is, they have been effectively formed in the past but are still active in the cultural process) or an emergent nature (that is, they consist of new meanings and values, new practices, new relationships and kinds of relationships that are being created), the alternative forms can develop as a real, vital opposition—a counterhegemony—to dominant forms. The potential (or threat) of contestation always exists and is always being realized in particular ways. Indeed, even incorporated or defeated counterhegemonic forms can have great consequence. Herbert Gutman quotes Fernand Braudel to remind us that "victorious events come about as a result of many possibilities" and that "for one possibility which actually is realized, innumerable others have drowned." Usually these others leave "little trace for the historian," and yet "it is necessary to give them their place because the losing movements are forces which have at every moment affected the final outcome."[8]

Gramsci further postulated socialist transformation as not so much an event or series of events but a process. A politicized educational praxis, rooted in everyday political struggle, was an essential component of this transformation. In the advancing stages of capitalist development, ideological encounters with the ruling class would take on added importance. Distinct from the "war of movement" (the actual assault on state power), the "war of position" involved the building of *"new forms* of state life" that could organically transform social and authority relations.[9] As Martin Carnoy has put it, such a "war" was to be based on the idea of "*surrounding* the State apparatus with a counter-hegemony, a hegemony created by mass organization of the working class and by developing working-class institutions and culture." The norms and values of a new, proletarian society would be created. It would confront the bourgeois hegemony in a war of position—"of trenches moving back and forth in an ideological struggle over the consciousness of the working class."[10] Only when this proletarian hegemony was set in motion, when the outline of a new society had been in essence created and controlled by the working class, would it make sense to take over state power.

Marxism would, of course, "never gain ascendency simply because of the logical consistency of its analysis or the 'knowledge' it could supply, nor because of the theoretical contributions of great thinkers, important as these might be."[11] An active role in the long struggle for ideological hegemony would have to be played by revolutionary intellectuals. The problem was how to combat the elitist and often obscuring nature of intellectual work in bourgeois society. Gramsci viewed the proper and critical linkage between the intellectual sphere (where Marxism had originated) and popular consciousness as supplied by "organic intellectuals." They were grouped in three categories: disaffected bourgeois professional intellectuals, professional intellectuals from the working class, and organic proletarian intellectuals. The last group was seen as the most crucial and to be developed outside of mainstream institutions, in particular by the Party. Thus, the counterhegemonic movement itself would create its own organic intellectuals (in counterinstitutions, for example), who would in turn be active in "raising new questions and introducing new modes of thinking about reality, attacking the accepted wisdom of established intellectual authorities, and providing theoretical guidance to emerging mass struggles."[12] In other words, it was not to be simply a matter of one hegemony replacing another. Rather, the principle of hegemony itself was to be transformed, "from a principle that mystifies the social situation to one that exposes exploitation and supersedes it."[13]

My point here is not that Gramsci's hopes became reality, for clearly they did not, or that his ideas help to explain anything about our society more than half a century after his major theoretical contributions, although I think that they do. It is rather that the efforts of socialist educators between 1900 and 1920 can be understood more clearly in the light of Gramsci's political insights, and these efforts, in turn, shed light on the nature of his political strategies. Again, socialist youth activists never articulated their interests in precisely the same terms as did Gramsci. And he focused most of his attention concerning formal education on education for adults and was ambivalent, at best, about the value of a radical education

(such as for the young) that does not grow out of industrial experience.[14] Nevertheless, the weekend schools that socialist youth activists helped to organize can be viewed as representing a contribution
to the American socialists' war of position and the attempt to develop organic intellectuals who would help in the resistance to bourgeois dominance. The schools tried to transmit new norms and
values based on a still-emerging (if eventually largely vanquished)
proletarian culture, norms and values that would supersede the
mystification of patterns of exploitation that existed in the state-
sponsored schools of the period. These educational efforts were initiated with the expectation, or at least the hope, that their operation
would continue into the future and play a role in supplanting capitalist social and economic relations with a more equitable and cooperative form. Supporters did not and could not foresee that their
struggles to create such alternative school settings would meet with
a sudden end.

     These schools can be viewed as more than a historical example
of deliberate human agency and of the radical project to foster working-class consciousness, solidarity, and activism.[15] In fact, my interest in them is also fueled by debates about the academic canon and
the legitimation of particular ways of viewing the world, as well as
by efforts to formulate critical pedagogies to counter dominant ideologies and educational practices. As such, it was always my intent to
go beyond the usual institutional focus of educational histories to
explore the official curriculum that was used in these radical weekend schools. If school curriculum in essence comprises "stories we
tell ourselves about ourselves,"[16] what specific stories were told to
workers' children in the Socialist Sunday schools? Were they so different from the stories being told in the public schools that the children attended during the week? Were they so different from the
messages that are being taught to children in the 1990s?
     Such questions are related to work in curriculum that focuses
on the existence of a selective tradition in Western culture generally,
and in public schools in particular. That is, there is a virtually unlim-
ited range of human history and culture, and yet only certain historical and cultural traditions and meanings are kept alive and transmitted in social institutions such as public schools. The knowledge,
skills, and values that are legitimated are not random, however. A
selecting process prevails that is the result of, and at the same time
provides continuity and support for, dominant ideologies and contemporary economic and cultural relations. In addition, the particular knowledge and ways of knowing are generally presented as the
natural common sense order of things, rather than as deliberate and

purposeful choices with far-reaching consequences for social and cultural definition and identification. This selective tradition appears to many as a diffuse and widely accepted sense of tradition, culture, and history. Indeed, to question or contest this perspective in some educational circles is to appear to be "impractical" in one's concerns or to be "introducing politics" into schooling debates.

And yet, as Fred Inglis points out, the curriculum "is another name for the officially sanctioned and world-political picture which we produce, circulate and reproduce in our society." Indeed, "it *is* our politics," not merely implying but actually teaching particular versions "of how to live a good life," of not only what is "good" in life and what is not, but also who is good and who is not.[17] Not just schools in general but also the curriculum itself represent a kind of battleground in which contrasting messages of who we are and what we should become, both individually and as a society, are played out. As Michael Apple concludes, for educators it is the case that "our work already serves ideological interests. One has no choice but to be committed."[18] Do the stories we tell children in school emphasize democratic social relations, critical thinking, and caring, or do they instead stress competitive individualism, narrowly defined basic skills, and preparation for work?

Recent examinations of language arts and social studies curricula have revealed three tendencies in particular: First, text and trade books reinforce a selective tradition that favors the material interests and ideological perspectives of white, Anglo-Saxon, middle- and upper-class males. Second, by overemphasizing an ethic of individualism and by selecting out interpretations of our past that stress the role that grass-roots collective action has played in the improvement of social life, school curricula have provided a narrow understanding of the distribution of power and the possibilities for social change. Finally, by minimizing the role of conflict and disagreement in the advance of the social and physical sciences, schools have presented an overly consensual view of the nature of academic knowledge. Most pertinent to this study is the schools' role in fostering what Benjamin DeMott refers to as a kind of "class-erasing impulse," for example by substituting words like "gifted," "overachieving," "underachieving," "slow," and the like, and by ignoring or distorting the role of labor in American history and the structures of dominance that predominate in our society.[19] What this research points to is a "selective transmission of class culture as common culture" that at least partially "silences the cultures of the oppressed, and legitimates the present social order as natural and eternal."[20]

While this curriculum scholarship has provided considerable clarification and documentation of patterns of curriculum inclusion and exclusion that serve to reinforce dominant perspectives and unequal social relations, it lacks a clearer sense of the contested nature of curriculum development and concrete examples of what could possibly (theoretically) be included in school curriculum that is not. Perhaps this is in part because discovering the sources of alternatives to hegemonic practice is a very complex and difficult task, for the selective tradition is a powerful process that is linked to many practical continuities that we daily experience (such as family, language, and social institutions). Indeed, it may be the case that "the most accessible and influential work of the counter-hegemony" is historical in nature: "the recovery of discarded areas, or the redress of selective and reductive interpretations."[21] One example may be the curriculum that Socialist Sunday School activists struggled to develop, which comprised materials and activities that explicitly sought to oppose the dominant ideological values, beliefs, and meanings that have been promoted in our public schools and other social institutions. It represents a body of alternative knowledge that in large part has been excluded from elementary and secondary classrooms in the United States but that once actually existed, albeit outside public schooling.

In essence, then, the focus of this study is not on the winners of the conflicts over school practice or the imagined losers, but the real losers, both people and curriculum, in the struggle to establish legitimate school knowledge. A familiarity with this discarded history may help to dispel the myth that what constitutes school knowledge in the 1990s has been the result of a consensual and neutral selecting process. The activities of these radical educators underscore the political nature of schooling, reminding us that what is presented in schools is not "reality" but a particular version of it. Moreover, one does not have to teach only children from working-class families or even embrace socialist principles (especially those from well over half a century ago) to view these weekend schools as representing a heretofore neglected radical tradition of social education from which educators attempting to formulate critical pedagogies may draw. After all, as E. P. Thompson has observed, "The past is not just dead, inert, confining; it carries the signs and evidences also of creative resources which can sustain the present and prefigures possibility."[22] The concluding chapter of this study briefly examines the Socialist Sunday schools, clearly outdated as they are, in the light of late twentieth-century efforts to promote a more socially informed and responsible curriculum.

CHAPTER ONE

American Socialism during the Progressive Era

Politics, Culture, and Education

On the morning of October 2, 1910, forty children and twelve adults gathered in the upstairs room of the Socialist Party headquarters in Rochester, New York, for the first session of the Rochester Socialist Sunday School. "The Red Flag" was sung, and short passages with titles like "Love One Another" were recited. The newly appointed superintendent, Kendrick Shedd, explained the purpose of the school, mentioning "brotherhood and good citizenship" as goals. In describing the event soon afterward, Shedd wrote: "We were to inspire the young to be true, to be brave, in a word, to learn to be good Socialists." More than three years later, his enthusiasm remained undiminished. He wrote to an interested Schenectady socialist that "the kids are learning to be good rebels," which would pay off in fifteen years, "when the revolution shall have waxed very hot."[1]

Kendrick Shedd was hardly some wild-eyed former "red diaper baby" who had never questioned the tenets of the radical cause. A dynamic and energetic man of forty-four in 1910, he was a professor of modern languages at the University of Rochester, active in social service for the past decade, and a recent convert to the socialist movement. While his middle-class background and experience in higher education was unusual among Socialist Sunday School (SSS) participants, the Rochester school itself was not unique in its attempt to foster a sense of "good rebellion" among the next generation of workers. On both coasts, and in the heartlands of America as well, at least one hundred Sunday schools, often enrolling many more than forty children, were established to teach the socialist perspective to children.

Socialist Sunday schools for children were organized for reasons and in ways that can be understood only by placing these educational experiments in their historical context. These schools were aligned with the Socialist Party of America and their fortunes were directly influenced by the Party's developments. A brief review of the history of the Socialist Party of America from 1900 to 1920 is necessary since the schools under study were inextricably linked to it. Moreover, these schools were one manifestation of a larger effort to create a radical culture in the early 1900s. They emerged out of a general criticism of the educational and social experiences offered to workers' children in the schools provided by the state, and in other aspects of American capitalist culture. In addition, the establishment of weekend schools was accompanied by other attempts by socialist youth activists to create social and educational alternatives for young children and adolescents. Socialist Sunday School advocates like Shedd could sympathize with these other efforts and still argue that children needed to be exposed to a more systematic rebuttal of capitalist ideology.

American Socialism at the Turn of the Century

The first two decades of the twentieth century were a time of rapid and widespread change within the United States. Immigrants flocked to its shores, assembly-line factories multiplied, urban areas became more densely populated and widespread, corporate empires were organized, and government and institutional bureaucracies became models for efficient service. All of these changes were evident in the second half of the nineteenth century but they became intensified during the early years of the twentieth century.[2]

The effects of these and other changes were far-reaching and complex. While no single industrial experience can be said to have existed, the result was an erosion of old norms and unprecedented demands for a wide range of services. Cities responded haphazardly, at best. The provision of facilities, such as housing, garbage collection, water supply, sewers, trolley lines, police protection, and schools, was clearly inadequate, and ghettos "came into being without plan."[3] Will and Ariel Durant summed up the situation in New York City during this time as "a bustling chaos of movement and energy, poverty and hope. . . . We talk now about the 'Gay Nineties,' but their reality included dirt, disease, degradation, and almost uncontrollable exploitation." Similarly, living in the heart of Pittsburgh in 1909 was described in an official city survey at the time as "very unfavorable, very disastrous," with the bulging central area of the city becoming unmanageable as the few were accumulating great wealth.[4] Tenement sweatshops and factories often were poorly ventilated, dimly lit, and overcrowded; work-related accidents and illness were common; child labor was extensively used; and most workers were defenseless against the anti-labor measures exercised by local employers (such as the use of lockouts, strikebreakers, injunctions, and the blacklist). Participants in labor disputes faced the combined force of capital and the state, often resulting in injuries, loss of jobs, and an increased feeling of intimidation in the workplace.[5]

American laborers dealt with such conditions in varying ways. Many immigrants held on to ethnic cultural traditions to maintain a sense of belonging in a bewildering and often disappointing new world. At the same time, they selectively accepted assimilation into the American way of life in order to be able to take better advantage of the promise that the United States still held for their children, if not for them. Other workers, immigrant and native-born, attempted to assimilate fully, and clutched fervently to the efficacy of Horatio Alger stories and "land of opportunity" arguments. The institutional pressures to believe were strong; the desire to believe, to have real hope for a better future, was perhaps even stronger. After all, as Jerome Karabel reminds us, for most immigrants to America, "life in the United States, however brutal and degrading it might have been, was better than life in the Old Country."[6] Still other laborers, like the Los Angeles family of Regina Karasick (later known as Peggy Dennis), outrightly "rejected the mores of capitalist America" and wore their poverty like a badge of honor.[7] For the Karasicks and others like them, the promise of significant progress in capitalist America was illusory. Only a new social order could significantly improve the living conditions of the masses of unskilled and skilled workers.

By 1910, increasing numbers of Progressive reformers were tackling the various social problems resulting from the transformation of American life. They also perceived the need to contain the spread of discontent among the poor and among frustrated laborers. The reformers' agenda included the establishment of social centers, settlement houses, social welfare agencies, political reforms, educational reforms, and various other programs directed at a general improvement of living conditions.[8] The person on the street hoped that these reforms would translate into newer and cleaner tenement buildings and streets, better transportation in and between cities, the opportunity to remove insensitive politicians from office, better schooling for children, and so forth. For many the Progressive reform movement represented new hope for improved living conditions. For others, like the socialist Karasicks, it appeared to be an insufficient response to the abuses and inequities of industrial capitalism.

Significantly, the social ferment of the period created the impetus and the opportunities for radical agitation. The most prominent radical political organization of the time was the Socialist Party of America, which originated in the summer of 1901 as a result of a split within the older Socialist Labor Party. While not a major national success, the Socialist Party was a significant presence on the American political scene, with about 40,000 members by 1908. In four years it could boast of 118,000, an increase of more than 1000 percent since its founding eleven years earlier. Socialists held positions of influence in organized labor, and in many of the local and national reform movements of the period. Moreover, in 1912 alone, about 1,200 socialists were elected to public office throughout the United States in 340 municipalities, including 79 mayors in 24 states. The Party could boast of the election of two U.S. Congressmen, Victor Berger of Milwaukee in 1910 (who lost to a fusion candidate in 1912) and Meyer London of Manhattan in 1914 (who was reelected in 1916 and 1920). Finally, over three hundred radical periodicals were being published in 1912, a 900 percent increase since 1900. One, the *Appeal to Reason* (published in Girard, Kansas), attained a circulation of over 760,000. Two local daily newspapers, the *Milwaukee Leader* and the *New York Call*, had circulations of 35,000 and 22,200 respectively during the same year.[9]

The membership of the Socialist Party from 1901 to 1920 was not an aggregation of like-minded radical activists who worked with unanimity for the end of industrial capitalism. Indeed, although predominantly working class, Party members came from every walk of life and every section of the country. Included in the ranks were old Populists who had clung to a radical vision of the future America; devout Christians, some of them clergymen, who viewed socialism as a polite way to bring a piece of heaven to earth; cooperative colonization group members who considered the Party as a political channel for their efforts; discontented intellectuals who sought an end to the alienation of American industrial society; followers of Edward Bellamy who perceived the expanding Party organization of the early 1900s as a logical and sensible outgrowth of the Nationalist movement; Marxist intellectuals and laborers, many of them immigrants or first-generation Americans, who naturally allied themselves with an overtly socialist political organization; and workers who had come to view the promise of the American Dream as only a cornerstone of the rhetoric of the corporate capitalist. Footholds existed in metropolitan areas, such as German-populated Milwaukee and Jewish-dominated sections of New York City, like the Lower

East Side, Harlem, Brownsville, and Williamsburg. But strong local bases emerged in other areas as well, including Massachusetts, up-state New York, Pennsylvania, Ohio, Illinois, Minnesota, Oklahoma, Texas, and Montana.[10] Of course, the vast majority of workers, whom radical activists believed were ripe for recruitment to the Socialist Party and allied organizations, were never attracted to radical principles and visions at all.

The character of the socialist movement in the United States between 1900 and 1920 reflected the diversity of its membership. All American socialists were united by the belief that the United States was essentially "a government of, by, and for the capitalists," but they differed over what to do about it.[11] The most fundamental ideological division involved those who tended toward an advocacy for evolutionary socialism (derisively called the "slowcialists" or "sewer socialists" by others because of their stress on sewers and related municipal improvements) and those who adopted a more revolutionary perspective (occasionally referred to as the "impossibilists" by their Party opponents). The former believed that socialism could only occur in a relatively democratic country like the United States by step-by-step, peaceful, and constitutional changes. The more revolutionary segment believed that piecemeal reforms would never result in a transformation of the ownership and management of the means of production and distribution. Thus they placed greater emphasis on organizing and agitating among trade unionists (as well as non-union laborers), instead of, for example, campaigning for votes in local elections. Disagreements over the efficacy of Socialist Sunday School work were more than matched by disputes over fundamental Party strategies.

During the first two decades of the twentieth century, the varied and sometimes deep divisions among Party members were bridged for the most part by a shared commitment to end "the irremediable wrong of industrial capitalism." While this shared vision did not prevent a major split in ranks from 1912 to 1914 or prevent defections of prominent members when the Party took a strong anti–World War I stand, the Socialist Party did seem to recover by 1917.[12] Support for a variety of activities appeared to be on the rise. (In the case of the Sunday schools, this was in part *because* of the split and the defections.) However, two dramatic developments that occurred after World War I destroyed the progress and precarious solidarity that had previously existed. The first development was the severe repression directed against all American radicals by local and national governmental agencies and private citizen groups. Many of the official acts of repression during the war stemmed from Congressional passage of the Espionage and Sedition Acts of 1917 and 1918, which, while primarily directed at treason, were "so construed and interpreted that [they] covered much lesser disloyal activity."[13] Scores of leaders from the Socialist Party, Industrial Workers of the World, and the anarchist movement as well as rank-and-file activists were indicted, many of them serving prison terms. Moreover, the radical press was seriously weakened and, in many communities, socialist journalists and activists had to contend with the wrath of local vigilante committees that were organized by local businesses and patriotic societies. These attacks on "disloyal" thought and activity continued when the war ended. If anything, the post-war climate, marked by severe economic troubles, resembled even more of a national hysteria. As Stanley Coben suggests about this post-war Red Scare, "Its objective was to end the apparent erosion of American values and the disintegration of American culture. By reaffirming those beliefs, customs, symbols, and traditions felt to be the foundation of our way of life, by enforcing conformity among the population, and by purging the nation of dangerous foreigners, the one hundred per centers expected to heal societal divisions and to tighten defenses against cultural change."[14]

Another dramatic development of the post-war years was a cataclysmic rupture within the Party. While the repression of these years no doubt exacerbated the tensions already existing within the radical movement, there were other reasons for this split. By 1920 the Party's membership was almost up to its 1912 level, with over 100,000 members. But now over half of its support came from the more radical foreign-language federations, which were less integrated into the Party's infrastructure. Thus, although its numbers were on the increase, the uneasy coalition that had always existed in the Party became even more unstable during an already tense time. Relatedly, the Russian Revolution and its aftermath "was like dynamite in splintering the whole movement" in the United States.[15] The conflict was not so much over the relationship of the American movement to the new Russian regime as it was on the Party's fundamental division from 1900 to 1920: the assessment of prospects for socialist revolution in the United States, an issue intensified by the success of the Russian revolutionaries and the force and counterforce associated with the Red Scare and with a wave of violent labor disputes that had erupted. Moderates complained that their more radical comrades, caught up in the euphoria of the Russian Revolution, the 1919 strikes, and the increase in Party membership, were misguided in taking the Bolshevik success not just as inspiration but as a blueprint for action. At the same time, radical socialists believed that the understandings of moderates seemed at least a decade out of date in 1919. They accused Party leaders of failing to integrate new members into Party decision making and becoming overly defensive toward the events of the period. The effects of this factionalism could certainly be felt on the personal level. Peggy Dennis, a young girl at the time, remembers the atmosphere this way: "[The split] tore our family apart. . . . Aunts, uncles, and friends fought bitterly, dividing into Rights and Lefts; Kerensky versus Lenin; Brest Litovsk peace compromises versus permanent revolution; proletarian dictatorship versus social democratic parliamentarism. Marriages floundered, lifetime friendships were destroyed, and our Sunday family gatherings became embittered explosions."[16]

By the beginning of the 1920s, the terrain of American socialist politics and activities had been torn asunder. New radical political parties emerged and Socialist Party membership dropped from 108,504 in 1919, to 26,766 in 1920, and 11,277 in 1922. The Party spent the next decade regrouping and trying to figure out what was wrong. After a nationwide tour in 1921, Socialist Party stalwart Ida Crouch Hazlett reported that there existed "a vast amount of discouragement, listlessness, not to say hopelessness, both in the skeleton-like condition of the [Party] organization and in the attitude of thousands of the old rank and file."[17] Twenty years after its formation, then, the success of the progressives, persecution by government and mob, and the 1919 split, combined to leave the Socialist Party of America just a shell of what it once was. Sunday schools for children were the least of the concerns for those who remained loyal to the socialist movement.

The Role of Culture

Despite the divisions and open splits from within and the repressive actions by governmental bodies and private citizen groups from without, for most of the first two decades of the twentieth century the American socialist movement was strikingly buoyant in nature. The path of the coming socialist society was generally viewed as an inevitable one that lay just ahead. One former Party activist recounted years later, "In 1912 . . . we all thought that socialism was around the corner. And when Victor Berger and Meyer London were elected to Congress, hopes were high." Similarly, a 1930s activist, born into a Milwaukee socialist family in 1909, described the early movement as "rubicundly hopeful."[18] It is this optimism that underlies the radical watchwords of the period from 1900 to 1920: "Agitation, Education, Organization." With the energy born of enthusiasm, American socialists initiated a wide range of activities outside the strictly political arena that has been the typical focus of those who have chronicled the Party's history.

In New York City and elsewhere, Socialist Party locals in the early 1900s sponsored festivals (for example, to provide alternatives

to "bourgeois" holidays), concerts, bazaars, carnivals, picnics, en-
campments, dancing bands, singing societies, theater groups, debat-
ing clubs, literary societies, athletic groups, and many other cultural
activities. As one Party activist suggested at the time, such cultural
activities were initiated by rank-and-file members and Party leaders
to "lighten the lump of Socialist seriousness with the leaven of
sociability."[19] They were in large part directed at two needs: recruiting new members and (especially given the various internecine
quarrels and countervailing influences such as the capitalist press,
the Church, mass entertainment, and public schooling) fostering a
sense of camaraderie and solidarity among those already allied with
the socialist movement. Often the two concerns overlapped, and
many of the cultural activities that were sponsored served both recruitment and socialization purposes. They also helped to bridge potential tension between radical politics and family life by providing
activities for the whole family to enjoy and to bring together old and
young Party members. Moreover, these cultural activities could help
adjust immigrant workers to American society.[20]

Even if one did not join the many groups or participate in the
various activities sponsored by Party locals, or subscribe to a socialist newspaper or journal, it was possible to become acquainted with
aspects of the emergent socialist culture in other ways. Indeed, the
streets were an important cultural arena for socialist agitation.
There were numerous parades and marches, both spontaneous and
carefully organized, sometimes with thousands participating and
many more observing. Familiar songs were sung loudly, slogans
were chanted defiantly, banners and flags and placards were carried
proudly, and the radical spirit in general was publicly and vibrantly
displayed. Such gatherings also served to unite the various local
branches and organizations within a city. One New York City parade in November 1912 reportedly drew 40,000 participants and
150,000 onlookers, with a socialist band playing such songs as "The
Marseillaise" and "The Internationale."[21]

Another street activity that socialist activists often engaged in
were street corner or soapbox speeches and rallies. In some locales,
accompanied by a socialist lecture or reading van, one could even
make a small living from such activities.[22] In New York City, for
example, seventy to eighty rallies per week, covering all boroughs,
took place in 1916. In Manhattan, socialist street speakers reported
audiences ranging from 35 to 1,500, with the majority of them between 150 and 300. These street corner speeches and rallies usually
were held near branch headquarters in the evening (after work
hours), although they also took place at the noon hour, during
strikes, and in parks and streets where workers gathered during
lunchtime. Such activities were obviously political in nature, as well

as an extension of the Party's educational work. But they sometimes also took on a festive air, with whole families gathered about, and added to the impression that revolutionary culture was everywhere.[23]

It was thus not only union organizing, strike activity, electoral campaigns, and membership drives that attracted workers to the socialist movement. Socialism also gained followers during these years because of the existence of an emergent radical culture, one that Charles Leinenweber has described as "flourish[ing] in the neighborhoods: in the streets, tenements, cafes, taverns, dance halls, theatres, barber shops, church basements, settlement houses and union halls."[24] The initiation of these social activities by radical activists played a significant role in the perception of potential recruits and Party members that the socialist movement was indeed a dynamic and viable alternative to capitalist politics and culture. Drama, humor, sports, music, songs, stories, dance, drawing, and so on, as well as more directly educational endeavors for adults and children, played a role in these efforts.

The Role of Education

Party activists generally viewed the education of workers as of fundamental importance to the success of the American radical movement. They believed that if the worker could reach an honest and substantive understanding of the nature of the capitalist system and of the real promise of the socialist alternative, allegiance to the Party would flow naturally. In general, they viewed this process of educating about, and for, socialism as the province of the working class itself (or of those who strongly identified themselves with working-class interests). As a placard at the Party's founding convention in Indianapolis in 1901 admonished: "THE EMANCIPATION OF THE WORKING CLASS must be the WORK of the WORKING CLASS ITSELF."[25]

Not surprisingly, given their diversity, Party members differed on the extent and kind of educational activity that was needed. For some, the availability of appropriate reading materials such as articles, pamphlets and books, electoral activity, and participation in labor struggles provided the most appropriate measure of adult socialist education. The press in particular was crucial, consuming as much if not more of radicals' time and attention than strikes, demonstrations, and oratory.[26] There was a realization that much radical activity was ignored, let alone portrayed positively, in capitalist publications. The local socialist press integrated the broad framework of social and political problems with a socialistic perspective and informed members of the local radical community about social activities. At times, it also functioned more directly as an educational forum. For instance, the *International Socialist Review* printed Joseph Cohen's "Socialism for Students" series in 1909, and the *Appeal to Reason* published a "Socialism for Beginners" series in the fall of 1912. Such articles were designed to make more accessible, and to supplement, the ideas contained in various textbooks authored by prominent theorists, such as by John Spargo, William English Walling, and Jessie Wallace Hughan. The socialist press also publicized, and at times even sponsored, correspondence courses, for example one by Walter Thomas Mills in the *Appeal to Reason*. Mills's course focused on socialism and public speaking and consisted of ten weekly lessons, a final examination, and the awarding of diplomas upon successful completion of the course. Mills charged a small fee, but he waived it in return for work done for the newspaper.[27]

One socialist periodical was intended to spread the combined messages of progressive education and socialist politics among public school teachers. This little-known journal was the *Progressive Journal of Education*, which lasted from November 1908 until June 1910. It published articles written by John Dewey, Algie Simons, May Wood Simons, Katherine Dopp, Francisco Ferrer y Guardia, Benjamin Gruenberg, and John Spargo. For instance, a 1904 address by Dewey at the Francis Parker School in Chicago on the methods of "the new education" was reprinted in the journal's pages as "Education, Direct and Indirect." More overtly political articles included Charles Dight's "Economic Wrongs of Capitalism" and Algie Simons's "A New Interpretation of American History." The *Progressive Journal of Education* does not appear to have had any official relationship with, or to have received any tangible support from, the Socialist Party. Yet it emphasized that it sought to offset the "exaggerated patriotism and individualism" of the public schools by "IMPLANTING SOCIALISM IN THE MINDS OF THE SCHOOL TEACHERS OF AMERICA, thus opening the way to the training of the youth of the land along progressive instead of reactionary lines."[28]

Many socialist activists perceived the need to provide more formal educational opportunities for workers and their families as well. This took a variety of forms but most initiatives could be traced to the Party local. Indeed, as New York City Party activist Algernon Lee later recollected, "Every branch was a little school of Social Science, much more than it was a political club."[29] Virtually all Party locals sponsored lectures and debates for educational purposes. Some Party members viewed these efforts as too superficial, casual, and incomplete an educational form. A more systematic education for socialism seemed warranted. Socialist women's clubs in particular helped to organize more formal ventures, in large part because this was the kind of work deemed appropriate for them by Party leaders (most of whom were men). In fact, in all women's unions and branches, "education in the principles of Socialism was the first priority." Such efforts basically took three forms: educational activities for the general adult populace, for example in the form of ongoing series of lectures, debates, and informal talks; more systematic educational opportunities (such as classes) for interested women to learn about socialist principles and policies; and the organization of educational (and social) opportunities—such as Sunday schools—for the children of radical working-class parents.[30]

In addition, a number of colleges and adult schools were organized by Party members and other radicals from 1900 to 1920 to provide a more formal and structured socialist education. Generally speaking, these institutions were small-scale and short-lived endeavors. There were exceptions to this characterization, however. Perhaps the most prominent was the Rand School of Social Science in New York City. Closely allied with the Party during this period but not actually a part of the Party organization (for legal reasons), it was founded in 1906 and closed in 1956. The Rand School offered a vast number of courses, for example in elementary and advanced socialism, U.S. history, economics, history of socialism, public speaking, and methods of Party and labor union organizing, as well as in English poetry, composition and rhetoric, shorthand, science, and music. During the early 1900s the school was especially attractive to immigrant workers, who felt that they could take courses there and not be looked down upon because of the sense of international brotherhood at the school. Among the teachers at the Rand School were socialist and non-socialist radicals and liberals, such as Charles Beard, David Berenberg, Louis Boudin, August Claessens, Charlotte Perkins Gilman, Morris Hillquit, Jessie Wallace Hughan, Algernon Lee, Anna Maley, David Muzzey, Scott Nearing, John Spargo, Lester Frank Ward, and William English Walling.

In 1910, the Rand School initiated correspondence courses in American history, government, and socialism that were utilized by Party locals, especially in the northeast, and by other allied groups, such as the Young People's Socialist League. A year later, the school began a program for full-time students, with 10 students in the first year and 22 students in the second year taking courses and helping the Party by working for the *New York Call* and radical trade unions. In the fall of 1914, the Rand School also began operating five extensions, in Brownsville, Harlem, the Bronx, Jersey City, and Manhattan's upper East Side. At its own building it also sponsored a library, a book store, and the Bureau of Labor Research (which compiled the *American Labor Year Book*). From 1918 to 1919, about 5,000 students were enrolled in the school's programs (as compared to 221 in evening classes in its first year). In the same year, the school established a summer session, which was transferred in 1921 to Camp Tamiment near Stroudsburg, Pennsylvania, its recently opened recreational auxiliary.[31]

The Rand School served as a prototype for similar though much smaller and less successful workers' schools in many communities around the country, such as Brooklyn, Newark, Wausau, Milwaukee, Los Angeles, and San Francisco. Other radical adult schools organized during this period included Ruskin College (begun in Trenton, Missouri, in 1897 but moved to Glen Ellyn, Illinois, in 1903 and Ruskin, Florida, in 1907), the International School of Social Economy (founded by Walter Thomas Mills in Girard, Kansas, in 1902), the Finnish Work People's College (founded by Finnish immigrants in Duluth, Minnesota, in 1903 as a folk school but taken over by members of socialistic Finnish workers' clubs in 1907), and People's College (founded in 1914 in Fort Scott, Kansas, with Eugene Debs serving nominally as its chancellor). There were also various allied educational organizations, the most prominent being the Intercollegiate Socialist Society, which was initiated in 1905 by Upton Sinclair and later became the Student League for Industrial Democracy, the forerunner of the Students for a Democratic Society (SDS). By 1920, there were also a number of labor colleges being organized by radical trade unions, in places like Boston, Seattle, and Philadelphia.[32]

In general, however, Party members seemed unable to sustain long-term, systematic educational forums for adult workers. Indeed, the 1916 *American Labor Year Book* characterized the educational work of the American radical movement as "conducted for the most part in a haphazard way."[33] Perhaps this reflected a majority opinion that time, money, and energy could be better spent on newspapers, lectures, leaflet writing and distribution, electoral campaigns, union organizing, and more informal educational ventures.

American Socialists and Public Schooling

If educational activities did not draw the active support of most Party members, they were of paramount importance to some. Among this group, the public schooling provided to working-class children was of special concern. To be sure, there was considerable support for the institution and expansion of public schooling because many socialists viewed the development of public schools as partially a result of the struggles of the laboring class and, in effect, as a splendid democratic achievement. This perspective prevailed in particular during the early years of the Party and was certainly evident during its second decade as well. For example, in August 1913, the National Educational Committee of the Party adopted a "Socialist Education

Platform" that emphasized the need for a continued extension of free public education as "the root and foundation of American democracy."[34] It was vital to prevent a decrease in financial support for the public schools and to wage an aggressive campaign to convince working-class children to take better advantage of educational opportunities. In support of public schooling and more equitable educational opportunities for working-class children, socialists agitated for additional and better ventilated buildings, smaller class size, free textbooks, inexpensive lunches, playgrounds, and related reforms.

This support for the institution of public schooling, mixed with a demand for improved facilities and a narrowly conceived notion of equal educational opportunity, tended to distract the attention of Party members from the actual instruction taking place, especially during the Party's early years. Before too long, however, socialist critics, while perhaps embracing what seems a rather mechanistic view of the relationship between capital relations and schooling practice, initiated a closer, more critical examination of public school policymaking and the content and form of instruction. Indeed, it was becoming clear that the public schools were undergoing change in response to the emergence of corporate capitalism. Movements toward centralization, professionalization, and the segmentation of the curriculum occurred rapidly in Progressive America, particularly in the cities where socialists often had their greatest visibility. As large, ward-based school boards were increasingly replaced by smaller, at-large, "non-partisan" boards, socialists, ethnic minorities, and working people found it more difficult to gain election to local policymaking bodies. In responding to the latest corporate phase of economic development, the public schools seemed more and more capitalist-controlled and unrepresentative of the poor, of various ethnic populations, and of organized and unorganized labor. Radicals also noted that this situation was aggravated when local school boards, reflecting a board of directors mentality, hired superintendents who were trained in the values of "scientific" Taylorism in the nation's leading graduate schools.[35]

While clearly influenced by progressive critiques of public education, the emerging socialist perspective differed significantly. In particular, socialists linked the problems of the public schools more directly to the perceived growth of their capitalistic character, and maintained a focus on what was of most benefit to the country's skilled and unskilled laborers. They criticized the public schools as increasingly fostering knee-jerk patriotism, a division of manual and mental labor, and uncritical thinking in general. If left in the hands of the rising group of business-oriented educational experts, the public schools would help to preserve the unequal American class structure by emphasizing such middle-class virtues as respect for

private property, reliance on professional expertise, and the profit
motive. They also would assist the rapid expansion of industrial capitalism by supplying the needed training in skills, habits, and attitudes of potential workers, and by encouraging patterns of con-
sumption that would help to fill the mushrooming expectations of
capitalist suppliers. The schools needed to be transformed, socialist
critics argued, so that they could play a greater role in the elimination of the class structure and in the establishment of a more active
and truly democratic form of citizenship. In other words, classrooms
were viewed not just in relation to the wider society but also in
terms of the revolutionized society that radicals sought.[36]

To be sure, Party critics could assume at times what seems a
reductionist and conspiratorial view of school affairs. George Herron
expressed such a perspective in 1901: "The public schools of America, those institutions which men uphold to the eyes of the world,
which are spoken of with such pride and fervor on every Fourth of
July celebration, these same public schools are now in the control of
one great school booktrust and the trust is in the hands of the capitalists. These men are the ones who decide what your children shall
be taught. The teachers must do as they are bidden and they are
always told to do the will of the scoundrels who control them. Even
now histories are under consideration which teach the youth of this
land that the methods pursued by these scoundrels are good and
true, and that the poor laboring man must be kept down because he
is ignorant and has no business to interfere in the affairs of his country."[37] Similar concerns for the content of public school instruction
were increasingly expressed between 1900 and 1920. For example,
campaigning for County Superintendent of Schools in Milwaukee in
the spring of 1915, Socialist candidate George H. Bartlett declared:
"[The capitalists'] idea of our common schools . . . is to reduce them
to institutions to make of the children more efficient tools for profit
making." During the following fall, Milwaukee's socialist mayor,
Daniel Hoan, spoke at the annual Socialist Party picnic about the
importance of education and stressed the need "to see that the truth
was taught and not the ideals of the Carnegies and Rockefellers."
And while urging workers to elect socialists to the local school board
in 1917, Milwaukee Assemblyman H. O. Kent delivered a scathing
attack on capitalist control of public schools: "The capitalistic interests desire to continue their hold on the schools in order that the
workers' children shall not be taught the economics that will lead
ultimately to greater justice and freedom. They want the young
mind to be taught to respect the law and institutions under which
the present masters of industry may continue to exploit, rob and
oppress the many. . . . We must not allow the minds of our boys
and girls to be filled with capitalist class economics; we cannot af-

ford it; it will impede the way in securing speedier justice to our class. The working class must get control of the educational institutions—the grammar and high schools, the colleges, the universities, and likewise the schools for industrial and vocational education."[38]

A number of radical critics also suggested ways for American education to look different in a socialist society. William English Walling, for instance, specifically warned capitalist educational reformers against obscuring the class nature of the social system and of the need to advocate more fundamental social change. Scott Nearing stressed the need to inculcate a sense of social morality along with individual morality, of social responsibility and cooperation rather than intense individualism and competition. With implications for the emerging support for academic tracking in the public schools, Nearing also emphasized that although "the people cannot all be scholars," and in fact there was no necessity for that to be the case, "they can all be intelligent upon the great issues of life."[39] Charles Steinmetz of Schenectady added an important related point from the socialist perspective: "Under capitalism our children are taught that their main mission in life is to make a living,—under Socialism they will be taught that the only thing worth working for and worth living for is to make this a better world to live in."[40]

A *Milwaukee Leader* editorial illustrated one of the difficulties faced by radical theories of pedagogy. It criticized the public schools for being "dominated by the forces of standpattism and reaction . . . by men and women who have the stocks-and-bonds outlook upon life." In contrast, "Socialists do not want to teach the children Socialism. They only want them to think for themselves—to lead their minds out, which is the true meaning of education—and protect them from the deadening effects of prejudice and falsehood."[41] However, the dilemma of teaching children to think for themselves and at the same time guarding against their learning prejudice and falsehood was commonly left unexplored and, perhaps, unrecognized by many American radicals.

Once proud of the public school as an evolving socialistic institution, increasing numbers of radicals were thus denouncing what May Wood Simons referred to as "the tendency among educators to make the interest of society identical with the interest of the property owning class." The prevailing sentiment within the Party tended to follow a base-superstructure model. As Simons remarked, "These defects in the school system can only be abolished when the entire capitalist system is abolished."[42] But Party members by no means ignored the need for reforming existing educational facilities and practices. Party platforms, nationally and locally, often included "immediate demands" for educational reforms. For example, the "Socialist Educational Platform" in 1913 stressed the need to provide free books, more attention to the physical care of children, more and better playgrounds, penny lunches for students, better physical conditions of schools and classrooms, smaller class size, more vocational training, trade schools placed under the aegis of public school boards, and school buildings used more prominently as social centers.[43]

Radical activists were involved in critiquing and attempting to transform public schools in a number of ways. Some of them even ran for local school boards. Between 1909 and 1911, for instance, over 100 socialist school officials were elected to two- to six-year terms in small towns like Muscatine, Iowa, and Basin, Montana; small cities like Flint, Michigan, and Berkeley, California; and large cities like Cincinnati, Ohio, and Milwaukee, Wisconsin. The Party claimed 126 socialist school officials in 1914. In 1915 Meta Berger of Milwaukee became the first socialist, and the first woman, to be elected as the school board president of a large American city.[44] Many other Party members and allied radicals influenced educational debates by their unsuccessful school board campaigns as well.

Socialists also hoped to introduce significant educational and social changes by entering the teaching profession. The Party even established its own Socialist Teachers Bureau to provide a link between avowed socialist teachers and socialist school officials. Although the Woman's National Committee of the Socialist Party took credit for the initial idea, it seems that the Socialist Teachers Bureau was actually established in August 1911 by a male comrade, Terence Vincent. However, under the leadership of Winnie Branstetter, the Woman's Department of the Party soon after assumed responsibility for this socialist "teachers' employment bureau." In a 1913 letter to "Socialist Teachers and School Officials," Branstetter explained the Bureau's purpose: "to place Socialist teachers in those communities where Socialists have control of the school system, in order that we may take advantage of every opportunity to eliminate avarice, militarism, race hatred, and blind subservience from our curriculum and instill in the hearts of the coming generation a spirit of social-consciousness." The demand for socialist teachers evidently had "increased so rapidly" by 1913 that the Bureau gained support from the Party's national office.[45]

Although it underscores the attention that American socialists gave to the teaching profession, the Socialist Teachers Bureau was actually a modest enterprise. It claimed to have two hundred teachers listed on its rolls in May 1913 and to have helped to place twenty-five teachers for the 1913–1914 school year. In 1915, the Bureau reported that its services were being used by approximately fifty teachers and twenty-five school board members.[46] However, the Bureau, which seems to have been intended to serve a similar function as the New Schools Exchange of the late 1960s and early 1970s, was no longer operating by 1916, one of the many Party initiatives abandoned during the mid-decade retrenchment period (1913–1916). And, of course, the Bureau could hardly assure teachers who overtly identified themselves as socialists that once they were hired they would not soon be fired, especially if their political sentiments became known to local constituents. In fact, a report surfaced in May 1913 that school officials in the Tacoma, Washington, area were looking to hire fifty socialist teachers, only to be followed by another report during the following spring that radical teachers were being fired throughout the state of Washington, part of a general repression against Wobblies and their supporters.[47]

Socialists also were involved in efforts to improve the working conditions and salaries of schoolteachers, in part by helping to organize teachers into the emerging teachers' unions. The *Milwaukee Leader* editorialized, "What's the Matter with the Public Schools" was primarily that the teachers needed more control over their work, to be freed from the "humiliating restrictions" of school directors and superintendents who represented an "oligarchic rule by the sordid beneficiaries of capitalism."[48] But while radical critics were advocating improved working conditions for teachers, they were also becoming increasingly vocal about the fact that teachers were systematically excluding working-class viewpoints when they stood in opposition to the interests of capitalist relations. As one might expect, this was especially the case in the emerging social studies field. For example, a 1903 committee of the decidedly non-socialist American Federation of Labor demanded better social studies textbooks, and accused public schools of failing to teach the dignity of manual labor and to give due importance to the service of labor in American society. Too much emphasis was placed on workers' being content with their lot, and too much attention was spent on exceptional laborers who rose out of their class. Similarly, the Socialist Party's educational platform in 1904 included a curricular demand: "in history and economics, the proletarian standpoint to receive equal consideration with the capitalist standpoint."[49] Socialist garment unions, such as the International Ladies Garment Workers Union and the Amalgamated Clothing Workers of America, also perceived the public schools as having serious gaps, not only with regard to an ignorance of the economic foundations of American life in general but also of the existence and importance of such figures as Nat Turner, "Mother" Jones, and Eugene Debs. The valuable contributions of organized labor were ignored; in fact, schools seemed generally hostile to labor, often using it as a scapegoat for society's problems. Terms such as free enterprise went unchallenged and unanalyzed despite the realities of corporate business practices. And at the fourth annual convention of the Illinois Federation of Labor in 1922, a committee on schools called attention to the class character of much public school instruction. Its report stated: "The great majority of our textbooks on economics and civics are written from an anti-labor point of view, and the information given therein is often one-sided and misleading. . . . The unorganized teachers, being uninformed on labor questions, are unable to detect and combat this propaganda."[50]

Generally speaking, socialist educational critics expressed the idea that it was not the individual schoolteachers and administrators who were primarily at fault, just as it was not the fault of individual workers when they failed to embrace the radical cause. It was somehow "the system" that was to blame, that kept individual teachers or workers from seeing the folly, or evil, of their ways. This reliance on the system and the false consciousness of individual participants to explain the conservative content and form of school practice was typified, with hyperbole and condescension, by Bruce Calvert in the pages of the *New York Call*: "Most of [the teachers] know no better. They are themselves the ripe products of the system. They but do as they have been taught. They have never been asked or permitted to think. They have just blindly accepted what was fed to them and asked no questions for God's sake. Some, a very few, do know better. But they are about as potent as a grasshopper in the maw of an elephant to make any changes. They have to teach what they are told, at the cost of their jobs if they refuse. . . . All is cut and dried for them. They get their orders from the man higher up."[51]

But this reluctance to place responsibility for troublesome educational practices on the shoulders of teachers did not stop radical critics from complaining about the actions of individual educators. For example, a teacher in New York City was severely castigated in the pages of *The Worker* for allegedly informing her class, "All Anarchists and Socialists ought to be driven out of the country." A high school principal in Unionville, Connecticut, was roundly criticized by local radicals for teaching that socialism stands for free love and the destruction of the family unit. Local activists filed a formal protest with the Town School Committee and challenged the principal to a debate. In February 1910, the *Appeal to Reason* attacked teachers in Kansas City who used stamp books to teach schoolchildren to save in banking institutions. (The students bought stamps with pennies and were then given interest for their money by local banks.) The *Appeal* noted that the teaching of "the habit of saving" was acceptable; what was at issue was doing it for the profit of the banking business. The newspaper further denounced the hypocrisy of capitalist bankers who pretended to care whether children saved money yet rarely spoke out against child labor in sweatshops. In New York City, the *New York Call* criticized the district superintendent and principal of P.S. 72 for allowing the East New York Savings Bank to distribute to schoolchildren circulars and booklets that advertised the bank. The criticism was two-pronged: against using the public school system as a medium for the distribution of advertising matter; and against those involved in this incident who allowed a bank in particular to reap such privileges. Incidents of militarism and strident patriotism in public schools often came under attack by American socialists. In 1902, for example, the Yonkers Social Democratic Party and local labor unions protested the procurement of $1,100 by its board of education to buy guns for the high school cadet corps. Local radicals viewed the measure not just as a waste of money but also as a ploy to train students in the military spirit, in particular so that later they would be able and willing to help the state militia to suppress strikes.[52]

One example of an ultimately unsuccessful protest of public school activity by Milwaukee socialists involved a group of working-class parents who publicly expressed their discontent over a pageant that was presented at North Division High School. According to socialist news reports, "The Land of Opportunity" included "a vicious slam at organized labor and holds up to the approval of the children the ideal of militarism." One father commented: "It is amazing that they would dare to attempt such a thing in a district of the city [the 25th ward] populated by the very working class they are seeking to insult." Eventually, Elizabeth Thomas, a socialist school board member, introduced a resolution that called for an investigation of the incident. If it was found that the pageant "contained anti-labor sentiment, repetition of such entertainments [would] be prohibited." But the school board divided along political lines, with the anti-socialist majority maintaining that there was no evidence of anti-labor sentiments.[53]

The local Federated Trades Council conducted its own investigation and found that the pageant did indeed represent "a disgraceful attempt to blacken the local labor movement in the eyes of the school children, many of them from working class homes." At issue in particular, according to the Council, was the last of six scenes in the pageant. The previous five scenes depicted why people from other countries had immigrated to the United States, for example because of religious persecution, military oppression, and heavy taxation. The Council described the sixth scene as follows:

> The last episode was devoted to the United States, but instead of presenting a land of opportunity, it was devoted to the labor question. As a prelude, several girls, dressed in black, called

Frenzies and meant to represent discontent, came upon the stage and danced about, led by another figure dressed entirely in red, who was called License. Then Peace, all dressed in white and bearing an American flag, appeared and drove the Frenzies and License away. At this point labor came on the scene, labor being represented by a crowd of ill-dressed and hungry-looking workmen in the land of opportunity. A labor speaker stood upon a box and urged the men to commit violence, and another, called a loyal workman, answered him. The workmen became riotous, one of them shot another, and down the aisle from the front of the hall came a company of regulars, carrying guns. They rushed the stage, charged the workingmen at the point of their bayonets, and the workmen crouched down at the back of the stage. A judge-like individual, who was called Law and Order, appeared and made a long speech over the body of the dead workmen, telling the workmen to be good and "not to bite the hand that feeds them." This ended the pageant.

While the socialist-dominated Federated Trades Council expressed no quarrel with the rest of the pageant, even complimenting the rest of the scenes, the "natural acting," and the performance of the school orchestra, it lodged a strong formal protest with the school board concerning the last scene. Evidently, the protest "fell on deaf ears."[54]

Another controversy that took place in Milwaukee (and in New York City as well) centered on the use of the *Current Events* newspaper in the public schools. The Rules Committee of the school board, with two socialist members (Elizabeth Thomas and Meta Berger), voted 3 to 1 to ban the newspaper from the local public schools, asserting that its articles were too partisan and antagonistic toward labor. The Federated Trades Council also requested that the newspaper not be used in the schools. However, the chair of the committee claimed that the newspaper's editor was a "patriot" and that the school board would be unpatriotic if the newspaper was barred. At a stormy monthly meeting of the entire school board, the minority report was accepted by a 10 to 4 vote, leading Thomas to comment: "It is quite amusing to talk of a free press when *Current Events*, with only one side of the story, is allowed to circulate in the schools. If the papers which give the other side were allowed in the schools, we could begin to talk of free speech."[55]

With all the criticisms and complaints it directed against the public schools, however, the American socialist movement generally maintained a faith in their efficacy. The same curious blending of exaggeration and optimism led Party members to view capitalism as a monolithic force capable of crushing mankind and as a foe easily vanquished in a revolution that was "just around the corner." One observer of the public school system argued that "the greatest foe to any real progress in the art of human living today is our empirical, tyrannical educational system" and then referred to the necessity and distinct possibility of "capturing the schools . . . so that we may be sure of introducing truth and fairmindedness in the elementary grades in place of the false and distorted teaching that now goes on."[56] While it became increasingly evident that significant problems and obstacles to progressive change existed in the public schools, most socialists continued to view the public schools as an arena in which to work. Few radicals lost hope in the institution's potential to help usher in the Cooperative Commonwealth. If they had, it is quite possible that Socialist Sunday School work would have garnered considerably more support than it did.

Socialist Youth Activities

In their concern for the next generation of workers, socialist activists did not focus exclusively on critiques of the public schools and other social influences. They also struggled to sponsor a number of their own activities for the recreational, social, and educational benefit of working-class youth. Most of the ventures in socialist youth work were decidedly small scale, of short duration, and local in nature. Still, there were a significant number of activities and groups initiated by grass-roots activists, many of them women, for the purpose of providing enjoyable social and educational experiences for the children of radical, working-class parents. Capitalist influences were viewed as so predominant that the advantage some children had in growing up in radical, working-class homes (as "red diaper babies") seemed insufficient to ward off the possible subversive effects of such influences as the public schools.[57]

Indeed, there existed the danger that emerging non-socialist youth organizations could attract working-class youth and dilute support for the radical cause. The Young Men's Christian Association, for example, was identified in 1914 as "great opposition" to the Young People's Socialist League. The newly organized Boy Scouts of America was also of particular concern to those socialists who focused their attention on the possibilities and necessity of insuring a cohesive and committed future generation of Party members. Articles in the *Young Socialists' Magazine* attacked the Boy Scouts as "militaristic" and as containing "poisoning influences." The *Appeal to Reason* referred to the Boy Scouts as "The Murder Schools," and the *Christian Socialist* called the organization "the most dastardly attempt to enslave the minds of the people."[58] Especially from 1915 to 1917, numerous socialist young people's clubs opposed the Boy Scouts as part of their general anti-militarism campaign.

As public criticism by radical activists toward the public schools, Boy Scouts, and so on increased, so did their attention to the need for socialist youth work. During the first years of the Party, small-scale Party-affiliated youth groups were organized, and the most prominent and long-lasting one was the Young People's Socialist League (YPSL). It began in Chicago in 1907 as a social and educational group, sponsoring dances, concerts, musical groups, and sports teams, as well as study classes, lecture series, dramatic and literary societies, and debates. It was initially opposed by the Party local as unnecessary, but individual Party members, particularly women, lent crucial support. In addition, the *Chicago Daily Socialist* allowed the group to use the third floor of its building, which had an auditorium, a gymnasium, and a kitchen. Starting with thirty members, the Chicago YPSL circle soon had three hundred members, ages fifteen to twenty-one. Circles were soon organized in various other locales as well, so that by 1917 there were about five thousand members nationwide in 147 cities.[59]

The Young People's Socialist League of the United States was not as politically active as its European counterparts, whose members were primarily young trade union workers. Instead the American socialist youth organization emphasized social and educational activities for the children of Party members. In fact, older Party activists generally discouraged the organization from becoming politicized, much to the growing consternation of the "Yipsels." The major political venture for YPSL members before the outbreak of World War I was the sponsoring of fund-raising events for socialist campaign chests. However, the war resulted in considerable disillusionment within American radical circles in general and among young Party supporters in particular. The Young People's Socialist League became increasingly politicized and activist, especially regarding anti-militarism work. The members of the youth organization also became increasingly left-wing on important political issues, indicating their growing alienation from older Party officials. This alienation stemmed both from disillusionment over the involvement of European workers and socialists in World War I, and from the fact that national and state Party leaders provided minimal encouragement and support for youth activities. Indeed, despite the fact that YPSL membership was overwhelmingly working-class and consisted of the children of Party members and sympathizers, formal Party guidance and assistance was very limited. There was little central coordination during YPSL's first dozen years, except for the efforts of the *Young Socialists' Magazine.* The growth of the youth movement was primarily due to the efforts of the young socialists themselves, with help from small numbers of hardworking local Party activists.[60]

During the middle years of the second decade, while the Party in general was suffering setbacks, the Young People's Socialist League experienced a rapid increase in membership and activities. It reached a peak of about ten thousand members in 1919, with the majority of the circles in New York, Pennsylvania, New Jersey, Indiana, and Illinois. The Party remained ambivalent toward youth activities, however, and "never actually developed a clear policy on the youth question."[61] Indeed, the Young People's Socialist League was never an official part of the Party structure from 1900 to 1920, functioning more as a parallel group, conducted along the lines and spirit of the Party. At times this relationship became decidedly strained. For example, when YPSL activities reached a fever pitch in the summer of 1917 (during the first months after United States entered World War I and the beginning of conscription), many older Party officials reacted with considerable alarm at the increased politicization of the youth organization, viewing such activity as further proof of the danger that young activists could become in effect "undisciplined radicals."[62] By 1920 the Young People's Socialist League was torn apart by the Socialist Party split.

Despite its uneven history, it is clear that the Young People's Socialist League could have a major impact on the lives of its young participants. The organization's potential social and educational role can be gleaned from the recollections of Maurice Malkin. Born in 1900, Malkin emigrated from Russia in 1914 and lived in the densely populated, vibrant Lower East Side of Manhattan. His favorite brother was a fervent Marxian socialist who influenced Maurice to become active in the radical movement. (Malkin later was a charter member of the Communist Party of America but eventually became an ardent anti-communist and government informant.) A few days after Malkin arrived in the country, his brother, who had come to the United States earlier, signed him up with the local YPSL circle. "After school I would rush to the third-floor club room—an auditorium with adjoining small rooms for class instruction," Malkin writes. Public lectures "were given twice a week," by prominent local socialists like Morris Hillquit and Abraham Cahan. The young radicals "journeyed frequently in groups by subway to Van Cortlandt Park, in the Bronx" when school let out for the summer. "We would carry our lunches and sit on the grass singing revolutionary songs. *Red Flag*, sung to the tune of *Maryland*, was a favorite." These outings occasionally included instructors, such as August Claessens (also involved in the Socialist Sunday schools and the Rand School) and Algernon Lee (executive secretary of the Rand School). Malkin and fellow Yipsels also attended lectures and night classes at the

Rand School. In 1917, at the age of only seventeen but seasoned by his experiences with the Young People's Socialist League, Malkin became the educational director of the 8th Assembly District Socialist Club and became more directly involved in Party affairs.[63]

Besides the Young People's Socialist League, many other smaller-scale socialist youth groups and activities were initiated between 1900 and 1920. For example, in such cities as New York City, Milwaukee, Chicago, and Pittsburgh, Junior YPSL clubs were formed for fourteen- to seventeen-year-olds. These Junior YPSL groups were organized during the later part of this twenty-year period. Supporters conceived of them as providing a link between the Socialist Sunday schools and other young children's groups, and the more politically active Young People's Socialist League. Manhattan, for example, had six circles of YPSL Juniors in May 1919. The Chicago groups held weekly formal classes, sponsored simple talks and discussions on socialism and related topics, staged plays, and sang labor and radical songs.[64] Both the Yipsel and the Junior Yipsel groups survived and grew during the late 1920s, and in 1932 there were 117 YPSL circles with 2,499 members and 18 Junior circles with 295 members in fifty-one cities and twenty-one states.[65]

Another youth group was the Inter–High School Socialist League, which had members in New York City and Philadelphia. It was initially organized in March 1910, with 50 girls and boys from twelve New York City high schools joining. By 1911, the League claimed to have 130 members in good standing. Meetings were held at the Rand School and the group publicized as its purpose "to study and spread the principles of socialism among high school students." The Inter–High School Socialist League sponsored lectures, debates, and social events, helped to distribute radical literature, and issued a monthly newsletter, *Searchlight*, which claimed a circulation of two thousand. As near as can be ascertained, little support was provided by the Party organization, and the League did not last beyond a few years.[66]

Generally speaking, despite periodic public support from state and national organizations, youth work was met with ambivalence at best, and opposition at worst, from Party officials. With all the other existing Party activities and the Party's constant financial and internal difficulties, youth work seemed an extravagance to many members. The establishment of the Young People's Department in 1913 is certainly an indication that the national office recognized the need for more coordination and assistance for youth work (such as financial aid and dissemination of information). But as indicated by the complaints made by the Department's director, Joseph Rogers, Jr., in a 1915 report to the national office, little tangible support had been forthcoming by mid-decade from most Party locals or from the national office.[67] Moreover, by the end of the decade, most of the Party's time and energy was devoted to the severe problems facing the entire radical movement. Although socialist youth activities continued during the 1920s, they were largely isolated ventures and functioned on an even less prominent and extensive scale than they had earlier.

In addition to serving as an overview of the history of socialist politics in the United States during the first two decades of the twentieth century, this chapter highlights two significant points: First, Party members generally viewed American culture as primarily functioning to undermine the radical cause among adult workers and their children. In particular, although they viewed the institution of public schooling favorably, they grew critical of the content of classroom instruction. Second, this perspective impelled a number of Party activists to devote themselves to providing alternative cultural and educational experiences for adult workers and their families. They hoped that such activities would encourage workers and their children to become more knowledgeable about and appreciative of radical tenets. A relatively small group of Party members successfully, but with great difficulty, organized youth groups and other educational and recreational activities for children. They viewed such work as crucial to the fortunes of the American socialist movement. Some of them argued the need for a more formal, systematic education for the children of radical working-class parents, quite unlike the education available in the schools sponsored by the capitalist state. Thus, the idea for Socialist Sunday schools was born.

CHAPTER TWO

Socialist Sunday Schools and Related Schools

Historical Overview

Between 1900 and 1920 grass-roots Party activists used Socialist Sunday schools to supplement the daily education working-class children received in the public schools (and in the press, the Church, and so on) and to provide these children with an alternative political and social vision. Neither of these goals was unique to the SSS movement. Numerous other kinds of schools attempted to supplement (or, in some cases, substitute for) the education provided by the state. Some of these schools were in fact allied with the efforts of American Socialist Party activists.

In all, approximately one hundred English-speaking, Socialist Party–affiliated Sunday schools for children were founded in the United States during the first two decades of the twentieth century. They were organized in sixty-four cities and towns in twenty states and the District of Columbia.[1] Information about most of these schools comes from reports that were published in the radical press. These reports appeared sporadically, however, and often contained bits and pieces of information rather than detailed summaries of school practices. Overall, except for Rochester, New York City, and Milwaukee, whose Socialist Sunday schools are discussed in Chapter Three, the available data is relatively sparse. In most cases, we have to be content with approximate life spans and numbers of students and teachers, and rather vague descriptions of school activities.

Precursors and Related Schools

The weekend form of supplementary schooling had a long history by the early 1900s and appealed to radical educators who
wanted to provide an alternative education to the children of working-class radicals without threatening support for state-run schools.
Throughout the nineteenth century, for example, Sunday schools on
both sides of the Atlantic tried to foster greater literacy and Protestant morality. In the United States, Lyman Beecher, Edward Eggles-
ton, and other religious and educational luminaries promoted the
schools as a way to civilize and to uplift morals on the Western frontier. Sunday school teachers brought the word of God into many
citizens' lives, placed bibles and religious tracts in the hands of
countless children, and established basic libraries for those who
were starved for new reading material. Sponsored largely by Whigs
and then Republicans during the nineteenth century, at the turn of
the century Protestant Sunday schools gained the support of major
corporate figures such as John D. Rockefeller, H. J. Heinz, and John
Wanamaker.[2] In terms of their form and their challenge to free
schooling provided by the state, these religious schools can be
viewed as precursors to the socialists' efforts.

Experimental or progressive (child-centered) schools from 1900
to 1920 also influenced Party activists even though progressive educators differed from contemporary socialist educators, for example,
in their attempts to appeal to children from non-working-class families and to replace the public schools with private day schools.
Moreover, as George Counts suggested a decade later, many of the
progressive schools were highly individualistic in orientation and
lacked a commitment to a more collectivist perspective.[3] Still, the
progressive schools and publications did provide an important forum for alternative educational theories and practices. Bertha Mailly,
secretary of the Party's New York State Committee on Socialist
Schools during its early years, strongly recommended John Dewey's
School and Society to SSS teachers. A series of books authored by
Katherine Dopp, a former student of Dewey's at the University of
Chicago, was utilized in many of the schools. An important SSS organizing manual authored in 1918 by William Kruse, director of the
Party's Young People's Department at the time, recommended that
socialist school libraries include the works of Dewey, Dopp, Edward
P. Thorndike, Charlotte Perkins Gilman, and Ellen Key.[4] Finally,
teacher training classes offered to socialist educators included discussions of progressive educational ideas.

More overtly and radically political in nature were anarchist
schools. Like other radicals, anarchists were a diverse group, and
the differences between anarchist political groups and socialist, syn-

dicalist, and other radical groups were not always clearly delineated in the late nineteenth century. In her memoirs, Jane Addams recollects visiting what she referred to as "a so-called anarchist school" on a Sunday afternoon in 1889.[5] This school was probably one of four such Sunday schools in Chicago that were reported by a police official at the time to be of both "Socialistic and Anarchistic origin." Estimating that five hundred children attended the four German-language schools, the Chicago police official referred to the schools as "the most conspicuous feature of the propaganda of the Internationale [*sic*] in Chicago to-day[,] . . . organized for the purpose of sowing in the minds of innocent children the seeds of atheism, discontent and lawlessness." The curriculum was described by a teacher as including lessons in "reading, writing, natural history, geography, literature, general history and morality, . . . [that is,] the great principles of right and wrong," as well as music, singing, and drawing. Although no direct teaching of "Anarchistic or Socialistic principles to the pupils in our Sunday schools" took place, the teacher made clear that the intent of the schools was for "the children to grow up into Socialists, that they be worthy successors of their parents."[6]

In the early 1900s, schools more clearly identified with the anarchist political movement were established. These schools gained inspiration from the ideas and practices of the Spanish educator, Francisco Ferrer y Guardia, who was influenced by the writings of such diverse figures as Jean Jacques Rousseau, Johann Heinrich Pestalozzi, Friedrich Froebel, Peter Kropotkin, and Leo Tolstoy. Ferrer helped establish the Escuela Moderna in Barcelona in 1901 and other similar schools for children throughout Spain. The Modern Schools of Spain were intended to serve a dual purpose: as instruments of self-development, and as levers for social transformation. On the one hand they were expected to encourage self-expression, individual freedom, and practical knowledge; on the other hand children were expected to embrace particular social values. Ferrer emphasized brotherhood, cooperation, and sympathy for the downtrodden and oppressed, along with anti-militarism, anti-capitalism, and anti-statism.[7]

By World War I, a network of Modern schools was established in the United States. Most of the schools were shortlived, however, and, despite intentions to be converted into day schools, remained as Sunday schools. Counting day schools and Sunday schools together, the Francisco Ferrer Association and its successor, the Modern School Association of North America, included about twenty-two schools during their lifetime. The most well-known school, at an anarchist residential colony in Stelton, New Jersey, began in 1915 and survived until 1953. Anarchist educators usually allied with socialists in their heightened concern for social injustice and inequality, and their hatred for capitalist America; and they shared with progressives an emphasis on individualization, spontaneity, creative self-expression, and self-realization. In practice, it was not always easy to decide when attention to social causes intruded upon (or should limit) creative self-expression and spontaneity. The anarchist schools tended to resolve this dilemma on the side of an extreme form of educational freedom, with a relative absence of external constraints on children as a guiding principle.[8] Still, socialist educators like Kendrick Shedd generally supported the Ferrer schools, and anarchist schools would occasionally join socialist schools for May Day demonstrations and other radical gatherings.

As the Protestant Sunday schools, the child-centered schools, and the anarchist schools testify, American Socialist Party activists and allies were not alone in adopting supplementary schooling for the purpose of providing alternative educational content and activities. What was different about the socialists' efforts were their exclusive appeal to the children of the working class and the socialist ideological perspective that infused their teaching. This perspective produced a curriculum for children unlike that offered by professional public school teachers, Protestant ministers, middle-class progressive educators, and anarchists.

Allied Radical Schools

The Socialist Sunday schools described in this study were organized by grass-roots activists from the Socialist Party of America. Three other groups of schools in existence between 1900 and 1920 served as allies and to some extent as inspiration for the American SSS movement: the Socialist Sunday schools of Great Britain, radical (often socialist) ethnic schools, and Workmen's Circle schools.

The British Socialist Sunday School movement began in the Battersea district of London in 1892 and in Glasgow, Scotland, in 1896. By 1901 the movement had produced its own specialized journal, the monthly *Young Socialist*, and by 1907 dozens of schools had been founded across Great Britain. Some of the schools may have originated as social clubs, such as the Clarion and Cinderella clubs initiated by Robert Blatchford, and then proceeded to adopt a more direct educational purpose. By 1909, five Unions of Socialist Sunday schools from Glasgow, Edinburgh, London, Lancashire and Cheshire, and Yorkshire united to form the National Council of British Socialist Sunday Schools. Throughout the next half-dozen years, as industrial militancy in Britain intensified, the SSS movement witnessed further expansion. According to historian Fred Reid, new schools at this time "were being opened everywhere and old ones were increasing their membership in spite of bitter attacks from anti-Socialists." By 1912, there were six Unions (Tyneside being added) with at least 96 affiliated Sunday schools and an additional 12 un-affiliated ones. By 1921, there were 153 schools, and 96 of them had officially affiliated with the National Council. In 1923, approximately 5,268 children were attending Socialist Sunday schools every week. Up to the end of the second decade, many of the schools seem to have been associated with the less orthodox, non-Marxist wing of the British socialist movement. Clearly anti-capitalist in their political ideology, they tended to adopt the language of traditional Christian ethics and portrayed socialism as a kind of agnostic religion.[9]

Although the American Socialist Sunday schools were by no means continuously influenced by the practices of the British schools, there is ample evidence from the socialist press and from personal correspondence of some direct borrowing of European materials and ideas. For example, when Kendrick Shedd and Bertha Vossler of Rochester attempted to form a Socialist Sunday School federation in early 1915, 20 American schools expressed interest. Shedd and Vossler sought a membership of 50 to 100 schools, comparing their effort to the National Council of British Socialist Sunday Schools, which had about 130 member schools at that time. In addition, the *Young Socialists' Magazine* in the United States informed readers on numerous occasions that it used materials from its British counterpart, from which it probably took its name, and the *New York Call* printed a series of SSS lessons that had originally been published in the *Young Socialist*. Local SSS participants visited England and shared their personal impressions of the Socialist Sunday schools there when they returned. In 1907, for example, Corinne Brown of Chicago visited several schools in London and eight years later so did Gladys Dobson, secretary of the Jamestown, New York Socialist Sunday School.[10] The radical press occasionally published brief reports of socialist schools for children in other countries as well, including Australia, Hungary, Belgium, Switzerland, and Canada, and Kendrick Shedd knew of a school in New Zealand.[11] Despite sporadic contact, then, SSS activists in the United States were aware of other Socialist Sunday schools and were influenced and inspired by them.

In the United States, there were a number of Sunday schools for children established by radical immigrant groups. Direct communication occasionally took place between those active in the English-speaking Socialist Sunday School movement and those who taught in these foreign-language schools. Most of these radical ethnic schools seem to have served as a source of comradely support for those active in socialist youth work, rather than as an influence on SSS organization and pedagogy.

The radical Finnish community of Minnesota and neighboring states was particularly active in the realm of children's education. Books published by the socialist press were often used to help teach simplified Marxist theory in the form of essays, stories, poetry, and songs, often using Finnish peasant heroes who led uprisings against rich landlords. Graduates of the Finnish Work People's College in Smithville, Minnesota, assisted in the summer and Sunday schools, where children were taught "the Finnish language, most of the grade subjects of the common schools in the localities, and also the simple fundamental facts of Socialist economics."[12] Other radical ethnic schools included Ukrainian Workers Schools for Children in such places as Harlem, Cleveland, and Minneapolis; Hungarian radical children's schools in New York City; and Lettish Socialist Sunday schools in New York City and Minneapolis.[13]

But it was the late nineteenth-century German socialist immigrants, who formed the Forty-Eighters, the Turn Vereins, and the Sick-and-Benefit societies, who pioneered efforts to educate the children of radical laborers. Some of their schools were no doubt the "so-called anarchist schools" discussed earlier. Organized in such places as the Bronx, Manhattan, Brooklyn, Paterson, Philadelphia, Boston, Chicago, and Milwaukee, German-language children's schools were established "to provide free or cheap educational opportunities unavailable to workers elsewhere and to counteract the domination of the public school system by the 'rich' and the 'clerics,'" whom German radicals accused of "systematically spreading ignorance among the people."[14] The schools mixed the teaching of the German language with folk songs and stories in German and English, gymnastics, and a brand of radical theory. By the 1880s, German immigrant women took the initiative in establishing and staffing most of these German schools. The increased involvement of foreign-born radical women, and the influence of the writings of Adolf Douai, a pioneering activist in the kindergarten and progressive primary movement, may have had a somewhat liberalizing effect on what was initially a rather stern, discipline-oriented educational approach.[15]

Information concerning the radical ethnic schools for working-class children was occasionally published in the socialist press. The activities of the German Free schools in particular were noted and the schools frequently joined the Party-affiliated Sunday schools for festivals and parades. However, the exact relationship between the German Free schools and the socialist movement is unclear. In New York City, for instance, it is apparent from local Socialist School

Union reports, and the maintenance of the German Free schools' separate names, organizational structure, and activities, that the German-language schools were wary of becoming absorbed by any socialist organization, including the Socialist Party. They sought to maintain their ethnic identity and their political autonomy, and to remain as institutions of the German-speaking community. Moreover, when World War I broke out, the attraction of having the German-language schools affiliate officially with the Socialist Sunday School movement lessened considerably. Even so, the heritage of the German Free schools as a precedent in the struggle against capitalist domination was not lost on SSS activists. In December 1918, for example, the *Young Socialists' Magazine* referred to the Freie Deutsche Schule of Yorkville, which had been established in 1884 and had about one hundred children learning schoolwork in both German and English by the early 1900s, as "the oldest S.S.S."[16]

In some communities, Workmen's Circle (Arbeiter Ring) schools were even more closely allied with the English-speaking, Party-affiliated SSS movement during the 1900 to 1920 period. The Workmen's Circle of New York had been founded in 1892 by two Jewish garment workers in New York City as a fraternal order for local Jewish workers. Members were expected to be opposed to capitalism but no sides were taken on the various schools of radicalism. The Workmen's Circle was reorganized in 1900, with a national convention in 1901. In 1905, the organization had 6,700 members and by 1924 it had 85,000 members in 698 branches in thirty-eight states and Canada. The Workmen's Circle became increasingly concerned with the education of workers' children. In the first decade of the twentieth century, Workmen's Circle branches in such places as New York City, Philadelphia, and Chicago helped to establish and staff Socialist Sunday schools in Jewish communities. Their efforts were sporadic and limited at first, as there was little money and a lack of qualified teachers available for ventures that were considered to be a luxury at this stage in the Jewish radical movement. The establishment of an educational bureau in 1908, however, helped to centralize and finance educational activities for adults and children.[17]

Some Workmen's Circle–sponsored schools from their start were referred to as Socialist Sunday schools. Others began as autonomous Workmen's Circle schools and evolved to become identified as Socialist Sunday schools formally allied with the Socialist Party. And other schools strove to maintain their separate allegiance to the Workmen's Circle while providing a supplementary radical education to the children of the working class. Many of these schools are easily confused with the attempts of Socialist Party members to establish their own children's schools. Indeed, many activists of the Workmen's Circle schools were also members or close allies of the

Socialist Party, and the financial and organizational support of the Arbeiter Ring was crucial to the formation and development of several of the Party's Sunday schools.[18] Also, Workmen's Circle schools founded before World War I had scant, if any, specifically Jewish component to their curriculum. They existed primarily not because of Jewish nationalism or culture but because of radical political motives. They were supported by the Arbeiter Ring because it was the belief of members that the children of workers "should from childhood on become accustomed to the radical thoughts."[19] However, these schools intentionally had a Jewish constituency. In keeping with the Party's general position not to give particular attention to ethnic or religious concerns, the Party-affiliated Socialist Sunday schools generally eschewed any such identification.

The differences between the Workmen's Circle and Socialist Sunday schools could occasionally strain their close alliance. For example, an organizational dispute occurred in 1911 in New York City, when members of the Party's State Committee on Socialist Schools (Bertha H. Mailly, Bertha Fraser, Frances Gill, John Weil, and John Storck) clashed openly with the chairman of the School Board of the State Committee of Workmen's Circle (Samuel Fine) over the extent to which the radical (but not officially socialist) Workmen's Circle was providing more support to certain Sunday schools than the Socialist Party. The dispute broadened to include a proposal by Mailly et al., that "hereafter the work in the schools will be carried on under a form of organization which will . . . insure a vigorous and harmonious control and direction of the schools by Socialists." Fine countered that such a proposal "reflect[s] badly on the party, and may ultimately result in antagonizing an element which the Socialist party cannot afford to lose just now. We'll take good care not to be captured next year."[20]

Clearly, some Workmen's Circle members, who did not feel their primary allegiance was to the Socialist Party (or even to the socialist movement as a whole), sought to maintain autonomy from the Party structure and were alarmed by the perceived encroachment of the Party organization. But the dispute in 1911 was resolved quickly, in a way that highlighted the usually close working relationship between organizers of the Party schools and Workmen's Circle schools. Within two months, a Workmen's Circle school on the Lower East Side was publicly conveying appreciation to Frances Gill, the State Committee on Socialist Schools, "and in particular Mrs. Bertha H. Mailly, . . . for helping us to get teachers, [and] also by organizing the Teachers' Training School which our teachers attended." And Mailly left no doubt in an article in the *Little Socialist Magazine for Boys and Girls* that the Workmen's Circle had helped to establish the Party's East Harlem School and other Socialist Sunday schools in New York City.[21] However, the 1911 incident might have added fuel to the fire of those Workmen's Circle members who wanted the radical fraternal order to organize a system of schools more explicitly identified with Jewish culture, which it began doing by the end of the second decade.[22]

1901–1907: A Fledgling Movement of Socialist Sunday Schools

Schools that referred to themselves explicitly as "socialist schools" were organized before 1900, often by the radical ethnic groups discussed earlier. In May 1879, for example, at the peak of activity for the Socialist Labor Party, a school announced as "the First Socialistic School" was founded in Chicago, with about 100 children attending. In the next year, socialist women in New York City helped organize district party-run schools that enrolled 255 students within five years. In fact, historian Mari Jo Buhle suggests, well before the twentieth century, from "the major urban settlements to the small industrial towns, Socialists introduced wherever feasible their own schools, a link in literature and language to the Old World, in free thought to the free society."[23]

The Socialist Party of America was founded in 1901 and soon afterward Sunday schools for the children of laborers were being organized by grass-roots Party activists. One of the first Socialist Sunday schools was organized in San Jose, California in 1902. The school was initiated primarily by women activists, in particular Josephine Cole, who has been described as a "movement veteran."[24] Chicago socialists opened Sunday schools for children in early 1903, although it is unclear how many were established. They were described in *The Worker* as "under the management" of May Wood Simons, a prominent Party organizer. Simons took a special interest in educational (as well as women's) issues and published articles on the topic in such journals as *Coming Nation* and *Progressive Journal of Education*. She also was actively involved in the Party's educational committees and at one time ran for county superintendent of schools in Girard, Kansas.[25]

Another Chicago school, the Cook County Socialist Sunday School, was organized in 1907 by the local women's branch of the Socialist Party, with Mary Livingston serving as its superintendent. By the following year the school had four classes focusing on such topics as nature study, the early people, the history of the human race from the standpoint of economic determinism, and the history of socialism. In 1909, Livingston published several articles about the school in *Progressive Woman*, but little else was reported about it.[26]

A socialist children's club was operating as a Sunday school in Omaha, Nebraska, by late 1903. The club probably owed its existence to the fact that Omaha had a significant German immigrant community, an active Woman's Socialist Union, and a key organizer in Bertha Mailly (née Howell), who was active in the Omaha socialist community at the time. It was still in existence in 1908 but little else about it is known.[27] A school in Boston also was organized in 1903 by the Socialist Women's Club, which had been formed a year earlier specifically to advance socialism through the education of women and children. Ironically, the school's first teachers were mostly men and its superintendent was identified as a former secretary of a branch of the Young Men's Christian Association. Sixty-five children and adults attended the school's first session at the Party local headquarters. Elizabeth Porter, referred to in the socialist press as "the first Socialist woman elected to public office in America," played the piano, and Dr. Antoinette Konikow addressed the assembly on "The Purposes of the Socialist Sunday School." The Boston school was still meeting in 1905, but monthly instead of weekly. Later in that year, it changed its name to the Young Socialists' Club of Boston, evidently appealing more to older youth. In 1906, the club claimed to have seventy-five members and to be meeting weekly again. After the summer of 1907, it renamed itself the Boston Socialist Sunday School, met every Sunday afternoon, and was intended for children four years and older. Mention of a Boston school participating in a "Moyer, Haywood and Pettibone" demonstration surfaced in December 1909. Except for a brief reference to the establishment of a Sunday school by the "Independent Arbeiter Ring of Massachusetts" in the West End section of the city in 1911, no other reports of socialist schools for children in Boston were issued until later in the second decade.[28]

At least three other schools were founded between 1900 and 1907. One was the Arm and Torch League Sunday morning school for children in Cincinnati, which was conducted by the local women's branch of the Party. Another school in Paterson, New Jersey, was organized in October 1907 by several socialist teachers from New York City who taught at the Paterson school until local activists Ruth Harrison and Frank Hubschmitt were found to take over. It reported an enrollment of 125 children during its first month. In March 1909, the school had 100 children registered, with 60 attending regularly. Hubschmitt had earlier taught at another socialist school in nearby Passaic. Little is known about the Passaic school except that it ordered one hundred copies of the *Young Socialists' Magazine* in early 1911.[29]

To summarize, over the first half-dozen years of the Socialist Party's existence, no more than a dozen English-speaking Party-affiliated Sunday schools were established in scattered parts of the country. They were fundamentally grass-roots efforts that operated on a shoestring. Little official support was given by the Party organization except for the use of district Party headquarters in some locales, and the frequent involvement of women's branches.

1908–1918: Slow but Steady Growth

The 1907 to 1908 years were noteworthy for three events. First, the *Socialist Woman* began publication in 1907, providing socialist women with a forum for their own ideas and activities. Second, the *Little Socialist Magazine for Boys and Girls* (later renamed the *Young Socialists' Magazine*) was initiated in 1908, encouraging socialist youth work and providing interested radical activists with excerpts from recommended reading materials, activity ideas for their clubs and classes, and news of similar endeavors taking place elsewhere. And third, election results in 1908 indicated a slight (though temporary) setback in socialist fortunes, causing concern in the radical press and at meetings about a socialist slump. The first two developments helped to provide a limited sense of a communications network among radical youth activists, and helped to spread ideas about organizing, staffing, and teaching in the Socialist Sunday schools. The third development probably served to convince a few reluctant Party members that such educational ventures were necessary for the future well being of the radical movement. The arguments of socialist educators of children may have gained a more receptive audience at a time when support for the radical cause among adult workers seemed stalled.

By the period from 1910 to 1912, success at the polls, an increase in Party membership, and an expansion of the socialist press created an atmosphere of considerable optimism about the future of American radicalism. Support for a broadening of the scope of Party activities followed. The SSS movement began a period of steady growth that increased despite still-limited visibility, with articles about youth work by Kendrick Shedd and others appearing more frequently in the socialist press. The 1913 to 1916 years, on the other hand, were generally a period of retrenchment for the Party. Splits in the movement and disagreements over the Party's anti-preparedness stand during the outbreak of hostilities in Europe resulted in a loss of membership and funding. However, this development only served further to convince SSS advocates of the need to offer a systematic alternative education to the children of radical working-class families. The Sunday school movement in fact continued to expand during the middle years of the decade, even though most Party officials were reluctant to offer tangible support for its efforts.

The Trenton, New Jersey, school was begun in December 1907, with staff members expressing gratitude to "workers" from schools in New York City, Cincinnati, and Oak Park, Illinois, for their informational help. The school soon enrolled ninety children and included a staff of five women teachers. A school in St. Louis was organized by the Woman's Socialist Club in January 1908. By the next summer, it had added an adult class, which was studying Walter Thomas Mills's *The Struggle for Existence.* The school was still functioning a year later and was listed in the St. Louis City Directory.[30]

In Los Angeles, the Children's Socialist Lyceum was founded in 1908 by the Woman's Socialist Union and apparently remained in existence, although on a small scale, throughout the second decade. A photograph of the school was published in the December 1909 issue of *Progressive Woman,* showing twenty-five girls and boys and sixteen adult women and men. A socialist school had been initiated earlier in nearby Pasadena, with its student body referred to as the "Boys and Girls of the Red Flag." It was originally headed by Ethel Whitehead, who later moved on to teach at the school in Los Angeles. Peggy Dennis (then known as Regina Karasick and later a prominent member of the Communist Party of America) attended the Children's Socialist Lyceum from 1914 to 1916, when she was five to seven years old. At that time, the school was meeting at the Labor Temple in central Los Angeles. Dennis lived in the predominantly Jewish section of Boyle Heights in East Los Angeles, and she and her cousins were driven "downtown" to the school every Sunday morning. She remembers fifteen to twenty children in her class but cannot recollect whether or not there were classes for older children as well. While she cannot recall many of the activities and subjects that were adopted by the school, Dennis does remember the use of games and songs, "all of them with clearcut, simple themes."[31] In 1918, Rasa Smith reported that the Los Angeles school was under the direction of the Party local and offering classes for kindergarten-aged children to adults.[32]

The Socialist Sunday School of Haverhill, Massachusetts, issued numerous reports of its activities during the 1908–1909 and 1909–1910 seasons. In March 1909, the school announced that its attendance was "still increasing" and that Bertha Mailly had visited and offered "some valuable information and suggestions." Organized by the Reverend Roland Sawyer, whose three children were enrolled, the school utilized group recitations of "Golden Text of the Day" lessons (sometimes borrowed from Nicholas Klein's *The Socialist Primer,* which will be discussed in Chapter Six). The Haverhill school occasionally sponsored contests in which students were expected to recite from memory as many of these lessons as they could. Perhaps because of this traditional method of teaching, as well as the decreased fortunes of the radical movement in Haverhill during this time, it was reported a year later that the school was down to fifteen children. Still, the Reverend Mr. Sawyer must have been pleased by a published letter in *Coming Nation* from his eleven-year-old daughter Ruth, who announced that she attended the Haverhill SSS on a regular basis and was on her way to becoming "a red-hot Socialist."[33]

A school in Newark, New Jersey, was organized on January 17, 1909, by Branch Seven of the Social Democratic Women's Society. Meeting at the Labor Lyceum, it had an initial enrollment of 15 students but grew to 60 over the next six months. In 1919, the school was still in operation, with 50 children in regular attendance and divided up into two classes. Joseph Julich, who also was involved in a Ferrer school in Manhattan and another Socialist Sunday School in Brooklyn, and Frederick Krafft, who had written a revisionist version of early American history for the *Young Socialists' Magazine,* were the school's directors. In Cleveland, a school was started in November 1910, with 30 children attending. Within a year, there were 125 students enrolled. During the following year, it was reported that two Socialist Sunday schools were in operation and that they provided entertainment at the Party's May Day celebration. In 1914, one school announced that it was holding a primary class, an intermediate class that focused on stories of evolution, and an advanced class that studied principles of "scientific socialism." The Cleveland schools continued on a shaky basis for the next several years, with occasional pleas for financial contributions, more teachers, and additional students. In 1919, a Cleveland school joined the newly formed national federation of Socialist Sunday schools and reported that it had four teachers and eighty-five students. A former participant in the Cleveland SSS movement during this period, later a Communist Party activist, recalls that there were three small schools in Cleveland during this time, one meeting at Party headquarters, another at Woodmen's Hall, and the third at the Labor Lyceum. The first school accepted children who were five years of age and older, while the other two were primarily for older children.[34]

Other cities where schools were organized during these years included Auburn, New York, which had sixteen children and three teachers at its outset in 1910; Jersey City, New Jersey, with eighty-eight students in 1910 and fifty in 1916; and South Haven, Michigan, in 1912. Another school in Garfield, New Jersey, was actually an outgrowth of the Passaic Socialist Sunday School. It had thirty students and two teachers in 1911, which seemed to local activists to be a good showing for such a small community. In March 1909, a school in Newport, Kentucky, started with five children, but it had thirty-five students attending and two teachers by the summer. The West Hoboken, New Jersey, SSS began at a member's home in 1909 and then moved to the Italian Silk Weavers' headquarters. Bertha Fraser of Brooklyn helped in its initial organization and the *New York Call* announced its establishment with the headline "Hoboken Opens New Socialist School: While Jingoism Reigns on Hudson, Children Are Taught Principles of Brotherly Love." The eighty children were divided into four classes. Besides the regular classes, gymnastic exercises, classes in dancing, singing and physical culture, and socials also were offered. There is evidence that the West Hoboken school was in operation for several years. Schools in Mystic and Stonington, Connecticut, also opened in 1910, with about fifty students in each. Edward Perkins Clarke was identified as an instructor at both schools.[35]

The years from 1910 to 1912 were banner years for the SSS movement. In addition to the schools already mentioned, the New York City and Rochester schools were now in full swing. Schools in four other locations that enjoyed a certain visibility within the national SSS movement were also established during these years. In April 1911, fourteen children, six to fourteen years of age, showed up for the first session of a school in Washington, D.C., that was conducted by the Party's northeast local. A year later a second school was organized by the central Washington local. Meeting at the Typographical Temple on Sunday mornings, the school announced that it offered "instruction in principles of Socialist thought." Julia Parks served as the school's superintendent from 1913 until she moved to New York City in early 1916. Despite some complaints about narrow-minded staff members who argued, for example, that baseball playing was an inappropriate activity for a socialist school, Parks apparently enjoyed her SSS work very much. She wrote privately to a friend, "We've had a lovely time organizing the school." In 1913 the school reported its regular attendance as varying from twenty-five to forty children, who were divided up into three classes. In 1914, when it was not holding "open air" sessions, the school met at the Party headquarters. Its motto was taken from Francisco Ferrer: "Give me the children and I will rule the world." By 1916, during the general downturn in Party activity, attendance was reported to have decreased and the school probably closed soon afterward.[36]

The first session of the Hartford, Connecticut, SSS was held on April 22, 1911. The school began with thirty-five students but had one hundred on its rolls by the end of its first term. Copies of the *Young Socialists' Magazine* were given out for use in the classes. A year later, the school celebrated its first anniversary with a Friday evening masquerade ball. Admission was ten cents and prizes for best costumes were awarded to SSS students. A girl dressed in a "Votes for Women" outfit with a red mask won Upton Sinclair's *The Jungle* and a boy dressed as "Trusts," with common foodstuffs (such as bread, meat, eggs) strung all over his black suit, was awarded Jack London's *The Call of the Wild*. The opening of the school's fourth year in 1914 saw sixty children register for classes, with six teachers, led by Edward Perkins Clarke, to conduct classes. The school was still in operation in 1919.[37]

Efforts to establish a Socialist Sunday School in Philadelphia had taken place before 1910. Bertha Fraser, who was already involved in SSS work in New York City and elsewhere, had visited Philadelphia in 1908 for such a purpose. But it was not until 1910 that a school in Philadelphia was organized. Reports are unclear, but it appears that two schools were in operation by 1911. The first was organized on October 9, 1910, with forty children initially registered but with over one hundred students by the end of the school year. One of the teachers was Simon Libros, who was also director of the Inter–High School Socialist League in Philadelphia. The second school was established in the fall of 1911 with help from a Workmen's Circle branch, which furnished a building and donated a piano. One hundred and fifty children, six to fifteen years old, enrolled in the school. By the following spring, the school announced that it had more applicants than it could accommodate. The Philadelphia SSS movement continued an active existence throughout the decade.[38]

As early as 1907, a women's branch of the Party in Buffalo, New York, was reported to be trying to establish a Socialist Sunday School in the city. However, the first School of Social Science in Buffalo was not actually established until May 5, 1912, which not coincidentally was also the birthday of Karl Marx. The school was visited more than once by Kendrick Shedd from nearby Rochester and used a number of his curriculum materials. By 1918, there were two well-established Schools of Social Science in Buffalo. One met at the East Side Labor Lyceum on Sunday mornings and the other met at La Touraine Hall on Sunday afternoons, with students from the two schools occasionally visiting each other. By 1920, however, only one school was still in operation.[39]

From 1913 to 1916, the Party cut back on many of its activities, especially those that did not deal directly with anti-preparedness agitation and electoral campaigning. For example, a proposed national tour in 1915 by Kendrick Shedd on behalf of socialist youth work was cancelled.[40] These developments may have had a negative effect on the SSS movement. Yet there were still reports of new schools being organized and old ones continuing. The information about the schools during these years is particularly sketchy, primarily because the *Young Socialists' Magazine* temporarily stopped most of its regular publishing of school news, and the *Progressive Woman* suspended publication altogether after its July 1914 issue. But the American SSS movement was healthy enough during this period to function and to expand into new locations.

In addition to the schools being organized in Milwaukee, other schools mentioned for the first time in the socialist press from 1913 to 1916 included those in Montello, Massachusetts; Meriden, Connecticut; Schenectady and Troy, New York; and at the Fellowship Farm in Stelton, New Jersey. And Brockton, Massachusetts, socialists held the first session of their Socialist Sunday School in June 1914. The school continued in existence through at least 1918. One of its teachers was Thomas Heath Flood, who wrote several SSS curriculum materials. Like the Brockton school, a shortlived school in Jamestown, New York, was in close contact with the Rochester Socialist Sunday School and made use of Shedd's lesson outlines. The Jamestown school was initiated on January 16, 1916, with fifteen students, from six to thirteen years of age, in two classes.[41] Schools were also founded in 1915 and 1916 in Yonkers and Syracuse, New York, and in Rockford, Illinois. The Yonkers school met at Party headquarters and was still meeting in 1917. The Syracuse school referred to itself as a Social Science School and was under the auspices of a committee elected by the Party local. In 1919, the Syracuse school joined the newly created national organization, and at the time claimed that it had five classes of instruction, including one for adults. The Rockford SSS was established in 1915, with a registration of 125 children. By 1919, 60 students were regularly attending, six teachers were on the school staff, and classes were conducted in both English and Swedish because of the large number of students from Swedish immigrant families. The school was staffed in large part by members of the local Young People's Socialist League and it also joined the national federation founded by William Kruse of the Party's Young People's Department.[42]

Schools that were organized in three other locations deserve mention as well. Two schools were begun in Pittsburgh, one in 1915 and the other in 1916. At the first school, twenty-five students attended the initial session, forty-one the next, fifty-six the next, and seventy at the school's fourth session. This rapid increase in attendance led Martin Weber, director of the school, to write enthusiastically to Shedd: "Why if we keep this up at this rate then Socialism will surely come faster and much quicker than any of us really could imagine!" Pittsburgh Socialist Sunday School No. 2 (of the North Side) was organized in January 1916. By December of that year, the school reported an enrollment of 104 students and in 1918 it was the first school to join the national federation.[43] Socialist Sunday schools were also organized in Racine and Kenosha, Wisconsin, in 1915, in part a result of the influence of Kendrick Shedd, who by that time had begun socialist youth work in Milwaukee. The local Socialist Women's Club of Racine donated fifty of Shedd's songbooks and raised money for a piano. The school's average attendance was reported to be forty-five children and twenty-five adults. The Kenosha school was initiated by local activist Ira Yingst, who had visited one of the new schools in Milwaukee and was "so favorably impressed" that he convinced Shedd to help organize one in Kenosha. By November 1915, it had enrolled eighty-five students. Plans were made to expand the school's activities and enrollment, and the Kenosha school (renamed a School of Socialist Science) joined the national federation in 1919.[44]

Between 1917 and the Party split in 1919, a renewed spirit emerged within the Socialist Party that stressed that after several years of retrenchment, and despite a repressive climate from without and tensions from within, the radical movement might once again be on the ascendency in the United States. Within the SSS movement, schools continued to close in some locations but open in others. For example, a school opened in Wilmington, Delaware, with forty children attending, and schools were organized in Prather, California, and Baltimore. A New Haven SSS was described as "very active," with over one hundred children enrolled and a school library started. In Providence, Rhode Island, fifty children were attending a new school that was staffed in part by Yipsels. Aided by the Party local and the Workmen's Circle, two more schools opened in Providence, with another one hundred children enrolled. On one occasion, the SSS children from the three Providence schools went on a joint picnic and, according to the schools' report, they "came down in a truck and . . . made people sit up and take notice along the road with singing, waving flags, etc. . . . With races, singing, free ice cream and peanuts, the kids had the time of their lives. It was a day that will be long remembered."[45]

By early 1919, the Rochester SSS had closed its doors, but schools in New York City, Milwaukee, and elsewhere continued to be active. Two other cities even witnessed a revival of sorts. In Boston, with Antoinette Konikow once again involved, three schools were organized in the fall of 1918. In Chicago, ten schools were operating in 1919, and a summer picnic attracted several hundred children and adults.[46] While it continued to be a considerable struggle for grass-roots activists to keep these weekend schools for workers' children afloat, the SSS movement entered the last years of the decade showing no signs of dissolution. Before too long, however, the fragile solidarity of the American radical movement was torn apart and with it went the fortunes of the American Socialist Sunday School movement.

1919–1921: Recognition and Rapid Decline

Official recognition of the work of the Socialist Sunday schools finally came from the Party's national office in 1918. Increased interest developed for four reasons. First, the continued growth of the SSS movement no doubt convinced some reluctant socialists of the viability and importance of weekend schooling for the children of workers. Second, increased criticisms of the messages being transmitted by public schools and other aspects of American capitalist culture provided further evidence of the need for supplementary schooling to advance the radical cause. Third, some graduates of the Sunday schools now entered the Young People's Socialist League and the Party organization and they were more favorably disposed to support the schools than their predecessors. They also viewed Sunday school work as a significant arena in which they could serve the radical movement, as Yipsels gradually became unhappy with their role as members of a separate and relatively de-politicized social organization. And fourth, the United States's entrance into World War I, and specifically the "patriotic" reactions it provoked among some socialists, reinforced the arguments of SSS proponents. In 1916 a significant number of Party members and sympathizers voted for Woodrow Wilson's reelection bid and endorsed the preparedness campaign despite the strong opposition of the Socialist Party. This may have been due, it was argued, to the fact that radicals who dissented from the Party had not received as children the kind of socialist education that was needed to withstand nationalistic and capitalistic pressures for war.

Efforts to form a national Socialist Sunday School organization were accelerated in 1918. Journals like the *Young Socialists' Magazine*, which had ceased to report on SSS activities during the middle years of the decade, reported on the schools more frequently again. The Young People's Department of the Party issued William Kruse's organizational manual on "How to Organize, Conduct and Maintain the 'S.S.S.'" The Young People's Socialist League officially endorsed the schools in a resolution at its first national convention in May 1919: "We regard the S.S.S. as much as a necessary adjunct to the Yipsel organization as the league is to the socialist movement as a whole. Yipsels can do not [*sic*] better work for the cause than to train themselves to act as teachers of this movement and then to take an active part in the work of the S.S.S."[47] More journal and newspaper articles praised the efforts of SSS organizers and stressed the need for additional teachers, as a network for socialist youth was increasingly envisioned. It would connect cities through a national union of Socialist Sunday schools and would link the children's schools with the Junior Yipsel groups, the Young People's Socialist League, and the national Party.

But these national office initiatives were shortlived, for the war and its aftermath proved to have contradictory effects on the fortunes of the Socialist Sunday schools. The war increased interest in the schools among socialists, so that new ones were organized and plans were made for systematizing and coordinating the work of the movement. At the same time, though, the war also undermined the continued operation and expansion of the SSS movement. Several draft-age teachers and activists submitted to conscription, went into hiding, or went to jail. Some of those involved in the work of the schools left the Party, in part because of its continued strong anti-war stand. It is perhaps the ultimate irony of the SSS movement that its most outspoken advocate, Kendrick Shedd, who had often argued that the schools could prevent the kind of desertion from the radical community that a crisis such as war can cause, was a prominent example. Ensuing government repression crippled the entire physical and financial resources of the Party. William Kruse, for example, was imprisoned for violating the Espionage Act. Frederick Krafft of Newark and Ira Yingst of Kenosha were also arrested. Numerous newspapers, which the schools counted on heavily to publicize their efforts, were forced to suspend publication. Finally, people whose commitment to radicalism was uncertain, including some SSS teachers and parents, were intimidated as the Red Scare continued after the war. Physical violence against radicals at parades, rallies, and meetings increased markedly. Schools continued to function and several new ones emerged at the end of the decade, but the hopeful atmosphere in which they were conducted, as a result of the Party's wartime electoral success, became more tense and uncertain.

The most devastating blow for the American SSS movement came in the summer of 1919, when differences that had divided the Party for several decades exploded into the open. A factionalized radical movement emerged by 1920, including the original but severely weakened Socialist Party, the Communist Party, and other radical splinter groups. Many other radicals retreated entirely from active participation. The Young People's Socialist League, which had become increasingly involved in SSS work, was shattered as a Party organization, with many members joining the more radical communist movement. Socialist Sunday School teachers and parents in such places as Chicago and New York City also split ranks. The Los Angeles family of Peggy Dennis, mentioned in Chapter One, serves as an illustration. It was even the case that SSS teachers in New York City ran against each other in the city's primary elections in 1919, with little love lost between the two factions, the Regulars and the Left.[48] In this fractionalized atmosphere, the weekend schools for children became a low priority for those who still called themselves socialists.

The split in ranks was devastating for the whole radical movement, and many Socialist Sunday schools, already struggling to survive, were forced to disband. Favorable mention of the work of this radical educational movement continued to appear in a few socialist journals and newspapers, and several schools, especially in New York City and Milwaukee, continued an active existence during the early 1920s. But they did so on a much smaller scale and with much less hope for the future of this socialist educational movement. Indeed, the combination of the split in the Party, the effects of World War I, and the Red Scare essentially dealt the Socialist Sunday schools their death blow.

CHAPTER THREE

Case Studies

New York City, Rochester, and Milwaukee

The Socialist Sunday schools in New York City, Rochester (New York), and Milwaukee were the most active and visible ones in the United States between 1900 and 1920. The first socialist schools for children in New York City were organized in 1907. They lasted throughout the first two decades and several schools continued in existence until the mid-1930s. The lone Socialist Sunday School in Rochester was founded in 1910 and closed in 1917. Milwaukee's first school was organized in 1915 and the last of its Socialist Sunday schools closed its doors in 1923.

It was not surprising that New York City and Milwaukee were homes to the most successful local Socialist Sunday School movements. Socialist youth activists in these two cities were part of a vibrant socialist community that elected Party candidates to political office, were represented by nationally prominent Party figures (such as Morris Hillquit in New York City and Victor Berger in Milwaukee), and sustained elements of radical political culture including daily newspapers, numerous clubs, classes and lecture series for adults and youth, and a host of festivals and parades. The weekend schools for children were an additional manifestation of this emerging culture. The same is not true of Rochester during the years that the Socialist Sunday School there was open. But Rochester SSS proponents had the services of Kendrick Shedd, whose energy and commitment to the idea of socialist youth work made up for the lack of a supportive radical community of the kind that existed in New York City and Milwaukee.[1]

These three cities are not chosen as case studies because they were somehow "representative" of the whole Socialist Sunday School movement. While all the schools nationwide gained support from, and were intended to support, the local radical community, they did so in ways that were usually less successful than the schools in these three cities. The schools in New York City, Rochester, and Milwaukee are examined more closely because materials are available that allow for a more in-depth look at their origins and development. Indeed, because of their relative success more notice was generated about them, not only in their local newspapers (in the cases of New York City and Milwaukee), but also in national journals and newspapers. While not fully representative of the movement as a whole, then, the New York City, Rochester, and Milwaukee Socialist Sunday schools help to illustrate the grass-roots nature of these ventures and the successes and failures that Party activists experienced in trying to organize them and keep them afloat.

New York City

More children attended Socialist Sunday schools in New York City than anywhere else. Probably more than twenty-four schools were organized at various times from 1907 to 1920 in Manhattan, Brooklyn, the Bronx, and Queens. Many opened and closed within a couple of years, so that there were no more than a dozen or so schools in existence at any one time, but several others maintained an active life for five years or more (and, in several cases, for more than twenty years). Because New York City contained pockets or neighborhoods with high concentrations of radicals, particular local communities were willing and able to provide sustained support for weekend schools for workers' children. For example, a former radical who grew up in the early twentieth century has referred to "the socialist citadels of Brownsville." Similarly, by 1900 the Lower East Side of Manhattan had become the most densely populated area of Russian-Jewish immigration in the country, acquiring a reputation as a habitat of "a vigorous, young radical movement."[2]

Radical Sunday schools for children were already in existence in New York City before 1907; for example, several were initiated by the Workmen's Circle.[3] However, it was in 1907 that local activists, who identified primarily with the Socialist Party, began to indicate a serious interest in offering a formal supplementary education to workers' children. Frances Gill, who had been active in the Party at least since 1905, and several other women met to discuss how to offset the deficiencies of the public schools, which Gill and the others believed "did not meet the requirements of the children of workingmen." Although aware that they were "without adequate preparation for such an undertaking," they decided to open a Sunday school. The school's first meeting took place on February 2, 1907, at the clubrooms of the Socialist Literary Society on East Broadway in Manhattan. With twenty children attending, songs were sung, games were played, Gill addressed the gathering, and Bertha Mailly was named temporary secretary of the "Socialist Sunday School Association." Gill described the school at its beginnings as "poor in everything but the zeal of its workers and their boundless faith in the ultimate success of the scheme." Plans were made to meet on Saturday afternoons but it was changed to Sunday mornings "for the convenience of teachers." Gill later contended that these early efforts directly benefitted the Party. She wrote: "From that first school there have graduated young lads who are now active in high school and young people's organizations and girls who have shown a splendid spirit of solidarity in the ranks of workers. Whatever of effort went into its creation has returned a thousand per cent on the investment."[4]

Gill also recounted the problem of reporters from "the lynx-eyed [capitalist] press" appearing unannounced at the school and then "branding" it in their accounts. The *New York Times*, for example, published an account of the first meeting of the school, incorrectly identifying it for "Jewish children" and reporting that fifty (instead of twenty) children had been at the session. It also quoted Gill as stressing that the children would be taught "natural science and ethics" and "the dignity of labor," and that "the course of instruction will, of course, be entirely secular."[5]

Serving on the organizing committee of the first Party-affiliated SSS in New York City were Gill, Mailly, and Theresa Malkiel. Gill was employed as a clerk by the New York City Board of Education. In 1907, as a member of the Party's New York State Committee, she publicly expressed her annoyance at socialists who seemed to imply that "the working class is not to be trusted to work out its own salvation." A year later she was involved in a local controversy over the establishment of a shortlived Proletarian Society, which Morris Hillquit fiercely denounced. Gill had joined the group and defended its attempt to offset what was perceived as the movement's drift toward becoming arrogantly intellectual and bourgeois. She stressed the need "to stay true to Marxian philosophy" and the self-development of workers so that they did not have to rely on leaders.[6] Perhaps she saw her SSS efforts in this light.

By 1907 Bertha Howell Mailly had already been involved in the organization of Socialist Sunday schools in Omaha and Boston. Born in LaGrange, Illinois, in 1869, she graduated from Cornell University and taught in the Chicago school system, the Milwaukee Normal School, and elsewhere for eleven years. In 1903, she married prominent Party activist William Mailly (who died in 1912) and between 1907 and 1909 she worked as a librarian in New York City. Besides writing for the socialist press on occasion (for example, she was editor of a "Children's Page" in the *New York Call* in 1912), Mailly is best known for having been the executive secretary of the Rand School of Social Science and then director of the school's recreational auxiliary, Camp Tamiment, in the Pocono Mountains of Pennsylvania, until she retired in 1941. Between 1900 and 1920, she also was elected to the Woman's National Committee of the Party, the local executive board of the Women's Trade Union League, and to the Party's National Executive Committee in 1920.[7] In 1907, Mailly brought considerable interest and experience in educational work to the fledgling New York City SSS movement. She took a direct role in the Sunday schools by helping to develop lesson outlines and authoring an organizational manual, and corresponding with and visiting Party activists in other localities who were interested in starting schools, especially before she began full-time employment with the Rand School. After 1912, she continued her active support for the schools by sponsoring teacher training classes and conferences and scheduling courses at the Rand School that might be of interest to SSS staff members.

Theresa Malkiel's involvement in the Socialist Sunday schools seems to have been more shortlived, as there is little discussion of her work in the schools after the first years of the New York City movement. Born in Russia in 1874, she came to the United States in 1891. Before long, she was a prestigious trade union leader and later served on the local executive board of the Women's Trade Union League. She also became a prominent Yiddish journalist and an organizer of socialist suffrage clubs.[8] It is possible that Malkiel's strong commitment to trade union and suffrage activities left her little time to devote to Sunday school work.

In the fall of 1907, four other Socialist Sunday schools were organized in New York City. The first was the Melrose SSS, under the auspices of the newly created Sunday School Association of the Bronx. Within a few weeks of its opening, ninety-five students were registered, with an average attendance of more than sixty-five. Another school, initially referred to as the "Children's S.S.S. of Manhattan," was begun at the Party's 8th Assembly District clubrooms on Grand Street. Information on both these schools does not appear after the fall of 1907, which suggests that they were either shortlived or moved to other locations and became known by other names. A third school opened in Borough Park in 1907. By June 1908, it claimed a regular attendance of seventy students, six to fourteen years of age. During the summer of 1908, children from the school went on an outing to Brighton Beach. The trip was noted in the *New York Times*, with the newspaper highlighting the school's role in "propagating class hatred." Another school organized in 1907 was the Williamsburg SSS, which was initially under the auspices of a Workmen's Circle branch in Brooklyn. Starting out with forty children, it reported having one hundred children and five teachers by the summer of 1908. During that summer, it joined two other schools, the Borough Park school and a newly organized Park Slope school, on a "Grand June Walk" to Prospect Park. The children sang songs, played games, and carried a banner that read "Universal Brotherhood."[9]

During July of 1908, two noteworthy events occurred. The first was the establishment of the Socialist Women's Society of New York to educate women in socialist principles and prepare them to join the Socialist Party. As the *Progressive Woman* suggested, women's study clubs were "a good way to prepare for lecturing and teaching in children's Sunday schools or lyceums." The second event was the founding of a Socialist Sunday School teachers' association in New York City. Twenty-one teachers from nine schools representing eight hundred children, no doubt some of them from schools under the auspices of Workmen's Circle branches, joined the organization.[10] Clearly, by the beginning of 1909, the SSS movement in New York City had begun to make headway.

At the beginning of the new year, Branch Twenty-four of the Workmen's Circle in the Bronx made plans to establish a new Socialist Sunday School. The difficulty of differentiating Workmen's Circle schools, with an explicitly Jewish constituency and perhaps even non-socialist, from other Socialist Sunday schools is illustrated in the case of this school. Despite being a Workmen's Circle initiative, Frances Gill was one of three individuals who volunteered to teach and the school appears to have become Party-affiliated. From an initial registration of 35 children, it had 105 students when it opened for its second year. Within a few weeks, the school had 150 students, separated into five classes by curtains. At the end of the 1909–1910 school year, the Bronx SSS sponsored a June Walk and reported that 350 children took part. A brass band played and transparencies held by the children contained the following inscriptions: "A Rebel Is No Coward," "Each for All and All for Each," "The World Is My Country," "Five Million Child Slaves in the Land of the Free," "We Want Play, Not Work," "Labor Creates All Wealth, Who Gets It?" "We Want Room to Grow," "A Wrong to One Is a Wrong to All," and "Workers of the World Unite." The children wore red sashes and red and white caps, sang songs, and were served lemonade, cake, and ice cream when they arrived at Claremont Park.

Such walks were described as not only enjoyable but also "effective methods of teaching the children solidarity, democracy and class consciousness." The school opened the 1912–1913 school year with 100 children attending. Several months later, attendance was back up to 140 and several teachers were needed.[11]

Four other Socialist Sunday schools were organized in 1909. One was the Flatbush SSS, which opened in April and appears to have lasted for only one year. Another school was the Yorkville SSS, which continued on a small scale throughout the next several years, with thirty-five children enrolled in 1912 and with Frances Gill having taken over as its director. A third school was meeting at the Brooklyn Labor Lyceum, conducted under the auspices of the Kings County (Brooklyn) Party local. It lasted several years, with John Weil serving as superintendent and Bertha Fraser visiting several times in 1911. For some of the time, the children who attended the school called themselves "The Merry Company." How "merry" the children really were is unclear, especially since Weil's daughter, who was first a student and then a teacher at the school, recollected with considerable bitterness years later that "it would be dignifying it" to call it a "school," and that it consisted of "a couple of classes" that were rather haphazardly conducted.[12]

A fourth school that was opened in 1909 was the Queens SSS, which continued to exist with different directors and at different locations throughout most of the second decade. One hundred and fifty children, seven to fifteen years of age, and six teachers were reportedly involved by the end of 1909. In 1914, the Queens school announced that its average attendance had dropped to seventy children but that it was starting a school library. However, the school apparently fell on hard times, reporting in 1916 that it was "in very poor condition," with "no regular rooms for the children . . . and unable to secure teachers," and desperately in need of a principal, who they would pay for the work. While most Socialist Sunday schools in a similar condition would probably not have survived the year, by the end of 1916 the Queens school was back on its feet, with Dora Lohse (who also was organizer of the Party local and women's organizer of the Brotherhood of Metal Workers) as its director and sixty children enrolled. In 1912 and 1913 one of the school's teachers was twenty-eight-year-old August Claessens, who was a very popular lecturer for the Socialist Party, the Rand School, and the Workmen's Circle. Five years later, Claessens was elected to the New York State Assembly and, after being reelected in 1920 at the height of the Red Scare, he and four other socialist Assemblymen were denied their seats because of their Party membership.[13]

As with the SSS movement nationally and the socialist movement in general, 1910 to 1912 were very active years for the New

York City schools. For example, a Children's Day celebration was sponsored by the Kings County schools on May 17, 1910. Held at the Brooklyn Labor Lyceum, six Socialist Sunday schools attended: Borough Park, Flatbush, Brooklyn Labor Lyceum, and three new ones (Fulton Street, East New York, and Ridgewood). Frank Bohn, a prominent socialist speaker and editor of the *International Socialist Review*, gave the main address, and Bertha Fraser spoke about the work of the schools. Publicity for the event, which reportedly drew a "big crowd," stressed the nature of SSS work: "The work done by these schools stands out in contradistinction to the influence of the capitalistic public schools, where the minds of the children are poisoned by conservatism and capitalistic jingoism. The lesson of brotherly love, of the dignity of labor, that profit is unpaid wages, that to live on the wage of others is immoral and similar precepts cannot but prove of great importance to the development of the minds of the children."[14] In September 1910, the Socialist Party of New York gave official recognition to the growth and necessity for Socialist Sunday schools by establishing a State Committee on Socialist Schools. Bertha Mailly was appointed its secretary and the committee made plans to develop lesson outlines and lists of books, and to help recruit teachers and organize new schools. A month later, a conference of SSS teachers took place at the Rand School. Thirty teachers, including several from Arbeiter Ring schools, attended. Significantly, the main point of difference during the teachers' discussion was "whether the ethical or the economic should receive the main emphasis in our Socialist teaching." During the same month, an article by William Mailly appeared in *Coming Nation* that highlighted the Socialist Sunday schools in New York City. Mailly claimed that over fifteen hundred children were attending the schools. At the end of October 1910, a *New York Call* editorial declared the outlook of the SSS movement as "excellent" and called for the "unswerving whole-hearted" support of Party members to insure a bright future. The editorial pointed out that more money, more pupils, and more teachers were needed ("there is work for every one"), and that the schools would soon be "one of the most important party institutions."[15] Intermittently, the newspaper published a "Socialist Sunday School Directory," although, with schools omitted one week and included the next, it is not a wholly reliable source of schools in existence at this time.

A new school organized at the end of 1910 was the Williamsbridge SSS in Manhattan. A photograph published in the *Young Socialists' Magazine* showed about twenty-five children and three teachers at the school, including Lucien Sanial, a long-time socialist activist. What is particularly noteworthy about this school, initiated by Italian socialists, is that it attracted considerable opposition from area Catholic priests. In fact, the local radical press claimed that this opposition played a significant role in the school's closing in under two years.[16]

In the spring of 1911, Bertha Mailly estimated that there were two thousand children attending the English-speaking Socialist Sunday schools in the Greater New York area, which did not count German Free schools and the schools of Lettish, Finnish, and other ethnic groups. On April 30, a Children's May Day celebration took place, with one thousand children attending and students from eight schools (East Side, Williamsbridge, West Harlem, Bronx, East Harlem, Yorkville, Second Street, and Fourth Street) contributing to the program. Other schools held their own May Day celebrations. The Borough Park school's program, for example, lasted three and a half hours, with singing, dancing, musical performances, addresses by Bertha Fraser and others, and refreshments. The program cost ten cents, with profits benefitting the *New York Call*.[17] It would appear that during the 1911–1912 school year, there were about fourteen Socialist Sunday schools in New York City, enrolling approximately two thousand children.

The following school year witnessed a continued burgeoning of the SSS movement in New York City. The East Side school, for example, claimed an average attendance of four hundred students and forty adults, and that it could take no more children because it did not have enough teachers. The East Harlem school reported that three hundred children and twenty adults attended regularly, and, like most of the schools, it needed additional teachers. The Williamsburg school had a staff of four teachers; this suggests a student body of sixty to one hundred children.[18] But the most significant event of the 1912–1913 school year was the establishment of a new Socialist Sunday School in Brownsville. Staff members at the Progressive Sunday School of Brownsville, which had opened the year before, protested that another school was not needed in the area. It is likely that this Progressive school had very loose ties to the socialist movement and that Party activists in Brownsville, who enjoyed great popularity in the area, desired a school that was more closely aligned with the Party organization. The Brownsville SSS opened in late 1912. More students registered than the school had room for at the clubrooms of the 23rd Assembly District branch of the Kings County local. For the short term, the students were divided into two groups; one was to meet on Saturday afternoons and the other on Sunday mornings. Before long, no mention of the Progressive Sunday School could be found in the local socialist press and the remaining Brownsville school became one of the most prominent Socialist Sunday schools in the city.[19] During its first several years, the school was headed by Abraham Shiplacoff, who had been a teacher at P.S. 84 in Brooklyn before becoming involved in labor union and socialist activities. In 1915, Shiplacoff became the first socialist elected to the New York State Assembly.[20]

In the spring of 1913, another SSS May Day Festival was planned, with Frances Gill serving as its organizer. A month before it was to take place, Gill and other SSS activists lodged a formal protest with the executive committee of the New York local about the lack of interest and assistance offered to festival organizers. Although no other tangible support was forthcoming, the committee did pass a motion endorsing the event and requested that Party members "see that their children take part in the demonstration." The program was held from 2:30 P.M. to 6:00 P.M., with about seven hundred SSS children and almost twice as many adults attending. The main speakers included Kendrick Shedd of Rochester and Algernon Lee of the Rand School. Shedd took the opportunity to urge the Party to provide more support to the schools: "It is necessary for the Socialist Party to take more interest in the children than it has done in the past, and I am glad to say that this work is now under way. The children must be started right, for they have to take up the work of Socialism in active life. They must be brought up to a realization of the fact that Socialism means the resurrection from the dead of the working classes. They must be brought up to understand what the red flag stands for, so they won't be afraid of it."[21]

During the next several years, there were fewer press reports about the schools but the SSS movement in New York City appears to have been stable in its number of schools and level of activity. During the spring of 1914, for example, sixteen schools were listed in the SSS Directory, although the list included two Finnish schools, one German Free school, and one Workmen's Circle school. The Socialist School Union of Greater New York claimed that four thousand children were enrolled in the schools. In February 1914, sixteen schools participated in an "elaborate program," which the *New York Times*, probably with some exaggeration, estimated as having drawn an audience of three thousand children. The *New York Call* reported on the various recitations, songs, dances, and musical performances at the festival and commented: "It was more than evident that the schools have grown tremendously. From all parts of the city—from Brownsville, from the Bronx, from Bay Ridge and the East Side—they came to take part in the festival. They packed the hall from wall to wall, and they enjoyed a glorious good time, as did their parents and relatives. Little ones were there from the ages of 2½ years and up. By the hundreds they were there, and in looks and in brightness they seemed to be the best hope for the ultimate success of the Socialist movement." With considerable hyperbole, another *Call* account claimed that "the demand for these schools is becoming so great . . . that it is impossible to get enough workers to go round. All you need to do is start a school in any part of the city and the children just flock to it, anxious to be taught in a simple way the Socialist ideals."[22] An estimated five thousand children took part in an SSS May Day parade, although not all of the children attended the schools. They marched up Second Avenue with red flags and placards, from the Labor Temple at 84th Street to the Harlem Casino at 127th Street, with the smallest children riding in a van at the lead. Their placards included a variety of political slogans, such as "The Future Belongs to Us," "Socialism, the Hope of the World," "Ignorance Is Our Greatest Enemy," "We Want More Playgrounds," "Children of Workingmen, Come Join our Ranks," "The Child of Today Is the Worker of Tomorrow," and "More Schools and Less Sweatshops."[23]

The mid-1910s were a time of transition for the city's SSS movement. Some old schools closed as neighborhoods changed, while new ones opened elsewhere. In addition, members of the Jewish Socialist Federation and the Workmen's Circle began developing plans for their own more Jewish-oriented schools for children. New schools being organized were thus more clearly identified as Workmen's Circle schools or Party-affiliated ones, although both kinds were overtly working-class and predominantly socialist. It was also a time when local Party members responded to the 1916 elections with anxious letters about another "Socialist slump." However, several schools seem to have strengthened themselves in numbers and organization. This was especially the case for the Brownsville SSS, which now met at the Brownsville Labor Lyceum on Sackman Street. By March 1916, the Brownsville school enrolled over six hundred children. In addition to classroom teachers, there were instructors for singing, elocution, drawing, and dramatics. The school was referred to as "the pride of Brownsville Socialists" and functioned as a social center for children and their parents. When the newly furbished labor lyceum was built in mid-1917, two thousand children registered to attend the school, forcing the staff to send half of them away.[24]

The East Side SSS, now officially identified as under the auspices of the 2nd-4th-8th Assembly District branches of the Socialist Party in Manhattan, was meeting in 1915 at the Forward Building at 175 East Broadway. At its first session of the 1915–1916 school year, 125 children attended. Nine months later, 180 children were enrolled and the school desperately needed additional teachers. When it reopened for the following year in December 1917, the East Side school claimed a registration figure of 720 children and noted that it was using the first five floors of the Forward Building for its Sunday morning sessions. It had fifteen teachers and urgently requested additional help.[25]

The SSS movement continued to expand in the Bronx as well. The Branch One school, meeting at 1792 Washington Avenue, held eight classes in 1915, with two hundred children enrolled. Because the building they were meeting in had only a hall and two rooms, classes had to be staggered. In early 1916, a Bronx SSS conference was held and a teachers' union was established. A motion was passed that reaffirmed that, despite the difficulty of finding suitable teachers, SSS teachers had to be Party members, except under "special circumstances." A new school, the Lower Bronx SSS, also was organized. It paid twenty dollars per month to rent the Finnish Hall on 149th Street and had an active Parents' Association. By the spring of 1917, the Bronx SSS Committee reported that the two schools were "practically self-sustaining now" and plans were initiated to establish new schools in the borough.[26]

Despite the defection of numerous Party members and some of its leading theorists in 1917 and 1918, there is little sign of a dissipation of energy among those involved in the Sunday schools of New York City. In fact, the work of the schools received increased attention. For example, the executive committee of the Kings County local, worried about reactions against the radical movement, voted to extend more aid and encouragement to the Young People's Socialist League and the Socialist Sunday schools. Moreover, although prominent SSS activists were no doubt distracted by the events of 1917 and 1918, such distractions were not new for many of them. Over the lifetime of the SSS movement, many teachers and helpers were also busy making street corner speeches, distributing literature, running for political office, teaching classes and directing clubs at the Rand School and elsewhere, serving as secretaries and organizers of their Party locals, as well as earning a living and taking care of a family. In fact, delegates to the Party's Kings County convention that voted for the majority report of the national Party's St. Louis convention in 1917 included SSS directors and teachers like Abraham Shiplacoff, Bertha Fraser, Benjamin Glassberg (who taught one of the older classes at the Brownsville school), and Rachel Ragozin (who had become principal of the Brownsville school when Shiplacoff left).[27] The increased anti-war agitation of these years did not prevent many schools from continuing to operate and new ones from being organized. One new school, for example, opened in the Bushwick section of Brooklyn. Within a few months, it was reported to be "making rapid progress," the students had formed their own association, and Andrew DeMilt, a well-known street corner speaker, had joined the staff. A new school in East New York, which opened in the fall of 1918, reversed the practice of the 6th–8th Assembly District school in Manhattan. At the 6th–8th Assembly District school, a Junior YPSL group had formed as an outgrowth of the oldest class of the school. In the case of the East New York school, the initiation of a local Junior Yipsel group had provided the impetus to organize a Socialist Sunday School. Sixty children enrolled at the first session; within a few months, 150 children were registered.[28]

The East Side SSS continued to meet at the Forward Building, with three hundred children in attendance and many others turned away because only thirteen teachers were available. Besides classes in U.S. history and socialism, instruction in dancing and arts and crafts also were offered. The latter included freehand drawing in water colors, embroidery, and basket making, with an emphasis placed on making "useful" things. A class on Elements of Socialism was made available to Yipsels. It was originally taught by Charles Solomon but when he was elected to the New York State Assembly in 1918, it was taken over by William J. Feigenbaum.[29] The Williamsburg school introduced a new initiative to their program, a summer Sunday school. Held in "the prodigious and flowery rear garden at the headquarters of the 14th Assembly District, 308 South 5th Street," it was supervised by Rachel Ragozin, who earlier had been in charge of the Brownsville school. (Shiplacoff returned as principal of the Brownsville school from 1918 to 1919 after he was no longer a member of the New York State Assembly.) Intended for children from the fourth grade and up, the Williamsburg summer school sponsored two U. S . history classes, as well as other kinds of classes, with "the history . . . taught from a different point of view than is customarily in public schools."[30] It was also in 1918 that the Rand School of Social Science sponsored an SSS conference where William Kruse, Bertha Mailly, Antoinette Konikow, and others formed a national SSS organization and made plans for teacher training classes, curriculum work, a speakers' bureau, a monthly bulletin, and a children's summer camp.

Along with the new energy in the Party as a whole, there was a sense within the English-speaking SSS movement during 1918 and early 1919 that this educational movement was "practically in its infancy" and that it would continue to expand.[31] Youth activists in New York City appear to have been looking with hope to the future, rather than nostalgically to the past. This was perhaps best expressed by the staff of the 6th–8th Assembly District school in Manhattan. Over three hundred children came to its sessions in December 1918. Samuel R. Slavsky, its educational director (and also educational director of the Brotherhood of Metal Workers), hoped to enroll two thousand children and enlist the assistance of one hundred teachers. In February 1919, he analyzed the current state of the SSS movement this way: "The trouble with the Sunday schools in the past is that they were considered temporary and were treated in a perfunctory manner. . . . It is time we considered our work among the youth seriously and strove toward stabilizing the institution." He wanted to extend his school beyond a Sunday school, to include after-school and evening classes so that the children could be taken away from "the 'charitable' settlement houses." His proposed school would offer courses in the history of the human race, the workers' contribution to human progress, the history of labor, organic and social evolution, an analysis of the process of thinking for older children, and arts and crafts, as well as clubs for writers, musicians, dancers, and painters. A "Children's Age Festival" was planned, with proceeds to go to "the $10,000 fund to create an interest in radical education for the young."[32]

In the summer of 1919, however, the landscape of the American radical movement underwent a striking transformation. In June, for example, both the Queens and Kings County locals had their charters revoked by the state executive committee for their support of the manifesto and program of the Left-Wing section of the Party, which had been formed in February. The state committee announced that the locals would be reorganized, telling the existing central committees in Queens and Brooklyn that they should disband because they had no authority. An editorial in the June issue of the *Young Socialists' Magazine* referred anxiously to the massive fighting that was taking place within the Party and suggested that its readers try to remain outside the fray and stay within the socialist camp. It was a futile plea, however, as the Left-Wing section was particularly strong among new recruits and young members. Opposition within the Party for the 1919 primary elections resulted, including participants in the Socialist Sunday schools. Regulars running for office included David Berenberg, Benjamin Glassberg, Gertrude Weil Klein, Bertha Mailly, and Abraham Shiplacoff. Candidates of the left who opposed the regulars included Rachel Ragozin (who ran against Klein and lost) and Andrew DeMilt (who won his primary election). Another member of the city's Left-Wing Committee was 30-year-old Jeanette Pearl, who had been involved in the Sunday schools since their earliest years.[33] By 1920, the radical movement had splintered and the Socialist Sunday School movement, while still alive, was one of its lesser concerns.

World War I and the repressive climate that followed also presented problems for the schools. For example, Yipsels had become more involved in SSS work. But in the summer of 1918, the New York State Young People's Socialist League reported that, "During the past year many of the most active members in the various leagues composing the federation have been drafted into the military service. Some of the leagues upstate have had to disband because of the draft taking away the major part of their active membership."[34] No doubt this adversely affected recruitment of staff members for the Socialist Sunday schools. Moreover, in early 1919 hall owners in New York City were pressured by police and other city officials not to rent to socialists, which may have exacerbated the constant problem of finding suitable school facilities. And the arrests, suppression of the press, and the prevailing intimidating atmosphere also took away time and energy from SSS work, as more attention had to be directed toward more pressing matters.[35]

Nevertheless, at times the post-war repressive climate could actually work to the shortrun benefit of the SSS movement. This can be seen in the case of Benjamin Glassberg, a teacher at the Brownsville school. Glassberg was an active Party member who ran for the State Assembly in 1917 and the State Senate in 1918, helped to found the Teachers' League, edited its newspaper, *American Teacher*, and taught classes at the Rand School. He was also a public school history teacher, first at Morris High School in the Bronx and Manual Training High School in Brooklyn for one year each, and then at Commercial High School in Brooklyn for the next six years. In November 1918, a new principal at his high school charged Glassberg with "conduct unbecoming a teacher" and suspended him without pay. He was specifically accused of having told his students that the Bolsheviks were not as bad as they were being portrayed but that he was not "free" to say much more about the topic. His trial was postponed until April 1919, at which time ten pupils testified against him and twenty-five for him. In May, a Board of Education subcommittee found him guilty of "seditious" remarks in the classroom and he was dismissed. Glassberg remarked: "Because I am a Jew, a Socialist and a member of the Teachers' Union I have been dismissed. Against these items the question of my guilt or lack of guilt did not matter." What is noteworthy here is that, following his dismissal, Glassberg became the principal of the Brownsville SSS when it reopened for the 1919–1920 school year. He also strongly supported the work of the Socialist Sunday schools in lengthy articles that appeared in the *New York Call* and *Young Socialists' Magazine*.[36]

But the SSS movement in New York City could not survive the cataclysmic split in the radical movement. Most Socialist Sunday schools in the city could not escape the drain on funding, the openly bitter disputes, and, finally, the massive loss of Party members (and their children) that occurred throughout 1919 to 1921. A few schools, for example those in Brownsville and Williamsburg, did continue to operate as the 1920s began. But they did so with little help or guidance from local Party officials, and they were virtually alone in their work.[37]

Rochester

Rochester during the early 1900s has been described as a city with squalid areas, obvious inequalities of wealth, long hours of work, and employers' use of various severe anti-labor measures. As was the case in other communities at this time, such conditions provided the impetus for the growth of a radical political movement. A Socialist Party office was founded in 1907 and a year later Eugene Debs spoke to a crowd of about five thousand. At the end of 1908, a women's study class in socialism was formed and endorsed by the Party local. By the summer of 1910, interest in the organization of a children's school led Mary Hammen of the women's club to write for information to Bertha Mailly, the newly appointed secretary of the Party's State Committee on Socialist Schools. Mailly responded in September, and by the end of the month a School Club was formed. Kendrick Shedd was asked to serve as superintendent of the proposed school. Shedd, a dynamic and energetic man of forty-four, was a professor of modern languages at the University of Rochester, active in social service activities, and a recent convert to socialism.[38] As it turned out, he was the perfect person for the position.

The first session of the Rochester SSS took place on October 2, 1910 at the Socialist Party headquarters on State Street. The assembly met in an upstairs room, which Shedd, with his characteristic flair, later described as "not splendidly adapted to our work, but . . . many times better than nothing." Forty children and twelve adults attended the first session. The program consisted of remarks by Shedd, songs (such as "The Red Flag"), and recitations. The school expanded rapidly and by its sixth session about ninety-eight children were attending, with an average of three dollars collected every week to help defray expenses. The school also received brief visits from two nationally prominent figures, Charles Edward Russell and Morris Hillquit.[39]

The school's enrollment doubled after its first month, owing in large part to the hard work and promotional abilities of Shedd, who was a tireless activist for socialist youth work. Additionally, in 1910 the socialist movement in Rochester, as elsewhere, was experiencing a surge of interest. The Party local moved to 10 Elm Street in November, where the main room was "larger and brighter" than the previous one and a back room could be used for cooking, committee work, storing books and other materials, and as a separate classroom. The new headquarters also was adjacent to Shoemakers' Hall, which the school was able to rent for a small sum. The hall had a long platform at one end, with a piano, and could seat two to three hundred comfortably. Gad Martindale, an active Party member whose wife was a member of the women's club that had initiated the school, was the Shoemakers' organizer and helped out at the school. General assembly was held in the hall, as well as all of the classes except the kindergarten and adult classes, which were held at the Local's headquarters. By November 20, the school had 166 students and fourteen volunteer teachers. The school's Christmas festival drew over four hundred adults and children, and included a large Christmas tree, ice cream, bananas, and a bag of candy and an orange for each child. During the next five months, the Rochester SSS averaged an attendance of 185 students, divided into fourteen classes. It also sponsored a "Play Night" and a May Day Festival, and the children sang songs at the Workmen's Circle convention that took place in Rochester. Two letters were sent to the school by Fred Warren, editor of the *Appeal to Reason*, thanking Shedd and the students for a letter and a song about him that they had sent. Another letter arrived from Eugene Debs, sent in response to the school's communication of birthday greetings to him.[40]

The Rochester school opened its second year at its third home, a three-story building at 27 Church Street, with the Party renting the two uppermost floors. "What a change!" Shedd later exulted. "Lots of room. It seemed a veritable paradise. But it costs to live in Paradise, for the Local was obliged to pay Fifteen Hundred Dollars a year for the joy of it all. That was 'some' price!" The top floor contained a large hall with a stage and an alcove, "splendidly adapted to [the school's] needs." To help with classwork, curtains were made that extended across the alcove, and separate rooms downstairs were utilized. Eliot White, a state organizer for the Party, visited the school when it opened. He reported that enrollment had quadrupled in a year, "with the 'liveliest bunch' of youngsters I remember to have been among. Rollicking, piping songs, shouted choruses of answers to questions in the ringing child voices, and mingled indignation in the young hearts against social wrongs, with keen enjoyment of the brighter phases of their teaching, mark this surprisingly successful organization of the youngest Comrades." White gave particular credit to Shedd, "who has the greatest genius for holding and delighting children that I have known, and I have had some experience with child instructors." He recommended that the national office of the Party hire Shedd to organize and develop similar socialist schools throughout the country (which it never did). By the end of the 1911–1912 school year, the school had increased its average enrollment to 250. Its "Red Flag Day" celebration in February involved the active participation of 120 students, with 600 children and adults attending.[41]

The most significant event for the Rochester SSS during its third year was the move of the Party local to the new Progressive Working People's Lyceum building at 580 St. Paul street, which was initially funded and maintained by members of the German socialist community in Rochester. The school remained at this location from December 1912 until its closing several years later. The building was situated outside the central area of the city but closer to the homes of active socialists, which helped to attract additional students and teachers. Alluding to the safety and health problems of many urban buildings at the time, Shedd emphasized that the Labor Lyceum building had fire escapes and a large hall with "lots of room and plenty of light and air." It also had a gallery, a dancing floor, a good stage for plays and pageants ("although not as large as we could wish"), and many rooms that could be used for classwork. A "Young People's Room" was set aside for the desks of school superintendents and the Sunday school library (which opened in 1914 and contained 250 books). The kindergarten class used a room that was referred to as the "Small Hall." Attendance was reported to be between two hundred and three hundred. Shedd continued as superintendent, with help from Bertha Vossler (who was twenty years old and active in the Young People's Federation of New York State) and two others, and the school paid about four dollars per week rent to the Party local. A "Red Flag Sunday" festival in February drew 425 people, the majority of them children, and a school picnic was held in July.[42]

The Rochester school experienced its most successful season in 1913–1914. Average enrollment for the year was about three hundred, with almost five hundred children showing up on picture day. Highlights of the year included the establishment of Boys' and Girls' Clubs and the formation of a shortlived Sunday school orchestra (which lasted for only a few months because, as Shedd put it, "those involved didn't seem to want to make the necessary personal sacrifice"). In a January 1914 letter to an interested Schenectady socialist, an optimistic Shedd wrote that "the kids are learning to be good rebels," which would pay off in fifteen years, "when the revolution shall have waxed very hot." Socialism would then "need all the intelligent defenders it can lay hold of, for the struggle is bound to be long and sore."[43]

In May 1914, Shedd was approached by Oscar Ameringer about coming to Milwaukee for several months to help organize socialist youth work and especially Sunday schools. Ameringer repeated the request the following October, while Shedd was visiting Chicago. At the same time, in the summer of 1914, the Party local decided (for reasons not recorded) that they would no longer pay Shedd's wages for his youth work, which no doubt were not substantial, and in return the Sunday school and the Young People's Socialist League no longer had to pay rent for use of its facilities. Members of YPSL then voted to pay Shedd, so that he would stay and continue "building up the league and the Sunday School." But

Shedd, who was often critical of the lack of support that he received from local Party officials, was no doubt upset by their unwillingness to continue to pay his nominal wages directly.[44]

The 1914–1915 school year began on September 7, with the school sending out neatly printed orange cards announcing the start of a new school season. The enrollment figure fluctuated between 175 and 200 during the next several months. Besides Shedd and the three assistant superintendents, the school also appointed a secretary, a treasurer, a pianist, an assistant pianist, a house committee, an auditing committee, and a librarian, and a "Teachers' Instruction Class" met on a voluntary basis. Staff turnover was obviously excessive, as Shedd estimated that by this time ninety-four different people had taught or in some other way helped out at the Socialist Sunday School.[45]

In early 1915, Shedd agreed to go to Milwaukee for several months to help organize Sunday schools there. The prospect of doing so in a city with a socialist mayor and thousands of children from socialist families was no doubt very enticing to him. The Rochester Socialist Education Federation and the Socialist Sunday School passed resolutions urging him to return to upstate New York as soon as possible. When Shedd left for Milwaukee in March, Bertha Vossler and Isadore Tischler took charge of the Sunday school. The school ended its fifth season with an outdoor session on May 16, with only 60 children present but with visitors from North Dakota, Ohio, and Troy, New York. A May Day Festival held two weeks earlier had attracted 250 children and adults.[46]

In August 1915, Vossler followed up a letter that she had sent out soon after Shedd left with a meeting to interest members of the local German branch of the Party in the work of the Socialist Sunday School. Vossler's efforts apparently met with little success. The school opened again the following year, but Tischler left, "with great regret," to pursue nighttime studies in New York City. Little else is known about the Rochester school between 1915 and 1917. It is likely that it continued until the summer of 1917, but on a smaller scale. World War I, governmental repression, and the splintering of the radical community may have taken its toll on the Rochester school as was the case elsewhere.[47] But the more direct reason for the demise of the Rochester SSS was the loss of its dynamic and energetic leader. Shedd was so heavily relied upon for leadership and ideas that his departure had a crippling effect on the school's continued functioning. Years later, Isadore Tischler remarked that "after Shedd left Rochester a decline in membership [of the SSS and YPSL] followed, for Shedd was a magnet for the young, well-liked, devoted to the work, and a wonderful organizer." Tischler's wife also recalled that "Sheddie" was "loved by all," was a great speaker and organizer, and indeed was "a great attraction" for the school.[48]

Kendrick Shedd is never mentioned in accounts of the American socialist movement. This is not surprising since he had little to do with Party politics on either the national or local levels. His contributions lay elsewhere, in a realm of radical culture and politics that remained on the periphery of the socialist movement throughout this twenty-year period. But his shortlived yet intense involvement between 1910 and 1917 reveals much about the temper of the times, the nature of the radical movement, and the incredible commitment displayed by some of the Party's unsung grass-roots activists.

There is little in Shedd's early background to predict the prominent role he was to play in the American SSS movement. Born in Lima, New York, in 1866, his father, a Civil War veteran, worked as an employee of the Civil Service. After attending public schools in Rochester, Shedd graduated from the University of Rochester, where he was elected Phi Beta Kappa. He taught school in upstate New York for two years before going abroad to study German and French at universities in Berlin and Paris. Shedd joined the faculty of the University of Rochester and became a full professor of modern languages in 1906. During much of the time that he was a professor at the University of Rochester, he was actively involved in civic affairs. He was secretary of the Good Government Club, which he had helped to organize, and was a speaker at various functions of the public schools, the churches, the religious Sunday schools, and the YMCA and YWCA. He lectured on such topics as the achievements of President Theodore Roosevelt, and in 1906 he attacked socialism in a speech at the old Labor Lyceum. But Shedd was also interested in social welfare issues; he taught languages in a settlement house; he managed a community social center in an immigrant neighborhood; and he directed a Boys' Evening Home for newsboys and bootblacks from 1904 to 1908 and a Sunshine Club for girls.[49]

At the University of Rochester, Shedd was an extremely popular professor. Rush Rhees, President of the University, remarked that Shedd not only performed admirably in the classroom but also did more to foster student spirit and loyalty to the college than any other faculty member. He wrote songs for the university and was known for inviting students to his home for Friday evening parties. Indeed, a former student remembered him sixty-five years later, noting that she still had "a warm spot in [her] heart for this excellent teacher." She described Shedd as "a great favorite, . . . [with] a zest and a flair for the unusual." German songs were sung at the beginning of his German classes, and "we sang them lustily." According to historian Arthur May, it was because of this sterling reputation as a university professor that Shedd received repeated raises in salary.[50]

His close association with immigrant working-class neighborhoods, and the influence of the growing radical movement in

Rochester, prompted Shedd to turn increasingly to the Socialist
Party as an outlet for his social concerns. In 1908, he attended an
address by Eugene Debs. An incident in January 1909 may have further convinced him to adopt a more comprehensive radical vision
and to affiliate with a national political movement. Shedd had been
chosen by Edward Ward, superintendent of playgrounds and social
centers in Rochester, to be director of the social center at Number 9
school. The school was located in the central district of the city, populated in large part by workers who had recently imigrated to the
United States, many of them Jewish. In January, the social center
sponsored a dance and masquerade on a Sunday, which Shedd
chaperoned. Local Catholic and Protestant clergymen, city officials,
and newspaper editorials criticized the day chosen for this event.
Rumors also abounded that women had masqueraded in men's
clothes, and that other "improper acts" had taken place. In a letter
to the mayor, Shedd denied the rumors and accused city officials of
blowing the incident out of proportion because of their general opposition to social centers.

Shedd had written the letter on university stationery and was
attacked in the local newspapers for having done so. Several university officials became concerned about the adverse publicity generated by one of its faculty members. A month later, Lewis Ross, President of the University's Board of Trustees, wrote to the school's
acting president at the time, Professor Henry Burton, strongly criticizing Shedd's attack on the mayor and his use of university stationery, and suggesting that Shedd "be taught 'noblesse oblige.'"
Shedd countered that it was meant to be a private matter between
the mayor and him, and protested against its being made public.[51]

By 1910, Shedd became more actively involved in the local socialist movement by becoming director of the Sunday school and the
Young People's Socialist League. However, several former University of Rochester students strongly assert that Shedd never mentioned socialism or his outside activities in the classroom and he
continued to be immensely popular with his students. The only evidence of Shedd's involvement in socialism on campus was his spon-
sorship in 1911 of a branch of the Intercollegiate Socialist Society. Of
course, this action only served to single him out even more, with
adverse comments being published in the local press.[52]

It was Shedd's continued involvement in socialist activities in
the community that resulted in his departure from the University of
Rochester, after more than twenty years of being a very effective
faculty member. He could easily have avoided the crisis that developed, but he evidently felt that he had entered onto a path from
which he could not (or would not) turn back.[53] In February 1911,
under the auspices of the Women's Civic Club of the social center,
Shedd spoke to nine hundred people on "Privilege's Fear of Democ-

racy." Two days later, the *Rochester Union and Advertiser* attacked the speech, claiming that Shedd had strongly supported socialism and the red flag. Indeed, to some extent Shedd had done so, but he had also made it clear that he was speaking only for himself and not for the University of Rochester or for the social center. Nevertheless, Mayor Hiram Edgerton and various civic and patriotic societies were incensed that Shedd had utilized one of the social centers to "insult" the American flag. The mayor barred Shedd from ever speaking again in a public building in Rochester, including the schools. In a letter to the *Rochester Union and Advertiser* a few days later, Shedd stressed that he was trying to provide a different political emphasis and that the newspaper had in fact distorted his speech by taking words out of context. He characterized the incident as "a tempest in a teapot," and emphasized that it was free speech that was really on trial, not himself. A committee headed by Herbert Weet, assistant school superintendent, cleared Shedd of trying to villify the American flag. Nevertheless, with Shedd present, the Board of Education passed a resolution disapproving of his speech as "essentially a plea for Socialism." Soon after, social centers in Rochester were closed down, perhaps as a result of the adverse publicity that had been generated during the previous two years.

Rush Rhees, President of the University of Rochester at the time, wrote privately that if Shedd were dismissed he would appear as a "martyr to the cause of freedom of thought and speech." Thus, the university, while critical of Shedd's involvement in the controversy, did nothing. During the next several months, however, Shedd addressed a "wildly enthusiastic" city crowd of two thousand on "The Right of Free Speech," and in April he ignored the Mayor's prohibition and spoke in the Shubert Theatre to a large, supportive audience on "Economic Patriotism." He continued to avoid discussing socialism in his university classroom, however, and was never accused of having done so.

By the fall of 1911, George Eastman, Rochester's most famous industrialist, had become increasingly interested in educational work. He and Rhees had become good friends and the university president asked Eastman to contribute more money to the university's endowment fund. Throughout his lifetime, Shedd maintained that he had been told soon afterward by a reliable source that Eastman dangled a possible contribution of one million dollars in front of Rhees, but at the same time told him, "That wild Indian [Shedd] must be fired before I give another penny to the University." Of course, Rhees had already become irritated by the continued unwelcome notoriety that Shedd had brought to the university.

In November 1911, Shedd addressed a pre-election crowd in Auburn, New York. Local Rochester newspapers reported that he was very critical of American patriotism and supportive of atheism and that he stated that the flag of Internationalism was greater than the flag of any single nation. The local press made a big story of the speech, with the *Rochester Post* editorializing that Shedd was unfit to be a university professor. Several weeks later, the university's executive committee of the Board of Trustees recommended that Shedd be asked to resign because his intemperate remarks had brought disrepute on the university and his activities in the community were interfering with his involvement in the higher intellectual concerns for which he was hired. Shedd met with Rhees and reluctantly submitted a letter in which he asked to be retained for two years, during which time he promised not to speak in public. This would give him time to change his vocation, save some money to support his three children, allow hard feelings to die, do his own resigning more honestly, and avoid embarrassment on both sides.

Perhaps out of a protective sense of loyalty to his alma mater, Shedd decided not to wait for the response to his letter and instead resigned "under pressure" on December 1, 1911, to be effective at the end of the academic year. On his own initiative, he promised not to speak in public again until his connections with the university were severed. Shedd declined offers from several university trustees to attempt to secure money to assure his children of a college education, despite the fact that his wife's health problems had left him financially insecure. Shedd's resignation became effective in the summer of 1912, but it became known during the previous spring. One former student later remarked that when the news became known, "the students were crushed." Another former student, stressing that Shedd "never mentioned or discussed his extramural activities on the campus," remembers that the students were "all shocked beyond belief and stirred to our bones to learn later that Sheddie was fired. It was surely a black day for all of us." Another former student recollects that students met at the chapel to give Shedd a gift, for "he was greatly beloved by the student body and a wonderful teacher." The *New York World* editorialized that University of Rochester officials had violated "every principle of intellectual liberty and every right of free speech." Money had exercised "a tyranny over university education worse than in any country outside of Russia." Three years later, Shedd provided his own version of what had transpired:[54]

> Yes, I was very popular in my own city just as long as I preached contentment and success and all the other stuff that the ignorant and designing capitalists so love to have speakers spread. I then had a "lead-pipe cinch" on my job at the university. . . . Just as long as I spread that sort of fool stuff; just as long as I spent my days and my nights (unconsciously) in the

blessed service of the capitalist system, keeping the innocent and the ignorant in beautiful darkness as to the actual conditions of life; just so long I was a "good boy," and a grand influence in the education and inspiration of the young, and my picture was often in the newspapers (outside of the police column). . . .

Then something awful happened. Somebody got me to reading something worth while. I like it. I read some more. I kept on liking it. I began to think; I began to tell of my new ideas, as occasion came—though not in my own class room. . . .

Not in two weeks was I put out of the university, nor in two months; but I was being watched. The enemies of Socialism were on the job with both feet and the rest of their anatomy. . . .

I made one speech too many. Auburn did me up. I spoke there one night with Frank Bohn. My innocent remarks were distorted and twisted in to crimes in the next morning's papers. The college groaned. . . . and I was duly called before the committee of the board of trustees.

After a few days, I was told that my resignation was desired. I wrote it—with a gun behind me, so to speak.

By mid-1912, Shedd was no longer associated with the University of Rochester. While this meant a severe financial loss for him, at the same time Shedd obviously relished the opportunity to devote more of his time to the cause with which he had become so enamored. Shedd's thinking about socialism, as indicated in his various writings and as interpreted by a former associate, was not of a typically Marxian kind.[55] Shedd represented a mix of Christian socialism, Fabianism, and a brand of Marxism that included a conception of the significant role of education and culture in radical change, a viewpoint that many other socialists at the time did not fully embrace. Between 1912 and 1915, Shedd became increasingly involved in all kinds of Socialist ventures. He ran for public office (for example, school commissioner), made numerous speeches, wrote many articles (including a weekly column in the *New York Call* on "Making Young Socialists" in 1915), taught adult classes, and directed the Young People's Socialist League and the Socialist Sunday School. He became so well known in the latter role that he was often invited to other cities and towns to talk about his work (including New York City, Buffalo, Milwaukee, Cleveland, Pittsburgh, Cincinnati, and Chicago) and he was one of the main speakers at a meeting of the Socialist School Union of Greater New York in November 1911 and at the SSS May Day Festival in New York City in 1913. He also received numerous inquiries and wrote many letters about his work at the Rochester school. In 1913, he was asked by Winnie Branstetter of the Woman's National Committee of the Socialist Party to write a special song for Children's Day, which was later used for a Women's Day Program, and he later served for a year (1915–1916) on the editorial staff of the *Young Socialists' Magazine*. Moreover, a participant at an Intercollegiate Socialist Society dinner in New York City wrote in 1914 that "so many people spoke to me in the loveliest terms about 'Shedd and his Sunday school.'" Indeed, Shedd began to perceive himself as a kind of "father figure" to the whole SSS movement. In 1914, he wrote to Thomas Heath Flood of the Brockton school: "Children are the very best things in this whole world. I have three of my own—of my very own—and about two or three thousand that are also my own, although I am not their real father."[56] He drove himself very hard in his work for the socialist movement; even the death of his first wife in 1914 (whom he had married in 1896) did not seem to slow him down in his desire to aid the radical cause.

In the spring of 1915, Shedd agreed to go to Milwaukee to organize young people's clubs and Socialist Sunday schools. What happened during the next two years is unclear, but it appears that five important developments occurred. First, although he was quite successful in organizing three Socialist Sunday schools in Milwaukee, Shedd was disappointed to find that the city's socialist community was neither as cohesive nor as harmonious as he had expected. Second, he faced the harsh reality of working-class life and had to find a way to support himself and his new wife. He tried several jobs, including selling Western Electric washers and ringers in Chicago. Third, he suffered illness and a serious injury, when he accidentally cut his knee with a hatchet, and had to return to upstate New York for treatment several times. Fourth, Shedd stayed in the Milwaukee area for longer than he had originally intended and never returned to work for the Rochester socialist community in any capacity. And fifth, as World War I dragged on, he came to believe that it was necessary for the United States to prepare to enter the conflict. When the Party voted to oppose aggressively United States entrance in the spring of 1917, Shedd left the Party, although he remained on good terms with many of his former associates (including Eugene and Theodore Debs). He left Milwaukee in the fall of 1917, in part because of his estrangement from the German Socialist-dominated Party there but also, he admitted, because he and his second wife (who was teaching public school in Milwaukee) were eager to return to New York State.[57] Shedd's intense career as a socialist organizer, begun seven years earlier, was over.

Later recollections of Shedd from those who knew him are glowing in their affection. Edward Friebert, who was a staff member at the International Socialist Sunday School in Milwaukee, described

Shedd many years later as "a man of rare qualities, a fine teacher and poet. He possessed a magnetic personality and his influence over children could not be exceled [*sic*]." Fifty-four years after Shedd left the Rochester Socialist Sunday School and 16 years after he died, Bertha Vossler remembered "Sheddie" as a man who "loved all children—young and old. He had a special way with the young and they adored and respected him. No *generation gap* whatsoever; Sheddie understood them—could be young with them, sharing their joys, hopes and ideals." Another former associate in Rochester revealed the kind of role that Shedd could play in maintaining and expanding socialist youth work. He recollected that Shedd "had a fine personality and was wonderful with young people. We adored him." Not only that, but "I suppose I stayed as long as I did because of him." Bertha Vossler added, " 'Sheddie' always had new ideas for activities, planned for and around the children—the music, short plays which he wrote, new songs, recitations, solo instrument talents, etc. etc. . . . No wonder children came to the Socialist Sunday School in droves! It was an outlet for their talents, their enthusiasm, their activities—and they loved the Director—'Sheddie!!' "[58]

Kendrick Shedd was a man of great passion, personal magnetism, and above all idealism. He had a deep love for nature and for humanity, and an intense sense of the follies and injustices of industrial America. His daughter has recently suggested that "he stood for what he thought was right, . . . although he lost everything in doing so." And his son believes that although he never complained, Shedd probably "felt he had messed-up his life for a cause that never reached fruition."[59] Such estimations are debatable, however. Clearly, Shedd felt that his talents had not been used to full advantage by the Socialist Party, which he felt was too stodgy and concerned with narrow political matters. It is true as well that in his quest to pursue ideas and activities that were not in the mainstream of Progressive America, he sacrificed not only a comfortable and rewarding career in academia but also the closeness of his family. But even in his old age, Shedd never seems to have displayed any bitterness toward his previous experiences in the socialist movement and the consequences of them. In fact, he expressed the belief that he would rather have been "a has been than a never was." Perhaps Shedd also received comfort in his later years from the many tributes sent to him by former students and friends.[60]

Milwaukee

In December 1914, the Milwaukee County central committee of the Socialist Party authorized Oscar Ameringer, county organizer, to call a meeting of Young People's Socialist clubs to discuss employing

Kendrick Shedd as director of the young people's movement in Milwaukee. Ameringer had visited the Rochester SSS and was interested in livening up the young people's movement in Milwaukee. Shedd seemed to be an ideal choice for such a task. Ameringer had approached Shedd during the previous spring and fall; the main problem was in convincing Party officials in Milwaukee of the value of the work and the suitability of hiring Shedd. While Shedd continued his work in Rochester, Ameringer held meetings in the early months of 1915, attempting to enlist support for his idea from various district branches, women's clubs, and the Young People's Welfare Commission. In January, a letter about SSS work written by Shedd, entitled "Ten Reasons Why," was published in the influential *Milwaukee Leader*.[61]

At a March 16, 1915, meeting of the Young People's Welfare Commission, a plan for socialist children's activities was proposed, "the purpose being to get the young people together systematically, with programs made up of talks by well known local Socialists, music by the Socialist young people's clubs and other features calculated to entertain and instruct." The matter was to be taken up "with the women's branches before definite steps are decided on." Two days later, the North Ward branch of the Party's Woman's Agitation Committee donated one hundred dollars to establish a Socialist Sunday School in Milwaukee. This action allowed Ameringer to finalize matters with Shedd, who arrived in Milwaukee ten days later.[62]

The day after Shedd arrived in Milwaukee, he explained the work of the Sunday schools to interested Milwaukee socialists. During the next several days, however, Shedd was confronted with the jealousy and friction existing within the Milwaukee radical community. Some members of the Young People's Welfare Commission disputed Ameringer's authority to give the go-ahead on organizing Sunday schools in Milwaukee. Shedd also found that the North Side and South Side clubs did not get along well with the West Side club. Nevertheless, efforts to establish Sunday schools proceeded smoothly. At a Party meeting on April 2, at which Eugene Debs spoke, Ameringer introduced Shedd as "the Sunday School man," gave a talk on the importance of SSS work, and urged Party members to attend the school's first session on April 4. One hundred and nine children, five to fifteen years of age, and sixty-three adults were at the first meeting of the Milwaukee Socialist Sunday School at Freie Gemeinde Hall on Fourth Street. Shedd spoke to the children about being "good rebels" and led the singing of radical songs. Greetings were sent to Debs, who had returned to Terre Haute, and to the Rochester Socialist Sunday School. Plans were discussed to establish schools in other parts of the city and seven dollars was collected. At the second session, 121 children and 109 adults attended, including Victor and Meta Berger. Oscar Ameringer played the flute while his wife played the piano, letters from Theodore Debs and John Schmidt of the Rochester school were read, songs were sung, a lesson on "internationalism" was conducted, nine dollars was collected, and plans for a May Day festival and a June Field Day were made.[63]

Although he was greatly encouraged by these developments, Shedd continued to face problems. On April 13, for instance, Emil Seidel, a former socialist mayor of Milwaukee, told Shedd that he was not in favor of Socialist Sunday schools being established there. He claimed that they would be an unnecessary antagonism to local religious and educational groups. During the same week, a mother informed Shedd that she would not send her daughters to the school because she feared that if they imbibed socialism at too early an age, they might become anarchists. (Shedd sarcastically noted that such a view was simply "wonderful logic.") In addition, while at first he could only "wonder when you come to think of it that such a thing [a Socialist Sunday School] was not established years ago" in Milwaukee, he soon realized that "the Socialists of that city have always had voters in mind. Voters are grown-ups. They are needed at once in order to 'win' a city. The training to Socialism has hardly been thought of." But Shedd also had problems with those Milwaukee socialists who took an interest in the schools. He found it necessary to argue in print that "old-time" comrades were wrong in thinking that a lot of singing was a sign of weakness, emotionalism, and sentimentalism. Two months later, he told SSS teachers about related concerns. He called their attention to "certain unenlightened criticisms which are being passed on our American Socialist Sunday School. . . . These people do not realize that we have a mixed population which is quite different from the homogeneous population in Germany, and must be appealed to and handled in quite a different fashion. They would have German cast-iron, military 'schulmeister' methods used. We don't want them. They would soon kill the spirit of the Socialist Sunday School." Perhaps Shedd's critics wanted to adopt the kind of "Golden Text of the Day" lessons that had prevailed in the short-lived Haverhill, Massachusetts, school. Finally, "turf" problems also continued in Milwaukee, as the Young People's Welfare Commission announced that it would devote itself only to the young people's clubs, not to children's activities, since the Sunday schools had been initiated "under other auspices."[64]

The first Milwaukee SSS continued in operation through the first week of July, when it closed until after Labor Day. Average attendance during May and June was about 175 students and 65 adults, with over 200 children attending several of the sessions. At the May Pageant, over 200 children and 30 adults took part, and so many people came to see it that "hundreds were turned away." The production was repeated two weeks later and again "the house was filled." One of the teachers, Eliza Taylor Cherdron, was so impressed by the pageant that she was moved to refer to Shedd as "a genius teacher of Socialism, using new and striking methods." She went on: "How new? How striking? By simply using his drama full of Socialist color, thought and action, to attract and teach the hundreds of kiddies and kiddies' friends. The big ideas of Socialism are impressively put into the minds and hearts of the children actors and they in turn pass on these big ideas in a way never to be forgotten. And what are these big ideas? The class consciousness of the workers of all nations, the causes and results of war and peace; the necessity of all workers to struggle for social and industrial justice!"[65]

Shedd also helped to organize two other Socialist Sunday schools in Milwaukee during the spring of 1915. Because the school at Freie Gemeinde Hall had grown so large, another North Side school was established at Bahn Frei Turn Hall, on 12th Street and North Avenue. Its first morning session on May 23 drew about thirty-five children and ten adults, with Shedd contending that it had not been well advertised. At the second session, sixty-three children and eighteen students attended, and, Shedd believed, "the spirit was excellent." By mid-June the second school had an enrollment of eighty children and eighteen adults. A third school opened on the South Side of Milwaukee, with thirty-two children and twenty adults registering at its first meeting. On June 20, a joint picnic of all three schools was held. Although she praised Shedd's efforts, a visitor from New Orleans later reported that she was surprised that the picnic had not been better attended and wondered if more publicity from the *Leader* and more support from the local socialist community was needed. Still, three months after Shedd arrived in Milwaukee, three schools had opened. While more teachers and funding were needed for the next school term, hopes were high that such problems would soon be resolved.[66]

With the new fall term approaching, a referendum was held in which Party members were asked whether or not the Sunday schools should be continued. Although most Party members did not bother to vote, the results were overwhelmingly positive, with a 511 to 67 vote in favor of continuation. The school at Freie Gemeinde Hall opened the 1915–1916 season with 141 children and 59 adults in attendance. Shedd was back in upstate New York but was considered to be the honorary superintendent who would be returning soon. He did return in mid-October with his wife and son, and immediately began presiding over the second Milwaukee school, the North Side SSS. Its first session drew 59 children; by the beginning of 1916, the North Side school had 260 children and 70 adults, although teachers continued to be "badly needed." It was not until the middle of March that the South Side SSS started up again. It is not clear why the opening was delayed. The school continued on a relatively small scale, with twenty-seven children and twenty-five adults attending its first session. In early April 1916, a newly-formed Milwaukee SSS Association sponsored a first anniversary celebration. Mayor Daniel Hoan and Sheriff Edmund T. Melms spoke, and each child received a socialist button. During the same month, three hundred SSS students, led by Shedd, sang for a large electoral campaign crowd that included the Ameringers, the Bergers, Melms, Hoan, George Lunn (mayor of Schenectady), and other prominent socialists. The three schools continued meeting until mid-June, when they closed for the summer.[67]

The North Side SSS opened the 1916–1917 school year with Eliza Taylor Cherdron in charge and Mrs. Oscar Ameringer and Edward Friebert leading the singing. (Shedd was in New York recuperating from illness.) At its third session, 255 children and adults were present, and Glenn Turner, who was running for State Assembly, addressed the children. By mid-November, the school claimed an attendance of 220 children and 80 adults and had adopted the slogan, "WATCH US GROW!" At about the same time, the South Side SSS started up again, and in November a third school, now directed by Edmund Melms (who had succeeded Ameringer as the Party's county organizer), also began meeting. Melms introduced lectures on "The A, B, C's of Capital," perhaps the kind of rigid educational drilling that Shedd had cautioned against when he first came to Milwaukee.[68]

In late December 1916, the North Side school changed its name to the International Socialist Sunday School, its name for the next half dozen years. Teenagers Tillie Hampel and Tynne Paalu (who, as a child, had been a student in Shedd's Rochester school) took charge of the kindergarten class, which they named the "Helen Keller class." A class of girls, led by Mrs. Oscar Ameringer, was called the "Charlotte Perkins Gilman class." A boy's class was referred to as the "Eugene V. Debs class." At an end-of-the-year Yuletide celebration, four hundred children and adults attended. One person dressed up as Santa Claus, a letter from Shedd (who was in New York State) was read, and the children were given candy, nuts, and fruit. A similar celebration was held at the Milwaukee SSS, with Melms acting as Santa Claus and every adult and child being given a stocking full of candies, nuts, cakes, and popcorn.[69]

Despite the growth of the SSS movement during 1915 and 1916, Eliza Taylor Cherdron, for one, was not satisfied with the level of support that the schools had received from local socialists. The year began with Cherdron, who was heading the International SSS, sharply criticizing "the Socialist members of the public school board for their failure to appear and co-operate with the Sunday school." More teachers and funding were still desperately needed. The International school initiated a membership campaign (with a slogan of "Five hundred at the beginning of 1918"), held a toboggan party in February to attract new recruits to both its teacher and student ranks, and placed a large advertising sign on the west side of Vizay's Hall, where the school now met. At the same time, Melms's school celebrated its second anniversary in April, with Melms optimistically announcing that in the very near future, "the Socialist Sunday schools would be an important factor in the Socialist movement in America." He urged Milwaukee socialists to provide more support for the schools in the community. The school on the South Side opened again, with Shedd identified as in charge but little else reported about it.[70]

The three Milwaukee schools continued to meet until the end of May. Beginning in the summer of 1917, tensions within Party ranks intensified over its strong anti-war stand and in response to the ensuing repressive climate. Some with ties to SSS work, like John Spargo, May Wood Simons, Lucien Sanial, and Kendrick Shedd, left the Party. Others, like Ira Yingst of Kenosha (and later Frederick Krafft of Newark, Abraham Shiplacoff of Brownsville, and William Kruse of Chicago), were indicted or arrested. While the Milwaukee schools must have suffered from these developments, they continued to operate much as before. One change that did take place in the fall of 1917 concerned the renaming of the Milwaukee SSS as the Milwaukee Socialist Propaganda School. Perhaps this change reflected a more overt declaration of the school's mission as perceived by Melms. One children's class was actually referred to as "ABC Socialist studies." The South Side school was now also being directed by Melms, and was renamed Socialist Propaganda School No. 2.[71]

The International SSS began the 1917–1918 school year in another location and with a new superintendent, Carl Haessler. Haessler was born in Milwaukee in 1888 and graduated from the University of Wisconsin-Madison. He became a socialist while he was studying as a Rhodes Scholar at Oxford University in England for three years. He received his Ph.D. from the University of Illinois and taught philosophy there from 1914 to 1917, during which time he helped to organize a chapter of the Intercollegiate Socialist Society. Drafted into the military service in mid-1917, he refused to serve, contending that the war was an imperialist and capitalist venture in which he would not participate. He was then dismissed from the University of Illinois. Haessler returned to Milwaukee, worked for the *Milwaukee Leader*, and with his wife Mildred, quickly became involved in the work of the International Socialist Sunday School.[72]

Enrollments in the three Milwaukee schools remained stable, with the two Propaganda schools reporting a combined total of 250 students and the International SSS about 200 students. There is no evidence of close cooperation among the three schools, however, and two separate May Pageants were held in 1918. At the International school's pageant, Richard Elsner, a local attorney who was soon to be elected Register of Deeds in Milwaukee, addressed the audience on "The Necessity of More Socialist Sunday Schools." It may have been difficult for SSS activists in Milwaukee to take the suggestion seriously that more schools could be organized when they were continuing to report that "the need for more teachers is being keenly felt."[73]

The Socialist Sunday schools in Milwaukee got off to an uncertain start in the fall of 1918, largely because of a nationwide influenza epidemic. At various times public school sessions and public meetings in Milwaukee were banned. In addition, the attention of local Party activists was diverted by several immediate crises, such as the indictment of Victor Berger, and serious financial difficulties for the *Milwaukee Leader*. Two schools finally opened on November 17: the South Side Socialist Propaganda School and the International SSS, now headed by Mildred Haessler. (Carl Haessler had been sentenced to the Fort Leavenworth, Kansas penitentiary for refusing military service.) The International school had ten classes and voted to affiliate with the national organization being formed by the Party's Young People's Department. Both schools continued meeting throughout the school year, holding their own May Pageants and summer picnics, but the third school never opened.[74]

During the fall of 1919, a time of severe internecine struggles and government repression, the two schools continued to operate. However, with no explanation contained in press accounts, the Socialist Propaganda School suddenly announced in early 1920 that its program was being "postponed indefinitely." Its closing was the result of insufficient staff and funding, but perhaps also a lack of interest from children who did not want to attend Sunday morning lectures on the "ABCs of Socialism."[75] This left the International SSS as the only school still functioning in Milwaukee. It was the result of Kendrick Shedd's first efforts in the spring of 1915, and it was in its sixth season. The school took a particular interest in supporting the work of the Prison Comfort Club, which helped the families of comrades in prison, but otherwise the school continued its normal operations. A February 1920 masked ball, sponsored as a school benefit, attracted 300 people, with 125 children attending an earlier afternoon event, and in May the school presented Carl Haessler's socialist version of "Jack and the Beanstalk."[76]

Milwaukee remained governed by a socialist mayor and the *Milwaukee Leader* continued to publish, but the Milwaukee radical movement could not escape the devestating effects of several years of repression and internal rancor. In the summer of 1920, for example, the North Side YPSL split into factions. In addition, Party activists and the *Leader* were experiencing less influence in city politics. Still, for the next three years the International Socialist Sunday School continued to meet. The school opened the 1920–1921 season with the good news that Carl Haessler was to be released from prison. When he returned to Milwaukee in late October, 250 SSS children welcomed him back, giving him a large basket of flowers and singing songs rehearsed especially for him. Haessler gave a short talk, explaining to the children "why a few people who think the government is wrong would rather be punished than do the wrong." While he worked full-time for the *Leader* and gave various speeches in Milwaukee and elsewhere, Mildred Haessler continued to take direct charge of the school. The "Jack and the Beanstalk" pageant was performed again at a Yuletide celebration and a new Haessler play, an altered version of "Aladdin and the Wonderful Lamp," comprised the school's fourth annual May pageant. The school ended its year in early June and a school picnic was held in Sherman Park that attracted about two hundred children and adults.[77]

The SSS movement in Milwaukee now functioned in a vacuum, with few other Socialist Sunday schools in operation nationwide and an association with a greatly weakened political movement. Buoyed by the continued though diminished socialist presence in Milwaukee, local activists struggled to keep alive the idea of socialist weekend schools for working-class children. The International Socialist Sunday School opened for another season on September 25, 1921, this time meeting at the Labor Lyceum on 8th and Garfield Avenues. Revenue to support the school was obtained by penny collections from the children, proceeds from the annual pageant and other entertainments, and donations from friendly organizations and individuals. General course lessons focused on "Geography and Socialism" and the school placed pictures all around of prominent socialists such as Karl Marx. Children representing fourteen different nationalities enrolled at the school. However, a headline in the *Milwaukee Leader* highlighted what continued to be one of the school's most pressing problems: "More Teachers Are Needed in Sunday School."[78]

In early 1922, Carl and Mildred Haessler moved away from Milwaukee and ended their involvement with the International Socialist Sunday School.[79] At the same time, another school was organized, named the South Side Worker's International School. It referred to itself as another "Party Sunday School" and traced its lifeline to Shedd's old South Side school. At its first session, thirty-four children and sixteen adults attended, and Leo Wolfsohn, its superintendent, led the assemblage in the singing of socialist songs and a discussion of the meaning of the phrase, "Workers of the World, Unite." This second school continued to meet throughout the year, but very little else is known about it and it probably never reopened.[80]

The final year of the SSS movement in Milwaukee was 1922–1923, with Leo Wolfsohn, who worked for the *Milwaukee Leader*, heading the International Socialist Sunday School. The school planned special activities every sixth week, for example "grand marches," festivals, and the like, and hoped to buy "a motion picture machine." At a November festival, one hundred children participated in the recitations, singing, and dancing, and a letter from the Haesslers was read. A school picnic was held at Lincoln Park in July, with an account of the affair, titled "Having a Pleasant Day at Sunday School Picnic," and an accompanying photograph appearing in the *Leader*.[81]

During the fall of 1923, the *Milwaukee Leader* carried an occasional announcement about the planned opening of the International school and its intention to attract more adult members. It appears that by the end of 1923, however, all that remained of the SSS movement in Milwaukee were the memories of its many former students, teachers, helpers, parents, and audiences. At the same time that Grace Wolfsohn and two other members of the local Commonwealth League protested against military propaganda in the Milwaukee public schools, in particular the glorification of war "heroes" in history textooks, there was no alternative formal weekend education available for children from the radical working-class.[82] While supporters reacted with some consternation and even bitterness about the closing of the last Socialist Sunday School in Milwaukee, there was no interest, energy, or funding left in 1923 to produce a different outcome.

CHAPTER FOUR

Organizing Socialist Sunday Schools

Rationales, Problems, and Governance

One of the salient characteristics of the American Socialist Sunday School movement was its lack of uniformity. Obviously, the schools shared a profound sense of the evils of capitalism and of the need for socialism in the United States, as well as a belief that the socialist vision needed to be communicated to working-class children in an educational setting. Jessie Wallace Hughan summarized the primary goal of this educational movement at the time as to teach "the value of the Socialist spirit and cooperative effort."[1] But the character of individual schools differed from place to place, with regard to size, facilities, teaching experience of staff members, and curriculum materials. Attempts to coordinate activities and centralize aspects of school life were usually limited and unsuccessful. In certain cities, such as New York and Chicago, steps were taken to encourage communication between schools in the same area, but most schools evolved so separately that they hardly noticed each other's existence. Some SSS supporters valued this autonomy. For many others, lack of coordination was a constant frustration.

For the historian, such a situation points to the difficulty of reconstructing a profile of the "ideal" Socialist Sunday School. Clearly, there was no such thing. But the evidence does allow for a description of the most important characteristics of this educational movement. It allows for the following questions about school life to be addressed: What specific reasons were given by socialist youth activists for organizing the Sunday schools? What serious problems did SSS advocates face? And how were most of the schools organized, governed, and financed?

Rationales for the Establishment of
Socialist Sunday Schools

Different reasons for opening Socialist Sunday schools were emphasized by SSS advocates. While one rationale may have been advanced with more passion than others at a particular school, supporters generally argued that the Sunday schools could fulfill three closely related needs for workers' children and for American radicalism: (1) to help counteract capitalist influences; (2) to help establish a sense of continuity and community; and (3) to help spread an intelligent understanding and acceptance of socialist principles and Socialist Party positions.

Virtually all elements of the American culture were seen by SSS supporters as "pernicious influences" on the children of the working class. The church and the press, for instance, were portrayed by Kendrick Shedd as "mainly in the hands of our enemies" and "doing their level best to educate [the children] away from 'us.'" Shedd often would repeat the biblical admonition, "As the twig is bent, the tree inclineth," and counterpose the efforts of such institutions as the Catholic Church to proselytize against socialist principles. Similarly, a SSS student entered a 1916 essay contest in the *New York Call* on "What Is New York's Most Helpful Institution," choosing the Socialist Sunday schools and highlighting their efforts to "break the false illusions which the papers, such as the Evening Journal and the Evening World [*sic*], create from false ideas the capitalists give to these papers."[2] Reminiscent of later cultural critics, mass entertainment also was occasionally villified for its effects on working-class youth. Shedd, for example, lamented the extent to which "the young are being systematically 'doped' into a condition of insensibility toward the vital things of life. They are being baseballized and funny-paperized and tangoized and pleasurized and motion-picturized until they have no thought of anything worth while [*sic*] in life." The Boy Scouts and Girl Scouts, the YMCA, and similar mainstream youth organizations were also a source of concern to SSS supporters. Indeed, E. J. Ross of New York City suggested that the Sunday schools constituted part of the "solution" to "the Boy Scout problem."[3]

Most of the arguments put forth by SSS proponents, however, focused on the anti-progressive influence of the public schools. Supporters of the socialist schools repeatedly pointed out that the education offered by the public schools, as William Kruse of the Party's Young People's Department put it, "is certainly not a working-class education." Indeed, Kruse argued, "we cannot expect it to be, we do not expect it to be. If the children of to-day [*sic*] were to be taught the truth about the history, resources, and conditions of their country, there would be some mighty big changes made by the men and women of tomorrow, the children of today." He criticized the "hero worship" approach to American history that prevailed in the public schools, maintaining that it amounted to "a fairy tale of impossibly virtuous heroes doing a lot of unbelievably wise and noble things." He concluded, "We must oppose their work with a counter effort that will be constructive and effective. . . . We must supplement Socialist education to that of the public schools if we would counteract the work of the masters."[4]

As early as 1907, Frances Gill, one of the first Party members in New York City to support the establishment of Socialist Sunday schools, forcefully criticized aspects of public school instruction. Sounding much like critical theorists of many decades later, she wrote:

> The relation of children to life and the truth about life—their life, the life which surges all around them—are not taught in the public schools. Even the dead and buried life of past centuries is never presented from the standpoint of the worker, and his children are compelled to accept the teachings of bourgeois educators, inoculated with bourgeois prejudices, in regard to what he holds to be a vital misconception of facts. They are taught to admire and reverence certain characters in history. Awe and respect for the great and deferential attitude towards superiority of rank or station is inculcated, if not directly at least by implication. But the collective name of the man—worker—who has borne all the burdens of the world and had made all its greatness possible, is never heard. Historically, Labor is utterly ignored, and contemporaneously, if considered at all, it is an aspect of inferiority.

Gill argued, "It is inconceivable that the children of the workingmen should receive their only education and preparation for life from schools whose every interest is bound up in the maintenance and perpetuation of their own oppression." It followed, then, that since "the educational system of the elementary schools is not adapted to the needs of the workingmen's child, it should be supplemented by an organized effort to correct its faults of omission and commission."[5]

Numerous other examples of the conservative nature of public school instruction were offered by advocates of Socialist Sunday schools. In 1911, the staff of the newly organized Philadelphia SSS contributed one of the most vitriolic attacks:

> Molded, twisted and unshaped in the furnace of the capitalist educational system that is filled with the poisonous gases of capitalist teachings and preachings, the minds of our children

become not the means for independent thought, but rather narrow chambers of matter and tissue with no capacity for that grandest and most profound of all things, Reason.

Our children's minds become the prey of wild patriotism and false conceptions of right and wrong. When they grow up they do not carry in themselves the thought and feeling that mankind is living for something better, but they are rather inspired with a mad desire to carry on the game of competition in society with a cold and merciless cruelty.

Our children become (if they ever become anything) the chemists, engineers, geologists and lawyers who merely form the instruments which the capitalist class employs in enriching itself. They merely become the tools which the capitalist employes [*sic*] in getting wealth. They do not become the vanguard of intellectual progress.

It should be part of the Socialist campaign of education of the working class to save our children from this.

Members of the 11th and 12th wards of the Party in Philadelphia therefore "decided to open a Sunday school for children where the beauties and truth of the Socialist teachings should be revealed to them. . . . [A] new road will be opened to the minds of the little ones. This road will not lead them to become austere thinkers, hiding the beauties of childhood from them, but it will bring them to a field set with the gems and flowers of the Socialist philosophy, while over their heads will rise like a shining rainbow the hopes and aspirations of a better mankind."[6]

Among the problems that SSS proponents faced from 1900 to 1920 was that not all radicals adopted such a critical view of public school instruction, or at least many chose to argue instead that the public school system should be supported, since it continued to represent a real advance in the fortunes of the working class. Supporters of the Socialist Sunday schools thus took great pains to emphasize their positive stance toward the public school idea while criticizing public school practice. The practices of the public schools, controlled as they were by the capitalist class (or state), necessitated the development of a supplementary socialist education in the form of Sunday schools. The very existence of hegemonic culture, then, created the force of counterhegemony: "If the Public School system were what it should be there would be no need for Socialist Schools."[7]

Socialist Sunday School activists sought not only to promote the contestation of capitalist culture but also to foster a greater attachment to the socialist movement. The Sunday schools could help to encourage a lifelong affiliation with the radical community, despite so many adverse influences. There were many informal ways to convey socialist culture and politics to the young, through familial influences, Party local affairs, parades, newspapers, and clubs. But SSS supporters stressed that the weekend schools could provide a more systematic effort in a more formal structure. Kendrick Shedd even discussed the possibility that a generation gap might develop between radical elders and the young, especially in the face of the overwhelming anti-progressive influences that dominated capitalist America. The Sunday school could help to encourage in the young an appreciation for the efforts of the old and could help foster in the old a willingness to "pass on the gavel" and thus "encourage the young." The staff of the West Hoboken school similarly worried in 1910 that "a large percentage of children of Socialists and sympathizers are lost to the movement every year. The parents, either through inability to render the subject interesting or from some other cause, allow the children to go astray as a result of the patriotic teachings of the public schools or the influence of the capitalist press."[8] The local Socialist Sunday School could assure a more promising socialist future by helping to prevent this loss to the radical community.

In many locations there was a concerted effort to develop a school into a community center, where parents and older siblings, as well as SSS children, could gather and feel part of a supportive group of like-minded people. One former participant of the Brownsville SSS remembers it as "fun" to attend and as resembling a "social center." Members of the school reported in 1917 that they were particularly interested in giving children "a place where they may come together while young and learn the principles of sociability, friendship and companionship." This approach would nurture an atmosphere in which allegiance to the socialist movement was natural and enjoyable. As Frances Gill pointed out, socialism was something to be acquired, not inherited. The next generation of socialists needed a forum for this acquisition to occur, spread, and be seen as an important and enjoyable aspect of their lives.[9]

It was also appealing to some radical immigrant parents to think that these weekend schools could not only teach their offspring to be "good rebels" for the working-class cause but also help them to become Americanized. This was the case for one family of children who attended a Socialist Sunday School in Manhattan composed mostly of children from immigrant families. The sisters who attended the school were the children of Lithuanian Jews who had immigrated to the Lower East Side in 1890. While their mother stayed at home to care for five children, their father made little boys' sailor suits and women's heavy cloth coats, working "12 or 14 hours a day, [in] sweatshop conditions." Years later, the eldest sister remembered that she and the other children practiced speaking English and learned English literature (such as the works of Charles Dickens) at the Socialist Sunday School, while also being introduced to such things as "white bread and peanut butter."[10]

By the middle of the second decade, a number of socialist activists envisioned a network of youth organizations that would feed directly into the Socialist Party of America: first, attendance at the Socialist Sunday School; then, membership in the Junior Young People's Socialist League and the Young People's Socialist League; and finally, membership and active involvement in the Socialist Party local. This formal network of affiliation would help to insure a continuity of socialist traditions. The Party needed to have "active, working members of the party" in the future, and the Sunday schools could help to realize this significant goal. Indeed, it was not unusual for enthusiastic SSS activists to refer to the children attending the schools as "little rebel folks," "the future revolutionists," or as Shedd, who often wrote with dramatic flair, put it, "comrades-in-embryo."[11]

Socialist Sunday schools in at least three locations were given credit for enhancing radical fortunes. At the 1911 meeting of the New York State Committee of the Party, it was reported that the Rochester SSS had increased the growth of the Party local. Delegates then passed a motion recommending that locals throughout New York State organize Socialist Sunday schools. In 1915, the East Side SSS in Manhattan reported that most of its graduates had become Party members and that they were usually "the most ardent workers" for the movement. And Martin Weber claimed that SSS work in Pittsburgh had resulted in "a new stimulus to the party. Every one is more active." Indeed, Shedd argued, working in the Socialist Sunday schools had quite a salutary effect on the older comrades: "They grow in the process. They themselves become inoculated. They grow enthusiastic. They grow in spirit and in purpose. They renew their youth and light anew the slumbering fire. . . . They grow less crusty. Their heart beats a little faster. They are helping. . . . Nothing so deepens and beautifies living like altruistic service."[12]

For the present and for the future, for adults and for children, the Sunday schools could foster a stronger and more integrated radical community. They could develop into centers of activity, where "people of all ages can find an application for their energies and a means of mental and moral advancement." The schools could help "to reach the fathers and mothers," that is, they could bring "parents into the movement" who may not otherwise have become involved.[13] At the same time, the voters of the future would develop a stronger attachment to radical politics.

A related rationale offered by supporters of the Socialist Sunday schools was that they could strengthen children's understand-

ing of socialism and provide "training . . . for the coming Cooperative Commonwealth."[14] Exactly what would constitute appropriate
training was not always made clear nor agreed upon, but the next
generation of workers would at least be exposed to a body of knowledge and a way of thinking that they would not otherwise receive.
Two former students of the International SSS in Milwaukee vividly
recall being taught the need for equality and democracy, put succinctly as "a better deal for the common man." Another former student at the same school remembers lessons on "some fundamental
ideas about socialism."[15] In 1909, the staff of the Los Angeles Children's Socialist Lyceum reported a similar emphasis on providing
the children of the working class with "a correct knowledge of history and economics." And Esther Sussman of the Hartford school
stressed that children there were taught "the fundamentals of scientific Socialism so that when they grow up they may be able to face
and overcome the social problems of the day with intelligence and
broadmindedness."[16] Whatever specific form the instruction took,
the children were given "some elementary understanding of what
the working class was fighting for."[17]

Activists like Shedd were aware of widespread rejection of socialist tenets by the working class despite the existence of conditions
at work and at home that seemed to favor a radical movement. Shedd
was "frankly more interested in the younger than the older generation" to correct this problem. It would take time and different conditions to implement a thorough socialist education for children of the
working class, but in the meantime weekend schools could be organized so that "the young may be led to thinking" and not "have to
be bent back into shape when they got older, as you and I did."[18]
While Shedd was particularly fervent about his work with children,
radicals generally perceived the child as "a symbol of incredible importance." They looked to the new generation with great hope that
it would "transform the world into a better place."[19] Sunday school
advocates argued that youth work was not the only important area
in which to devote one's time and energy. It was simply another one
that deserved support.

Problems

Opposition and Indifference within the Party

Supporters of the Socialist Sunday schools encountered many
problems. In fact, despite their earnest and emotional arguments,
their most serious problems resulted primarily from the apathy and
opposition of their fellow radicals. This meant not only a lack of
support to establish Sunday schools but also a lack of funds, mate-

rials, teachers, facilities, and so on to carry on their work once schools were organized.

During most of this twenty-year period, the Party's national and state leadership offered limited support at best to the schools, despite repeated requests from SSS advocates for financial, curricular, and organizational assistance. Party officials were even less supportive of the Sunday schools than they were of the Young People's Socialist League. At the national convention in Indianapolis in May 1912, for instance, a resolution of support for YPSL was adopted without debate, but there was no similar resolution concerning the Sunday schools.[20] In 1915, Kendrick Shedd, active in the YPSL and SSS movements, complained that "the Young People's Socialist movement is already established and has a national secretary in the national office at Chicago. The more fundamental and important Socialist Sunday school movement is still a homeless wanderer. Its true guardian will not own it, as 'the time is not ripe.' "[21]

During the first few years after its founding, the Socialist Party perceived the public school as an enterprise that would ultimately embrace socialist doctrine. Many Party members feared that Sunday school work might drain time, funds, and energy needed for other struggles, including making the public schools more democratic, electing Socialists to political office, recruiting workers to the movement, and providing for the education of adult workers. This feeling was well expressed by Anna Maley, who served as national organizer of the Woman's National Committee of the Party. Maley did teach for a short time in a Socialist Sunday School in New York City, believing that this field of work "seems a most fruitful one for practical and valuable service for the reason that the young minds so readily grasp the truths which we are trying to teach." But at the same time, she reacted angrily to a comment published in *The Worker*, about its being "imbecile to allow from eight to ten plastic, formative years to pass without an effort to sow the seed of our economic faith." She countered that although she was willing to give such Sunday school work a trial, it was not imbecile to "choose lines of Socialist activity that respond to the intimate present needs of the party rather than those that promise return in the remote future." She questioned spending too much time with children, suggesting that SSS supporters needed to "recognize our limitations" and to realize that every active Party member already "carries heavy burdens in addition to his daily grind."[22] Indeed, weekend schools could never be a serious alternative to institutions that educated the mass of working-class children, and thus they seemed to be a luxury to a movement struggling to become a viable alternative force in American politics. In 1913, despite (or because of) the prevalence of women working in the Sunday schools, the Woman's National Committee of the Party adopted a resolution that suggested that "these schools assume rather the nature of social centers, and that greater energy should be expended toward capturing the public school system and using it for the benefit of the working class."[23]

Several of the more moderate socialists, concerned with presenting a "respectable" face of radical politics, also questioned the establishment of Socialist Sunday schools because they seemed unnecessarily antagonistic to the public school system and to local religious groups. For instance, in Milwaukee, as elsewhere, Catholics frequently denounced socialists as atheists and infidels. So as not to alienate such groups further, Emil Seidel, one-time socialist mayor, refused to endorse the Sunday schools. Shedd described Seidel as "mortally afraid of offending some church" and unwilling "to listen to us when we assure him that we are not founding another church." Years later, Edward Friebert, former choir director of the International SSS in Milwaukee, recounted that many of the older Party comrades in Milwaukee were opposed to the school mainly for political reasons: "They were in fear of loosing [*sic*] . . . votes from the liberal religious people." He blamed local Party officials like Victor Berger for placing too much emphasis on election results.[24] Other socialists were suspicious of any youth work, arguing that if young people progressed along a socialist path too early and too quickly, they might become too radical and undisciplined, which would threaten the gradualist approach of the Party.

Some socialists also worried that it was, in fact, improper and perhaps counterproductive for inexperienced weekend teachers to attempt to educate children in the basics of socialism. At the National Socialist Party Congress in 1910, for example, Morris Hillquit of New York, a leading Party theorist, stated: "The mind of the child is too sacred to be made the object of rough experiments, and Socialist Sunday schools conducted with insufficient skill or method often do more harm than good."[25] Besides, older comrades had obviously become "good rebels" without such schools, and it was only in the experience of working, of being exploited each day by the capitalist class, that one developed a true appreciation for the merits of socialist agitation. Hence, a proper socialist education for children should follow, not precede, the creation of the Cooperative Commonwealth. Until then, socialists should work for industrial and political changes that would help usher in a socialist society. After all, neither Marx nor Engels urged the formation of such Sunday schools in any of their writings.

What exacerbated this problem of a lack of support was that SSS participants also found themselves criticized by those who endorsed the idea of weekend schools but who opposed the specific teaching that was (allegedly) taking place within them. Arguments proceeded from opposite directions. Some radicals complained bitterly about the prevalence of "soft" teaching. They argued that, because of unsystematic instruction, children would fail to develop into good socialists. Children spent too much time playing games, singing songs, going on picnics, and engaging in other frivolous distractions. Others similarly charged the schools with bourgeois or hazy sentimentalism, and with failing to provide a clear and realistic focus on class struggle. On the other hand, other advocates of the Sunday school idea condemned the fruitless and possibly alienating attempts in the schools to cram abstract economic concepts into the heads of the children. There was a feeling among these critics that many of the teachers understood socialism but not children, that they were "enthusiasts [who] ultimately succumb to lack of information in pedagogy and psychology."[26]

Socialist Sunday School teachers were thus being cautioned not to teach above the heads of their students and not to simplify political and economic matters to the point of superficiality. In 1920, David Berenberg of New York City briefly addressed the problem and in doing so expressed both kinds of criticisms: "Some have sought to teach 'Socialism' to immature children, entirely overlooking the fact that 'Socialism' as a system of political thought presupposes a great deal of historical knowledge and requires a thorough understanding of economics. Other schools, in an endeavor to avoid the dogmatic teaching of Socialism, have taught a watery reformism or a stupid and incorrect version of evolution and anthropology, totally unrelated to Socialism."[27] Such a pedagogical dilemma was not unique to socialist educators. What is important here is that such criticisms further lessened support for a movement that for most of this twenty-year period lacked the formal endorsement, let alone active assistance, of the Party's national office.

SSS activists took special note of the lack of tangible support provided to them and directly responded to the criticisms leveled against their work. In 1911, for example, E. J. Ross complained that "the Socialist party as such has done very little to further this movement. Instead of considering it as a most important factor in the rearing of future warriors to carry on the battle against exploitation . . . , this movement is officially practically disregarded. Lately appeals have been made through the editorial columns of *The Call* for help in carrying on this great work. Help has come, but not in the volume that it deserves. The reason of this neglect may perhaps be ascribed to the fact that the party members and others possessing the necessary qualifications and ability have not fully realized the importance of this movement." Likewise, the staff of a Washington, D.C., school urged Party members to "evince more interest in the Sunday school work of the party," and asked, "Why neglect our 'kiddies' during their most impressionable age?" And in 1915, William Kruse tried to explain that even by then, the Socialist Sunday schools in existence represented "little experiments that . . . do no more than point a way." The schools were only in their first stages of development, he argued, and Party members needed to "give more time and attention to them before passing judgment."[28]

Kendrick Shedd often expressed frustration with the blind opposition, apathy, and lack of seriousness that Party members exhibited toward the schools. He believed that some socialists, who seemed actually to "despise" the schools, were misinformed about what was taught in them and what could result from a weekend education for working-class children. They simply "do not realize what can be done with a lot of kiddies in a short space of time." Elsewhere Shedd wrote: "When will the party wake up? Is it going to sleep forever?" While he publicized the socialist schools as "Schools of Inspiration," it was painfully apparent to Shedd that most Party members were either opposed or indifferent to them, or supported them with words only.[29] In the summer of 1915, Shedd did receive a letter from Eugene Debs, the Party's most prominent figure, that "heartily congratulated and commended [Shedd] for the amazing success you have achieved in Milwaukee under not too encouraging circumstances." Debs expressed the hope that "in spite of all obstacles," Shedd would be able "not only to build up the child movement in Milwaukee but to widen indefinitely the field of your operation." During the same time, Debs wrote a short article on behalf of the Cleveland Socialist Sunday School, in which he suggested to readers of the local labor paper, "The Socialist father or mother who neglects the opportunity offered in the Socialist Sunday School to checkmate this work of capitalism in the mind of the child, neglects the noblest work in the entire field of Socialist propaganda."[30] And yet, except in these two instances, Debs appears to have taken no clear-cut public stand on behalf of the schools. Although his essay on "Children" was frequently reprinted in socialist publications and he was often described in terms of his love for children, nowhere else in Debs's speeches, or in articles by him or about his work, was the existence of the Socialist Sunday schools mentioned.

Perhaps the frustration felt by SSS supporters was best expressed in early 1918 by a staff member at one of the Buffalo Schools of Social Science. He no doubt summed up the feelings of many of his fellow teachers when he wrote: "The men and women of the Socialist Party seem to be about as much interested in the Socialist Sunday schools as they are in the price of champagne." The children themselves were going to have "to wake up the dead" if the schools were to be successful.[31]

Opposition from Non-socialists

Former participants of the Socialist Sunday schools who were interviewed for this study do not recall any serious interference in the operation of the schools from outsiders. For example, a former student at a Bronx school believes that the public generally knew very little about the school. Similarly, a former teacher at the Brownsville SSS described it as "tucked away" in the Brooklyn neighborhood, with its own building, and left alone.[32] It is possible, then, that attendance at a local Socialist Sunday School did not adversely affect one's public school experience or one's relations in the community.[33]

Occasionally, the non-socialist press did focus attention on the schools, portraying them in a negative, sometimes heinous light. One of the earliest mentions of the work of the English-speaking Socialist Sunday schools was published in a 1904 issue of the *Chicago Tribune*, an account that was prominently reprinted and commented upon on the front page of *The Worker*. The Chicago newspaper described the activities of the Children's Club of the Woman's Socialist Union of Omaha, Nebraska, focusing on a children's entertainment given at the local Party headquarters. In a headline titled "Children Insult Roosevelt," the paper reported on a part of the program in which "President Roosevelt's picture was torn from the wall of a room" by a girl of ten, who cried: "There is the man who wouldn't receive 'Mother' Jones and the children of Philadelphia!"[34]

The Omaha incident and the pride with which the socialist press publicized it was recounted in *Bolshevism: Its Cure*, a virulent attack on the American socialist movement by David Goldstein and Martha Moore Avery. Both Goldstein and Avery had been socialists at the turn of the century, but they spent the next two decades actively denouncing the radical movement in speeches and in print. In *Bolshevism: Its Cure*, as well as their earlier book, *Socialism: The Nation of Fatherless Children*, Goldstein and Avery gave prominent attention to the "blasphemous lessons" of the Socialist Sunday schools. They maintained that these lessons were turning out "a prolific crop of degenerate citizens" who attack all the things that good Americans hold dear: family, God, private ownership, decent morals, and so forth. Goldstein and Avery accused socialist teachers of trying to substitute Eugene Debs for Jesus. They provided examples from socialist press accounts, Party documents, and SSS curriculum materials to make their case.[35]

The *National Civic Federation Review* took special note of *Bolshevism: Its Cure*, and especially the authors' discussion of "the sinister work of the Socialist Sunday Schools." It also published several articles that attacked the work of SSS activists. An extensive piece by Martha Moore Avery that dealt specifically with "Socialist Sunday Schools" utilized essays written by SSS children (that were reprinted in *The Worker*) as evidence that "the Socialist dialectic" was being taught to the children dogmatically. Avery stressed that "there is no

monopoly in New York of Socialist Sunday school achievement."
She cited as evidence the work of schools in Chicago and Boston
along with the incident at the Omaha children's club.[36]

The Socialist Sunday schools were the object of vituperation in
other non-socialist publications as well. For example, in 1908 the
American Review of Reviews published a piece on "'Red' Sunday-
Schools and Child Socialists" that excerpted information from
Avery's May 1908 article in the *National Civic Federation Review*. On
several occasions, the *New York Times* also took note of the schools.
In 1908, an unflattering account of playlets presented by the Borough Park school was published, with Bertha Fraser, one of
Brooklyn's most active SSS organizers at the time, quoted as ac-
knowledging that the schools set out to teach "class hatred." A year
earlier, the *New York Times* published an extensive description of the
initial session of a school in Manhattan (mentioned briefly in Chapter Three). According to the *Times* reporter, many of the children
seemed uncomfortable, as if "they were going to be dosed with
some new and strange kind of medicine." In 1910, the paper also
gave prominent attention to the publication of Nicholas Klein's
"dangerous" *The Socialist Primer*, linking its appearance to the existence of "ten Socialist Sunday schools in this city alone."[37]

Another negative account of the Socialist Sunday schools appeared in the *Living Age*, which linked the schools to "the spirit of
irreligion and agnosticism which prevails among the lower strata of
democracy at the present time." It claimed that worldwide the
schools had enrolled about 120,000 children and that "the harm
these Socialist Sunday-schools are effecting is inestimable." And in
the initial issue of the *Common Cause*, its managing editor discussed
"The Menace of Radical Education" by focusing on the Socialist Sunday schools. While somehow having doubts about the purpose and
results of the Ferrer Modern Schools, it was clear to him that the
children in the socialist schools were being trained "insidiously . . .
to become active revolutionists and destructionists" against patriotism and high ethical ideals. If this movement was not stopped
soon, he warned readers, it would be too late to stop the spread of
socialism into the public schools and colleges. Several issues later,
another observer described the SSS movement as "a deliberate,
coldly planned, cleverly conceived device to capture the young for
the doctrines of spoliation, irreligion, and social anarchy."[38]

Of course, it was not just in the press that socialist youth work
was attacked. Speeches by anti-socialists occasionally focused on the
schools as well. The Socialist Sunday schools of New York City were
sharply criticized by the Reverend John Wesley Hill in a talk on "Socialism as a Peril to Childhood" delivered at the Metropolitan Temple in Manhattan. Hill informed his audience that little children

were being taught to venerate the "red flag" instead of the American flag and were being deliberately prepared to enter into "class warfare." And at least one school, started by Italian socialists in the Williamsbridge section of Manhattan, attracted considerable opposition from local Catholic priests.[39]

The impact of such adverse publicity is not clear, however. In the case of the Omaha incident in 1904, for example, the socialist press did seem to appreciate the national reputation that had been gained for the schools.[40] No doubt little good came from such notoriety, but the absence of evidence that printed and verbal attacks directly affected the work of the schools indicates that by and large they were able to ignore the opposition their efforts engendered.

Everyday Problems

Besides the absence of strong support from fellow radicals and the occasional attacks (mostly in the press) from opponents, additional practical problems plagued the SSS movement throughout its lifetime. Finding a suitable place to meet was often a formidable hurdle. Some schools were fortunate enough to hold their classes in the local Party headquarters or labor lyceum. However, for many radical schools, unlike their church-related counterparts, finding suitable facilities was a recurring problem. In Washington, D.C., for example, a school held its first meetings in an organizer's living room. The Newport, Kentucky, school met at a teacher's music studio. And the Williamsbridge school in Manhattan met in a rear basement that needed to be cleaned and furnished.[41]

Many schools were confronted with the inadequacy of the space afforded to them, even when halls and buildings were found. A school in Philadelphia, with 150 students, was similar to many schools when it announced that it had "more applicants than it has room for."[42] The quality of the facilities themselves also differed from place to place. In 1917, after a fire destroyed the original building, the reopened Brownsville Labor Lyceum gave the school that met there quite pleasant facilities, although half of the two thousand children who registered for classes had to be sent away "for lack of accommodations." On the other hand, a former student of the Socialist Sunday School on Claremont Parkway in the Bronx remembers the physical conditions of her school as "rather miserable," although at the time she did not mind at all. The organizer of a Pittsburgh school alluded to the same problem when he wrote that just because "a hole in the wall is thought good enough for old socialists to meet in (and of course it never really is) does not make it fit for a [sic] S.S.S." He suggested that school organizers try "to get a good sunlit hall, even if the rent is a little higher than you have been paying."[43] In some buildings used by the schools, separate class-rooms were unavailable, so teachers had to gather their age-divided classes in different corners of a large clubroom or assembly hall. In schools with classrooms, a small hall or auditorium might still be needed so that the entire student body could assemble for common exercises at the beginning and close of the school session.

Schools often had other mundane but troublesome problems as well, including a need for chairs, blackboards, song charts, a type-writer, and fuel.[44] In addition, there were three critical everyday problems that were cited repeatedly by SSS organizers in their press reports and personal correspondence: (1) a lack of adequate funding; (2) a lack of competent teachers; and (3) a lack of suitable lesson materials.

From its earliest years, SSS activists throughout the country complained that they were short of funds for printing, class mate-rials, school flags, transportation, and the other costs that were in-volved in running the schools. The lack of funding had, of course, a major impact on the character of the schools. Sometimes its influ-ence amounted to incorporating the open air idea during the nice weather to save the cost of renting a hall, as was the case for the forty-one students of the Washington, D.C., school in 1913. A more common effect was the absence of money to pay teachers and other school helpers. There was also a direct impact on curriculum, be-sides the obvious inability of many schools to pay for new readers, songbooks, and the like: Because of the lack of funding, the schools were forced to sponsor a number of fundraising festivals, entertain-ments, dances, and pageants that usually required that the children rehearse songs and plays during schooltime.[45]

Teachers and other SSS supporters spent an inordinate amount of time figuring out how they could raise enough money to cover their expenses. Kendrick Shedd, for example, strongly recommended that collections be taken at school sessions. Parents, visitors, and even children were asked to bring in pennies to help support the Sunday school. Shedd rationalized the practice by suggesting, "We must teach the children the art of giving for the sake of the working class." Other schools relied more on mandatory fees. A Bronx school asked parents to give two cents each Sunday to help defray ex-penses. A school in Rockford, Illinois, charged each student five cents for each quarter of the school year. And the Brownsville school charged a registration fee of twenty-five cents for each child to help pay for such items as registration cards, songbooks, and textbooks. On the other hand, some schools, like the Newport, Kentucky, school, reported that they did not take regular collections or, like the 2nd Assembly District Branch SSS in the Bronx, that they had no mandatory fee. Instead, they relied on voluntary donations from interested individual and group supporters, which could be books and equipment as well as money.[46]

Every school sponsored festivals, pageants, dances, concerts, and picnics for the purpose of raising money for their operations. Occasionally, more unusual fundraising ventures were adopted; for example, the Milwaukee SSS raffled off a Ford automobile and raised $450.[47] In most schools the money raised was at best barely above the minimum required to provide appropriate levels of staffing, supplies, and housing. This was especially the case before the end of the second decade, when the national office of the Party offered little encouragement to the schools' efforts. In fact, Edward Friebert later blamed the demise of Milwaukee's International Socialist Sunday school in large part on, "as all workers [sic] undertakings, the lack of funds."[48] Friebert's recollection reveals much about radical working-class endeavors, for it is one thing to theorize about the development of alternative working-class institutions but it is quite another to secure the funding to support them.

The recruitment of a sufficient number of competent teachers was a related and significant problem that supporters faced. No other problem so vexed SSS activists during the entire period from 1900 to 1920. As Benjamin Glassberg noted in 1920: "The Socialist movement has never been overburdened with capable writers, speakers, or organizers. Nothing, however, has been so difficult to get hold of as teachers for Sunday schools."[49] From all parts of the nation, there were recurring complaints about the need for teachers. The situation was perhaps best summarized in 1913 by the Socialist School Union Committee of Greater New York. It reported that "many new teachers are needed" and that some schools were "languishing because of the lack of [a] proper teaching force," while other schools were "all ready to open if suitable teachers could be secured." Such a situation evidently existed in "all boroughs of the city."[50]

There were enough Party members and allies sympathetic to the work to have helped lessen the extent of the teacher shortage. Why were supporters reluctant to become teachers in these part-time weekend schools? No doubt many did not feel qualified to take on such a role. Also, the realities of working-class life during the early 1900s included the six-day work week, long hours, fatigue, and illness. In addition, teaching positions in virtually all the schools were voluntary, or at best offering token payment. It is hardly surprising that organizers attracted and retained good teachers only with the greatest difficulty. In Rochester, so many staff members left the area for work elsewhere that Shedd was moved to comment: "Such is the uncertainty of the working class movement. Slavery drives them whither the work is." A clearly frustrated Shedd wrote:

"You know the well-known saying, 'Where the duty calls, I obey.' Well, for the working class it is 'where the Job, I obey—because I MUST.'"[51] Additionally, many grass-roots SSS supporters were active in other Party matters that took precedence over school work. Bertha Mailly, for example, withdrew from most of her active involvement in youth work in 1911 because she just "could not afford the time."[52] Finally, with members leaving the Party (Shedd, Simons, Sanial) or being arrested or indicted (Haessler, Yingst, Shiplacoff, Krafft, Kruse) at the end of the second decade, the problem of finding teachers became more intense.

The difficulty of attracting and retaining competent teachers greatly exacerbated the everyday problems that the schools faced. Staff turnover tended to be excessive in some schools, which undermined the quality of instruction and limited its effectiveness. In fact, many schools recognized the problem of attracting teachers and tried to impress upon interested observers that the qualifications for becoming an SSS teacher were not that demanding. The Socialist School Union of Greater New York made the following appeal in 1913: "We want teachers. We need them badly. Will you volunteer? . . . If you have had teaching experience, so much the better. But if you love children, if you have sympathy with and understanding of the child, you need not hesitate for lack of pedagogical knowledge. We cannot expect Normal graduates. Our teachers must get their training in the work." The national office of the Party similarly suggested in 1918 that "almost any big-hearted, broad-minded Socialist who is human enough to love children will make a fine teacher of the S.S.S."[53] This desperate attitude was criticized by Benjamin Glassberg (who had public school teaching experience): Too often, the schools used teachers who were long on enthusiasm and interest but short on knowledge of teaching children. In fact, a former participant at a Brooklyn school, a rather poorly attended and equipped one, claimed years later that "anybody you could grab—and could repeat what he [the director] said . . ." was used as a teacher.[54] On the other hand, in 1918 the national office had a different view, suggesting that although "the greatest trouble is to get qualified teachers, . . . thrown back upon their own resources our workers have developed splendid teaching talent right from among their own members—talent that never showed itself in ordinary Party work but that shone brilliantly in this S.S.S. setting."[55] The truth probably lay somewhere between these two assessments.

Another major problem that the schools had to confront was the scarcity of suitable curriculum materials. Because there was little coordination and dissemination, it was often the case that schools in one location knew very little about the materials used in schools elsewhere. Although numerous successful attempts were made to provide lesson materials, many SSS teachers felt they were inadequate to operate successful Sunday schools. In 1908 the Woman's Socialist Union of Los Angeles reported that the great need of the Socialist Sunday schools there was "the preparation of a series of lessons adapted to the understanding of children and very young people." Three years later, at a supper meeting for SSS teachers of Greater New York, it was reported that there was a great need "for lesson outlines in the schools." In 1916, John Spargo, a leading Party theorist, expressed his interest in helping the SSS movement and pointed in particular to "the utter lack of good materials in the form of suitable readings, songs and lessons." In the same year, in a discussion of the serious problems facing SSS work, the *American Labor Year Book* cited the need for "the formulation of a course of study that shall at once be adapted to very young children, and at the same time aim at a thorough understanding of the underlying principles of Socialism." And again in 1919, the staff of the Rockford school specified their principal needs as "1. Lesson material of all sorts. 2. A weekly story paper for the children. 3. Picture cards and similar materials to give away to children."[56]

The preparation of lesson materials often meant burdensome commitments of time and energy (and sometimes expense) for these radical youth activists, many with little or no experience in teaching. Since most Sunday school teachers worked full-time during the week and had their own family responsibilities, they did not have the time to develop exhaustive lesson plans and classroom readings, even for such part-time educational ventures. The lack of assistance provided by the national office caused particular bitterness for some SSS advocates. One participant blamed the demise of the Baltimore school on the unwillingness of the national office to assist in developing, printing, and distributing appropriate lesson materials. He argued that socialist teachers needed "actual TEXT BOOKS" and "not indexes of books" suggested by a national leader. Despite all the Olympian dreams of activists, "those who are willing to teach have neither the time nor the inclination to handle stuffy volumes in preparing lessons every week. . . . They are workers who must earn their living." Likewise, Edward Perkins Clarke of Hartford complained in 1914 that the national office should help out more with lesson materials, "instead of forcing us to go to capitalistic sources."[57] To be sure, suitable original lessons were prepared by some particularly active participants such as Shedd, while other teachers relied on adapting the work of progressive educators like Katherine Dopp. But the problem remained of finding detailed socialist classroom materials that would interest children.

It was only in 1918 that the Party's national office gave direct aid to the Socialist Sunday School movement. It was a case of too

little, too late. The Party appropriated one hundred dollars for curricular work and initiated a national organization of socialist schools.
But the money stretched only so far, producing only one songbook
and one organizational manual.[58] Within a year, the Party faced severe government repression and internal strife, and the fate of the
SSS movement became of minor interest to Party activists.

That Word "Sunday"

A less significant problem that created some tension among
those active in the schools involved the use of the word "Sunday."
As early as 1908, the staff of the Trenton, New Jersey, school was
"searching [their] minds for a better name," one that avoided "the
old-fashioned conception of a Sunday school." Seven years later,
William Kruse complained that the "Sunday" name connoted that
the schools were "seeking to rival the religious institutions in the
teaching of unintelligible dogma to immature minds." Perhaps
some other name was needed, such as "The Socialist Children's
League." Likewise, a young socialist in Milwaukee wrote in 1918 of
the false impression some sympathizers held about religion being
taught in these "Sunday schools."[59]

The issue of the use of the word "Sunday" was eventually
taken up at a conference of SSS and YPSL activists that was sponsored by the Rand School of Social Science in 1918. Among the delegates were Antoinette Konikow of Boston, Bertha Mailly of New
York City, and William Kruse of Chicago. It was decided that while
the "SSS" identity was strong and should be maintained, the name
"Sunday" should be deleted from schools' names because it "served
no useful purpose and only hampered our work in many cases."
However, no other name was agreed upon and a request for alternatives was made. During the following year, the *Young Socialists' Magazine* also recognized the strength of the "SSS" identity but began to
refer to the schools as "Socialist Schools of Science" instead. No
doubt Kruse was responsible for this attempt at changing the name
of the schools. In a pamphlet he wrote in 1918, he had called the
schools Socialist Schools of Science, adding that they were "sometimes familiarly called Socialist Sunday Schools." And at the first
national convention of the Young People's Socialist League held in
Chicago in 1919, with Kruse calling the meeting to order, the schools
were similarly referred to in the convention minutes as Socialist
Schools of Science.[60]

Kendrick Shedd, however, saw no need to turn the proper
name for the schools into a controversial issue. He pointed out in an
article on "That Awful Word Sunday," that "Sunday is the worker's
only holiday, the only day of the week that may be said to belong to

him. It is the only day in which he can really enjoy the Sun—hence, his Sunday." Since the school met on this day, "why not call it so?" He saw no reason why socialists should change the name simply because capitalists used the same name in a different way. Elsewhere, however, he agreed that there was no particular need to call a school a "Sunday school" if one did not want to.[61] In fact, several schools did adopt other names, for example the Arm and Torch League in Cincinnati (the emblem of the Socialist Party was an arm holding a torch), the Children's Socialist Lyceum in Los Angeles, the Schools of Social Science in Buffalo, and the Social Science School in Syracuse.

Organizational Features

One of the key characteristics of these schools was that they were grass-roots efforts functioning in most places as integrated (if not integral) elements of radical communities. If the Party local and allied organizations were doing well in a community, the chances of a school continuing in operation were greater. A dying socialist neighborhood meant a dim future for the Socialist Sunday School.

This relationship to the community can be seen in the activities of the schools as well. Children were not cloistered for a few hours on Sunday mornings, quietly and seriously engaged in a study of abstract socialist tenets. The life of a school included the people and the activities around it. This could be seen in the curriculum that was offered and the people who staffed and visited the schools. Unlike some of the anarchist schools, no thought was given to removing the school children to a more idyllic setting (other than a local park). These were socialist schools for children from radical working-class families, and they sprang from and were nurtured in the neighborhoods where these children lived.

The schools emphasized this aspect by involving students in the concerns of the radical working-class movement. At the end of the second decade, for example, the children of Socialist Sunday schools in Milwaukee and New Haven helped local Prison Comfort Clubs by writing messages to political prisoners and their families, collecting money, and sending clothes and Christmas presents to prisoners' children. And in a reversal of typical practice, students from the Newark SSS gave a benefit entertainment for the *New York Call*, and the children of the Mystic, Connecticut, school donated thirty-three dollars to the Party local. Similarly, a Washington, D.C., school donated money to the children of striking Colorado and Ohio miners, and the Brownsville SSS sent forty dollars to the children of Lawrence strikers.[62] It was particularly common for the students of a school to participate in the radical community's parades, rallies, benefit entertainments, festivals, and picnics. For example, 250 SSS children met Alan Benson, the Party's candidate for United States President, when he visited Milwaukee in 1916. They sang at a rally for him and made him an associate member of their school. And at the Party's New York State Convention in Rochester, arriving delegates were met at the train station by cheering SSS students, many "clad in white and red," carrying flags of all nations, red flags, and socialist banners. On the last day of the convention, the local SSS children performed a pageant for the delegates.[63]

The Socialist Sunday schools were not isolated institutions but were instead closely linked to the fortunes and character of the radical political movement. Sunday school activists believed that the schools could lend immediate and long-term support to their political movement, and they generally welcomed the opportunity to have the real world enter their classrooms. The schools were not just teaching about the socialist culture; they were part of it.

The organization and governance of the schools varied from place to place but they shared certain features. According to William Kruse, there were two basic organizational plans that had been followed by 1918. The first involved the establishment of an "S.S.S. Association" (or Club), consisting of people interested in organizing and promoting a local school. While members of this school club did not have to be Party members, the Socialist school committee operating the school was to consist only of Party members in good standing. (Bertha Mailly had suggested a similar plan in an earlier SSS manual.) The second plan involved the Party local more directly. A committee from the local was chosen, or in a large city each branch might elect delegates to a central committee, and the school would be run by this committee. "The school then belongs to the local, which is responsible for this educational work, for its maintenance and its financing."[64] Throughout the life of the SSS movement, most localities seem to have relied on a version of the first Kruse plan. It was only during the later years of this twenty-year period, when national and state Party organizations showed more interest in the work of the schools, that Party locals became more involved in their operation. In New York City, however, several Party branches did participate in the initial organization of schools, although their subsequent financial and other support was minimal.

In general, as Kendrick Shedd admitted, the Socialist Sunday schools were "conducted much the same as capitalist Sunday schools." For example, there was need for a superintendent, director, or organizer to take charge of the school. After all, "things don't run themselves. Every machinist knows that. There must be a motive power, and there must be direction." As Shedd had a strong desire for a well-organized, efficient, and dynamic Sunday School, and a seasoned awareness of the amount of work involved, he made sure that school officers or committees were appointed for specific aspects of the school's operations. A secretary and assistants were "to keep the card index of the school in order, to take the attendance, collection, etc., and make out the day's report." A treasurer was to handle all financial aspects of the school. A house committee was "to see that the building is ready for the session, that the song books are distributed and collected, that the school banner is set up, the piano open and ready, the chairs in place, etc." What was unique was Shedd's idea that a "Glad-hand" or welcome committee also be organized, because "the strangers, the newcomers, must, above all, be made welcome." Indeed, Shedd remarked, "Let it never be said of our Socialist schools, as is so often said of certain churches, that there is no warmth, no welcome there! The school should be made attractive to everybody. The superintendents, the officers and teachers can help in this, but so can the Glad-hand Committee!" People also were assigned to help in such matters as "the checking of hats and coats" and leading the school choir. The latter was particularly significant to Shedd because he believed that singing was a vitally important aspect of a successful Socialist Sunday School.[65]

Both Shedd and Kruse emphasized that teachers should be included in the governing body of the schools, and Shedd was adamant about this point. He wanted "to have the Sunday school work governed, as far as possible, by those actually engaged in it." He accepted the notion that school officers, teachers, and helpers needed to be Party members, but he believed that they alone should govern their school. He was concerned about the interference of Party officials who were not involved in the operation of the schools. Shedd claimed that he was aware of many Young People's Socialist League circles that had been "hammered and strangled by a lot of bosses appointed by the local to supervise them." He sarcastically asked: "Shall the party appoint a millstone committee to be hung around the neck of the struggling school? Shall there be a stumbling block commission to consist of certain ambitious and nosey delegates who don't care enough about the school to work in it as teachers or helpers or officers but who will be glad to dictate to the school as to what it may or may not do?" For Shedd, the answer was clear: "Some say Yes. We most decidedly say No!" If delegates from Party branches wanted input, "let them show it by participating in the actual school work."[66]

In some large cities, such as Chicago, central committees were formed to help run the schools. In 1918 the eight schools there formed a central organization to encourage more uniform and systematic instruction. Three delegates from each local SSS organization served on the central body. This central body was described as running "the S.S.S. agitation of the entire city. It is the real center of power." Within the districts themselves, SSS societies were formed, and "anyone is eligible for membership." These local bodies had a role in the operations of the individual schools but the central committee had the authority to hire teachers and decide on curriculum.[67]

While the schools were governed by a combination of school personnel and Party officials, there was also an effort made to involve parents and students in the operation of a school. In Pittsburgh, for example, parents of children who attended the school elected the school officers (superintendent, recording secretary, treasurer, librarian, and board of trustees). The Upper Bronx school reported that it was "democratically managed," with a parents association helping to run it. Other schools encouraged more informal parental participation, such as an early Boston SSS that invited parents "to offer suggestions and criticisms on the methods used."[68] In a few schools, children also were encouraged to participate in governing. Frank Wilt of the Cleveland SSS, for example, strongly advised that the schools should introduce "as much democracy in the affairs of the schools as possible." Thus, when three boys at the Cleveland school behaved "a little unruly," the students were responsible for hearing the charges against them and their defense, and then voting on their guilt or innocence. (In this case, the Cleveland SSS students voted not guilty.) Similarly, in 1918 the Buffalo "kid comrades" chose a fellow student each week to chair the regular business meeting. At one meeting, the school superintendent suggested the adoption of a new disciplinary rule, but it was rejected by the students. Students at the Los Angeles school were included more formally in school governance. The school was run by a board of education composed of the superintendent, two members of each socialist local in the area, teachers, as well as two student delegates from the older grades. Students also held regular meetings every two weeks or so, where "everything of importance . . . comes before the children themselves for their approval or rejection."[69] Of course, it is impossible to determine how much real authority the parents and children in these schools enjoyed.

Most schools met for two hours on Sunday mornings, typically from about 10 A.M. to noon. A few schools met in the afternoon or Saturday mornings, or for different lengths of time. Because of the uncertainty of facilities, staffing, and funding, it was not unusual for the beginning of the school term to vary somewhat from year to year for one school, let alone between the many schools. Still, Socialist Sunday schools generally followed a calendar similar to the public schools, although they often opened a few weeks later. There are cases, however, of schools starting at different times, even in the spring, especially when they were first organized. This happened during the first year of the schools in Milwaukee, but Kendrick Shedd believed that schools should begin whenever a sufficient number of children and teachers, and adequate facilities were found, rather than waiting until the fall term.[70]

In most cases, the schools stopped meeting during the summer months, in part because school rooms were too hot for classes. During the 1913–1914 school year of the Rochester school, for instance, the last session was held on June 28. Other schools completed their terms earlier, some using the May Day holiday as a convenient time to end the school year. Shedd and his staff in Rochester organized several summer activities, including school picnics and hikes, and also sent postcard reminders to the children, so as not to lose touch with interested parents and children, as well as teachers and other school helpers.[71]

The program that was followed during school sessions varied somewhat from school to school. Still, there was a general pattern that was encouraged by those who were nationally prominent in socialist youth work, and it was followed by most of the schools. The schedule of a Cleveland school in 1918 is illustrative: School started at "ten o'clock sharp" with a general assembly, a very important feature of most school programs. During this time, when all the children, teachers, and visitors were together, radical songs were sung, recitations were presented, and announcements were made. After about a half-hour, the school broke up into separate classes for one hour. General assembly reconvened after the class sessions, with more singing, announcements, and visitors' remarks. The session at this Cleveland school ended at 11:45 A.M.[72]

The number of classes within a school depended on the student enrollment. The smallest schools, like the Newport, Kentucky, school opened with just five students and had only one class, while schools in Brownsville and Rochester had twenty or more classes during their lifetimes. The majority of schools had an enrollment of between 50 and 150 students, divided into three to eight classes.

Centralizing Efforts

A general lack of coordination marked the American SSS movement. There were some advantages to this situation, primarily regarding the autonomy that individual schools enjoyed. For many participants this autonomy was a welcome by-product of the lack of cohesiveness between the schools. More extensive Party involvement only would have meant unwanted interference. But for most socialist youth activists, even those like Shedd who obviously were wary of direct Party involvement, the disadvantages of such a lack of coordination far outweighed the advantages. Interested persons in locales without schools could not be sure how to request information; staff in some schools complained about a lack of materials while school directors and teachers elsewhere had already developed suitable lessons; and a strong sense of being part of a growing network of socialist weekend schools for children was lacking. Teaching and curriculum development were highly unsystematic, with new schools often having to "reinvent the wheel." This lack of coordination seriously hurt the movement's efforts to generate widespread support for its work.

The reaction of one former SSS student to the news that there were dozens of other Socialist Sunday schools in existence across the country while he was attending one in Milwaukee represents the recollections of all of the former participants interviewed for this study. Expressing surprise at the news, he remarked: "I thought this was a unique kind of contribution to the whole picture by the people of Milwaukee."[73] Even within the same city, and even though they did see other children at radical parades and rallies, former SSS students that I interviewed at best could only vaguely recall the existence of other schools. For most youth activists, the blame for this lack of communication and coordination clearly lay with the unwillingness of national and state Party officials to invest energy and funding in Sunday school work.

Prominent SSS organizers were aware of the problems caused by this lack of coordination and did attempt to encourage closer collaboration between schools. Sometimes they would visit other communities to help organize new schools. Kendrick Shedd, for instance, traveled to such places as Buffalo, Pittsburgh, Cleveland, and Racine for such a purpose. Bertha Mailly helped organize new schools in Omaha, Rochester, Haverhill, and Boston, as did Bertha Fraser in Philadelphia and New Jersey. There were occasional exchanges of curriculum materials, apart from the more frequent sharing of materials in the socialist press. For example, one New York City school ordered 450 song cards directly from the International Socialist Sunday School in Milwaukee. And while Shedd was in Rochester, he sent lesson outlines, recitations, and song sheets to schools in Buffalo, Jamestown, New York City, Brockton, Hartford, and elsewhere.[74]

Efforts also were made to create centralizing committees and organizations to provide ways for the schools to communicate more directly with each other. On the local level, the previously discussed Chicago SSS central organization was one such example. Another local effort occurred in New York City, where a loose-knit SSS Association was initiated in 1908. During the following year, a teachers' club for SSS staff members and others interested in the schools' work was launched at the Rand School of Social Science. It was publicized as under the direction of the Woman's National Committee of the Party, but it was probably instigated by Bertha Mailly. The intended purpose of the club was "to bring about co-ordination in the work of the schools and closer co-operation among the teachers." By the fall of 1910, the Socialist School Union of Greater New York was in place, with meetings being held to help coordinate the coming school year, and lesson outlines being prepared for publication in the *Young Socialists' Magazine*. During the following spring, SSS teachers from nine schools met and elected officers, including David Greenberg as organizer and Bertha Mailly as secretary. Ambitious plans were made to help organize new schools in the Greater New York area; prepare and publish curriculum materials; arrange for music, songs, and dances for the schools; initiate classes for the preparation of teachers; arrange joint festivals and celebrations; obtain a vacation home in the country where groups of children could be sent; and coordinate efforts with the directors of the Young People's circles.[75] In the pages of the *New York Call* and occasionally in the *Young Socialists' Magazine*, an "S.S.S. Directory" appeared, with a listing of names, addresses, and starting times of schools in Manhattan, the Bronx, Brooklyn, and Queens.

The Socialist School Union of Greater New York continued in existence for the next several years, with monthly meetings held at the Rand School. It helped to promote curriculum materials authored by David Greenberg and Edith Breithut; arranged several festivals that were attended by children from as many as sixteen schools in the New York–New Jersey area; sponsored summer picnics; and initiated teacher training classes. However, by 1916, for reasons relating to the general retrenchment of Party activities during the mid-decade, the Socialist School Union of Greater New York had faded from the scene. Internal bickering may also have played a role in its demise. Party officials outside Manhattan sometimes resented city-wide coordinating efforts that were initiated by Manhattan organizers. Thus, after Bertha Fraser reported on a recent Socialist School Union meeting, the executive committee of the Kings County local (Brooklyn) passed a motion protesting "against the action of the SSU in electing a committee to take charge of the Sunday school work in Brooklyn and considering the electing of a paid organizer, and that we notify them that we can take charge of the Sunday school work in Brooklyn and have already elected an organizer for that purpose."[76]

There were also limited attempts to organize the schools on a state-wide basis. For example, in 1910 socialists in New York and

New Jersey established state committees to help in the organization of Sunday schools. And at the 1912 state convention of the Ohio Socialist Party, it was recommended that the Party's state bulletin help coordinate the schools' efforts in that state.[77] However, in most other states and localities, there is little evidence that Party officials devoted much time and effort to the funding and coordination of Socialist Sunday schools.

Kendrick Shedd and like-minded youth activists sought the more active involvement of state organizations as well as the national office. Indeed, there had been some support for a national coordinating effort during the early years of the SSS movement, which was part of the reason for the introduction of the *Little Socialist Magazine for Boys and Girls* (later renamed the *Young Socialists' Magazine*) in 1908. A year later, Anna Maley suggested that the *Progressive Woman* could play a similar role. And in 1912, the Woman's National Committee of the Party recommended the establishment of an educational committee to help prepare lessons and select suitable materials.[78] However, these efforts did not provide the schools with the coordination of activities, preparation and dissemination of materials, and funding that Shedd and others felt were badly needed.

Shedd was constantly frustrated by his lack of success in this area. Because of his contacts with school participants throughout the country, he was the most aware of the number of schools in operation and of the movement's potential for growth. He also was informed about the British Socialist Sunday School movement and in particular the progress of the National Council of British Socialist Sunday School Unions. And yet he could not convince Party leaders to provide substantial support for SSS work. In early 1915, while still in Rochester, Shedd finally attempted to initiate his own national organization of Socialist Sunday schools. He publicized the proposed national union in the socialist press and sent out letters to SSS activists around the country. His letter reveals much about his approach to Socialist Sunday School work and is worth quoting in full:[79]

Dear Comrade:

One of the greatest agencies for good yet discovered, to judge from the Socialist standpoint, is the Socialist (Sunday) School. The Party does not yet appreciate its vast significance and wonderful value. Some day it will; but we who already realize its worth must not wait.

These schools are being established in many parts of the land, and we ought to organize them into a federation or union for mutual benefit until such time as the Party itself is willing to take them under its care. In Great Britain there are various

"District Unions", besides a national Sunday School Union.
And be it noted by all, that these schools go under the title of
"Sunday" Schools over there, there being no disposition to
hide their real significance beneath any disguise. They meet on
Sunday—the workers' best day—and hence are known as Sun-
day Schools.

We have for some time been considering the idea of forming
a national organization of these Socialist schools, to be followed, we trust, by an international union. Are you with us in
this? Will you join us in this good project? Let us get together
at once. We may not be able to hold an actual convention for
some time yet, but let that not deter us from going about to
convene on paper, so to speak. This much we can do.

We are enclosing a list of questions which we ask you to
reply to briefly, and to return to us at an early date. Will you
also send a dollar to help with the expenses of organization?
Or, if you prefer, you may send it directly to the treasurer,
Comrade Edward Perkins Clarke, 226 Wethersfield Ave., Hartford, Conn.

Just a word as to the value of such a union of the Socialist
schools. It ought not to be necessary to put it on paper. If we
unite, we shall be much more likely to have a oneness of aim
and purpose. We should also have a central office whence sup-
plies may be obtained for school use. We should all feel free,
too, to offer our suggestions for the betterment or guidance of
the schools. And by our solidarity we should give notice to the
world that we were "in business", so to speak, to fight Capitalism to a finish. Other advantages might be named, which will
readily suggest themselves to your fertile mind.

It doubtless would be an excellent thing for you to bring this
matter in a simple way before your school children and get
them to vote on the proposition. This would teach them democracy.

With best wishes, and awaiting your immediate reply to our
questions, and your hearty assent to our proposal of a union,
believe us, for the Rochester Comrades.

The professionally printed questionnaire that was sent with the letter asked questions about the school's name, location, starting date,
average attendance, number of classes, kinds of lessons, songbooks
used, and suggested names for the proposed federation.

By April 1915, Shedd noted that there were about twenty
schools that were ready to join the federation of Socialist Sunday
schools but that so far no name had been decided on. Comparing
this effort to the British counterpart, which had more than one hun-

dred schools, Shedd hoped to have fifty to one hundred schools in his national organization. He had been in touch with about fifty schools, but at the same time he guessed that "there are undoubtedly as many more scattered throughout the country." Shedd sent out another letter asking for more cooperation and urging even the smallest schools to join.[80] During this same time, however, he moved to Milwaukee and reports on his national federation, both in the press and in his personal papers, ended abruptly in mid-1915. Unfortunately, whatever results Shedd may have gained from his efforts have not been located.

About a year later, another SSS activist attempted to establish a national organization of the schools. T. J. Mead of Washington, D.C. (and later Pittsburgh), promoted such an organization to help "standardize our methods" and to sponsor a national convention. He stressed that SSS work was just beginning to graduate from the experimental stage and now needed to exchange ideas more thoroughly and help less experienced supporters in setting up new schools.[81] It is unclear whether Mead was resurrecting Shedd's failed attempt or whether this was an independent initiative on his part. At any rate, there is no indication that Mead's effort met with any success.

But the agitation of Shedd and others, as well as the increasing concern of national and local leaders about the erosion of support for the Party during the middle years of the second decade, did result in a new interest in the coordination of SSS work by the national office. In the fall of 1913, the Party established a Young People's Department, based in Chicago. It was first headed by Joseph Rogers, Jr., with the focus of attention primarily placed on the Young People's Clubs. In 1915, William Kruse replaced Rogers as director. Whether or not the shift in leadership had any direct effect, in the fall of 1916 John Spargo reported that he had been asked by the national executive committee of the Party to help collect and prepare lesson materials for SSS teachers.[82] Spargo's own departure from the socialist movement a few months later (due to the Party's opposition to American entrance into World War I) meant a quick end to this effort, however.

The national office sought to become more involved in SSS work in November 1917, when Kruse announced that the Party was "anxious to collect the addresses and histories of all the various schools of this kind that have been started in this country." He asked "each local secretary in any community that has or has had a Socialist Sunday School" to answer a series of questions designed to gather basic information about the initiation, organization, staffing, and activities of the schools.[83] Unfortunately, here again, whatever data was generated from Kruse's detailed questionnaire has not been located. It is quite possible that his appeal resulted in little information being received from local secretaries, busy as they no doubt were with many other (including anti-war, electoral, and re-cruitment) activities. Kruse indicated as much when, six months later, he reported, "We have no list of such organizations in this country and from reports there must be hundreds of them." Still, Kruse's initial effort resulted in a new sense of the possibility of a closer relationship between the schools and the national Party or-ganization. Kruse announced that the national office was undertak-ing to supply a set of illustrated lessons for use in SSS classrooms and emphasized, "Our movement is, essentially, an educational in-stitution, and what more proper place could we begin than with our children?"[84] These were words that Shedd, no longer affiliated with the Party in 1918, had waited almost a decade to hear.

In July 1918, a conference of people interested in the education of children was held, later referred to as the "First American S.S.S. Conference." It included delegates from New York City, Boston, Philadelphia, Pittsburgh, Buffalo, and the national office. The deci-sions made at the conference included the following: The national office was to issue an organizational pamphlet about SSS work; schools were asked to delete the word "Sunday" from their names; and a temporary national executive committee was appointed, con-sisting of Antoinette Konikow as chairman, William Kruse as secre-tary, and Bertha Mailly, Rudolph Blum of Pittsburgh, and Elizabeth Baer of Philadelphia. The national executive committee of the Party was asked to give official recognition to this committee until a na-tional convention of SSS delegates could meet. In the meantime, all schools were asked to register with the national organization by sending a complete list of their officers, time and place of meeting, and other information to the Young People's Department in Chi-cago. Obviously intended to reassure SSS activists who viewed a national organization as a potential threat to the autonomous opera-tion of their schools, the conference report emphasized, "It is not at present the intention of making the S.S.S. an iron-bound Party af-fair, but there must be some central point of contact between the various school organizations and it is but right that, as in the case of the Y.P.S.L., this point be the Young People's Dept. of our Party. Details of finances and management will be worked out later, the first step is registration."[85]

By October 1918, an organizational manual authored by Kruse was offered "FREE to Sunday School organizations registering with the national office." In it, Kruse stressed that the first tasks were to supply the necessary materials for existing schools and then to or-ganize new schools. After all, Kruse wrote, "there ought to be an S.S.S. in every town and hamlet of this land, for any number of children with any number of teachers have a fair chance of success." City and state organizations were to be organized, with monthly reports, including photographs and samples of lesson materials sent to the *Young Socialists' Magazine* and other socialist publications. Within the next several months a new song book, a monograph of games for children, and mimeographed copies of about a dozen short plays were being prepared. The *Young Socialists' Magazine* began devoting more space to the work of the schools and an SSS emblem was even being considered. Schools were beginning to sign up with the national organization, including ones in Chicago, New York City, Milwaukee, Pittsburgh, Buffalo, Rockford, and Kenosha.[86]

It is one of the great ironies of the American Socialist Sunday School movement that it finally attained a significant measure of attention from the national office at the same time that the Party was splitting apart. The last mention of the national organization was contained in the January 1920 issue of the *Young Socialists' Magazine*.[87] With the Party and its youth organizations in disarray, the socialist youth periodical halted publication after its May 1920 issue. And nothing more was ever reported about a national federation of Socialist Sunday schools in the United States.

CHAPTER FIVE

Teachers and Students

As is the case for other grass-roots radical movements in American history, the vast majority of those involved in the SSS movement are not easily identified. Of the hundreds of teachers and the thousands of students who participated in the socialist schools from 1900 to 1920, relatively few were described in the pages of the radical and non-radical press, in Socialist Party documents, and in personal correspondence. In addition, the Socialist Sunday schools existed so long before this study was initiated that most teachers and students have died. Those who have not are very elderly and not easily located (for example, they have moved from their hometowns and women changed their last names if they married).

Biographical sketches of prominent activists have been included in previous chapters. In addition, the available evidence allows for a summary of the most important characteristics of SSS teachers and students. This discussion has been aided by interviews with several SSS participants. Most were involved in schools in Milwaukee and New York City. They were interviewed not because they were especially active members of the schools or shared some other special personal characteristics but because they were traceable. Mentioned in brief and infrequent accounts in the socialist press, they were located through local telephone directories or information provided by others. They also were willing to talk about their socialist weekend school experiences that occurred more than sixty years before they were interviewed.

Teachers

Many of those involved in the Sunday schools were the "Jimmie Higginses" of the Socialist movement, active in countless Party ventures besides the schools and serving to link the Party leadership with the rank and file.[1] These were the men and women who distributed Party leaflets at the factory gate, who met in meeting after meeting in taverns and labor meeting halls, and who knew the abuses of the capitalist system first hand. They experienced what others only vicariously felt through the muckraking, sometimes socialistic tracts of the day. Teachers and other staff members were often from the ranks of these "amateur agitators." Some remained relatively unknown figures within radical circles, while others were more prominent (such as Josephine Cole, May Wood Simons, Anna Maley, Frederick Krafft, Edmund Melms, Bertha Mailly, Antoinette Konikow, Edward Perkins Clarke, Lucien Sanial, Carl and Mildred Haessler, William Kruse and Abraham Shiplacoff). However, for perhaps an equal number of those who served as teachers, SSS work represented their major contribution to the socialist cause. Although not the case for Kendrick Shedd, they may initially have become involved because they had children or siblings attending a school.

The main characteristic of SSS teachers was that they were radicals who affiliated with socialism and were from working-class backgrounds (or, for a few "disaffected bourgeois intellectuals" like Shedd, they were not, but identified themselves strongly with what they considered to be the interests of the working class). In most cases, they were also members of the Socialist Party. This comes across in all discussions about the staff and in the backgrounds of individual teachers. Although Haessler and Shedd had been college professors and Mailly had graduated from college, they were the exceptions in this regard. Indeed, Shedd expressed the common belief that a college degree was not necessary to teach in the Socialist Sunday schools. (He pointed out that "fishing in those waters doesn't as yet seem to yield great returns.") Much more important was that teachers should feel a strong allegiance to the working class, have an interest in learning more about socialism, and want to teach working-class children. "Slummers"—those who were condescending and felt or acted superior to working people—were not to be used. In fact, Shedd argued, "the average Socialist school boy or girl can scent a 'slummer' seven blocks away. They know the real from the false." Socialist teachers needed not only to come from the working class but also to "realize that they belong there," that is, to be class conscious. As was the case for the British schools, it is likely that many American SSS teachers or their spouses were active trade unionists.[2]

At times these essential qualifications were made quite explicit. For example, the Woman's National Committee of the Party recommended that a SSS teacher "shall have the right point of view . . . [and be] . . . a member of the Socialist party, which will indicate at least a willingness to accept the Socialist principles." Frank Wilt of Cleveland was similarly forthright in suggesting that teachers should be "Marxian students . . . who know, first, what to teach and second, how to teach."[3] But a number of prominent activists, especially those who had prior teaching experience or were familiar with the work of progressive educators like John Dewey and Caroline Pratt, also urged that teachers exhibit a warm personality, enthusiasm, creativity, and loving and tactful ways. "Learning may be alright [*sic*] in its place," Kendrick Shedd argued, "but it must be thoroughly mixed with a passion for human souls or it will reap no great harvest." Teachers needed to be able to "get down to the child's standpoint."[4] No doubt, as in the public schools too, the extent to which Shedd's suggestions were adopted in socialist schools varied from place to place.

The qualifications of teachers at times became a matter of dispute. In 1911, for example, staff members of a school originally founded by a Workmen's Circle branch in New York City were identified as non-socialists (that is, anarchists and progressives). Party supporters of the schools argued that Socialist Sunday schools should be clearly "socialist" in nature and aligned with Party positions. There was enough non-socialism elsewhere.[5] However, differences between "Left" and "Right" Socialists that were enunciated in other realms of Party life never became an issue with regard to staff qualifications for the Sunday schools.

It should be clear that it was not just women who taught in the Socialist Sunday schools. A number of men were actively involved, some of whom, like Shedd, Greenberg, and Haessler, developed important curriculum materials. Still, there was a preponderance of women involved in SSS work. Indeed, women activists were strongly encouraged by national and local Party officials to become involved in certain areas of activity more than others and youth work was clearly one of them. What this led to, according to Shedd, was Party members thinking that teaching children was "women's work." He repeatedly called for male comrades to become more involved: "Get over the idea, if you ever have it, that Sunday school work (especially Socialist Sunday school work) is a thing for women only. . . . Let no man think it beneath his dignity to teach Socialism!"[6] How narrow-minded the perspective of Party members could become was well expressed by George Gobel of New Jersey. As a delegate to the Party's national convention in 1912, he interrupted May Wood Simons's discussion of a Woman's National Committee report on vocational education by saying, "I do not believe that this comes properly within the province of the Woman's Committee. Anything relating to Socialist Sunday schools might. In my judgement this other matter does not."[7]

It is true, however, that radical immigrant women did seek to become involved in ventures like the Sunday schools. Such efforts represented a way to aid the radical movement within an autonomous environment. The *Socialist Woman*, for example, suggested, "Since the attitude of the next generation toward Socialism will mean much for its success or failure, it would probably be one of the best services women could render to the movement if they pushed the work of establishing Sunday Schools all over the land."[8] A number of socialist women and men did attempt to contest the Party's limited role for women and to agitate for a more prominent place to be given to "feminist" concerns. Such efforts to expand the scope of activities for socialist women may have intensified the constant problem that the Socialist Sunday schools faced anyway in attracting competent people to their staffs, as women qualified to teach sought to involve themselves in other radical activities. Additionally, while many schools (for example, in San Jose, Los Angeles, Omaha, Milwaukee, Chicago, Newport, St. Louis, Cincinnati, Rochester, Boston, Hartford, New York City, and Washington, D.C.) were initiated by local socialist women's clubs, a good estimate of school directors is that a disproportionate number of them were men, further evidence of the secondary role women played in socialist agitation.

It is unclear how this preponderance of female teachers affected the schools. Perhaps it can be seen in the inclusion of certain topics in teacher training classes and SSS curriculum materials (for example, sex hygiene). There was also at least one reported episode of girls at a school being "very shy" and allowing "the boys to overrule them in committee," and the woman school superintendent being aware enough of the inequity involved to work with the girls so that they "have come at last . . . to understand that they are a part of the organization as much as are the boys."[9]

While SSS teachers shared an allegiance to the interests of the working class and to socialist politics, and a great many were women, there was a wide range in their ages. There were old-time and middle-aged radicals like Lucien Sanial and Bertha Mailly of Manhattan, Bertha Fraser and Abraham Shiplacoff of Brooklyn, Edmund Melms and Eliza Taylor Cherdron of Milwaukee, and Nell Martindale and Kendrick Shedd of Rochester, as well as youthful participants like Gertrude Weil and David Greenberg of New York City, Edna Peters and Louis Hampel of Milwaukee, and Isadore Tischler and Bertha Vossler of Rochester. At some schools, such as the International SSS, many teachers were the parents and older siblings of students. In most cases, however, teachers were simply members of the local radical community who were willing and able to volunteer their services and receive very little remuneration for the cause of promoting weekend socialist education for working-class children.

In some places the Young People's Socialist League played an active role in a school's operation. Kendrick Shedd perceived his work with the YPSL as "completely intertwined" with his work with the Sunday school and was a strong proponent of the involvement of Yipsels in the schools. From his experience as director of the Rochester YPSL circle, he believed that the constant teacher shortage could be alleviated by Yipsels. In June 1915 he argued that "Yipsels make natural teachers and helpers. They are not so learned as to be technical. Their vocabulary is still smaller and more easily compre-hended than that of the old-liner who has drunk in Marx for years. They are therefore nearer to the child-mind. Also they are not so set in their ways as the older comrades, and are more adaptable. Be-sides, they are still fresh and young and hopeful and full of life. They are natural optimists." To Yipsels themselves, Shedd stressed that the schools could serve as a "feeder" for the League, so that "even intelligent selfishness would command the Yipsels to work in these schools, in order that the future of their Clubs or Leagues might be more secure." Such work could also serve to "deepen the worker's own life," and would be fun, make them stronger and more confident in their own abilities, and provide them with an op-portunity to assist the socialist movement in the present instead of waiting "for years wondering just what you might possibly be fitted for." In fact, the main reason that Shedd on occasion hesitated in his endorsement of the requirement that SSS teachers had to be Party members was that they might be under age (that is, Yipsels). In 1918, William Kruse also suggested, "None are better fitted for this kind of work than the Yipsels."[10] However, aside from reports about schools in Milwaukee, New York City, Rochester, and Rockford, there is no evidence that YPSL members were heavily involved in the work of the Sunday schools.

Teacher Training

Recruiting qualified individuals to teach in the Socialist Sunday schools was a constant problem. Many schools were forced to use supporters who had little or no training as teachers. This lack of experience was especially noted when discussions of the schools fo-cused on the need for better instruction. Even the movement's strongest advocates recognized the need for teacher training, not because the instruction taking place was so desultory but because the relatively inexperienced teachers needed to learn relevant psychological principles and pedagogical skills, and become better able to identify and develop suitable curriculum materials. As Benjamin Glassberg pointed out, "Although a good many Comrades still believe that all the equipment necessary for a good Sunday school teacher is vim and enthusiasm and an interest in the work, the children quickly discover that more than that is necessary. Teaching, like everything else, requires more than good intentions. It requires, in short, people who also know how to teach, especially in the case of children."[11]

While the extent of teacher training within the SSS movement was quite limited, it did take a variety of forms, from informal get togethers and lectures to more formally developed series of classes. For example, teacher training lectures for SSS teachers in New York City included Sidonie Matzner Gruenberg's talk on "The Teacher's Attitude toward the Child" and Alexander Fichandler's on "The Second Year Curriculum." Teachers at a Chicago school met every Saturday afternoon in 1908 at the home of Mary Livingston, the school's superintendent, to "go over the outline for the next day's lesson, try over the songs together, play the little games, and rehearse the story that is to be told." Such meetings were intended to ensure that "when the children come together, there are no hitches, and everything passes off smoothly and intelligently."[12] Shedd was a strong advocate of such teacher meetings. He stressed that they were to be simple and voluntary, and specifically not business meetings: "All of us get, alas, too many of those things." They were to be "instruction meetings, in which the lesson of the coming Sunday is talked over [and] . . . teachers get acquainted. They come to know and to like one another."[13]

More formally structured classes also were sponsored by Party locals and the Rand School. In 1908 and 1909, for example, the Rand School offered a twelve-week "Teachers' Training Course" that was advertised as especially geared to the work of the Socialist Sunday schools. The instructor, Edith Breithut, was a public school teacher. Publicity for the course indicated that Breithut planned to bring a group of day school children to the class for demonstration lessons. In 1911, the Rand School offered another teachers' training class that was under the direction of the State Committee on Socialist Schools and provided free of charge. The course's first two sessions were on "The Psychological Basis of Modern Methods" and "The Curriculum," with a particular focus on the interests of the child. Recommended readings included those by William James, G. Stanley Hall, and William Kilpatrick. Both of these sessions were taught by David Greenberg, a teacher at the Brownsville SSS and a student at Teachers College of Columbia University. Subsequent sessions were taught by Henrietta Rodman, a public school teacher who had worked with Edward Thorndike at Columbia University. Other Rand School courses in 1911–1912 that were advertised as of particular interest to SSS teachers were Dr. Cecile Greil's "Sex Hygiene and Sanitation" and Edith Breithut's "Methods of Teaching."[14]

From 1913 to 1918, the Rand School did not advertise any of its courses as of special interest to SSS teachers. In early 1919, however, several Rand School courses were announced as such, including A. A. Goldenweiser's "Ancient History," Laura Garrett's "How to Teach Nature Lessons," Lucy Retting's "Social Recreation," Alexander Fichandler's "Methods of Teaching," and David Berenberg's "The Socialist School." The course taught by Berenberg, who had public teaching experience and who at the time was teaching at the Brownsville school, is of particular interest because it was directly related to SSS work. It covered eight topics: The Aim of the Socialist School; The Child; Theories of Child Development; Classification; Psychology and Its Relation to Teaching; How to Outline a Course of Study; Teaching Aids and Equipment; and YPSL and Sunday School Problems. During the following year, Berenberg offered another course at the Rand School on "Methods of Teaching."[15] Unfortunately, no further indication of the content of Berenberg's courses has been located. In 1920, the Rand School reported that it had been commissioned by the Party to prepare a textbook for the Sunday schools. It was to be written by Berenberg, but it was never completed, as other more pressing matters facing the radical movement overshadowed the need for SSS curriculum materials and SSS teacher training classes.[16]

Recruitment of Students

Socialist Sunday schools ranged in student enrollment from a handful to several hundred. While it was never discussed as a major problem in the same way as the shortage of teachers, schools needed children in order to function. For many students, who occasionally accompanied parents to the local Party headquarters or labor lyceum for meetings, rallies, festivals, or special children's programs sponsored by the Party or another radical group, attendance at the Socialist Sunday School was a natural activity. While in some cases interested parents undoubtedly insisted that their reluctant children attend, the available evidence indicates that most children went willingly: with a sense of purpose, to meet friends and to have fun.

Still, student turnover, like staff turnover, was common, and as long as there were enough teachers and classroom space, many schools sought to increase their enrollment. The usual way to do this was by word of mouth and through announcements and reports in the local radical press and Party local bulletins. Another strategy used in Omaha was for SSS teachers to go door-to-door in the neighborhood to look for interested families. In Newport, Kentucky, two SSS teachers distributed all their "Socialist magazines and papers after reading them, very often with marked passages," in order to interest parents in the work of their school. Although it was rarely done, some schools even paid for formal newspaper advertisements. In addition, in several schools the students themselves helped recruit other children. For example, students from Milwaukee's International SSS sold flowers and distributed literature pertaining to the school at a socialist festival in an attempt to interest parents and their children in the work of the school.[17] Sometimes prizes were even offered to the students who brought the most new students to a school.

Kendrick Shedd also sent out letters to parents, appealing to them to enroll their children in the Rochester school. One letter contained exceptional detail from Shedd about what he saw as the reasons for sending one's children to the Rochester SSS and the nature of the education that was being offered there:[18]

Dear Comrades and Sympathizers:

Of course, you want your children to grow up filled with the spirit of intelligent rebellion against the present system of injustice and favoritism toward a privileged class;

Of course, you desire that those children shall understand the world they live in, and what is wrong with it, and why;

Of course, you would not have your little ones grow up with a feeling of satisfaction with things as they are;

Of course, you want them to be class-conscious, and filled with a longing to help emancipate the working-class from its bonds of wage-slavery;—

Well then, if this is so, what are you doing to bring it about? Do you find that they learn these much desired things in the public or parochial schools? Or in the Churches? Or in the Capitalist Sunday Schools? Do they learn what you want them to learn from reading the Capitalist papers, or books or magazines?

Where then, can they learn these things? Where can they imbibe the spirit of intelligent opposition to wrong conditions?

Where can they learn why these conditions are wrong, and what is the remedy for them?

We have here in Rochester a Socialist Sunday School. It is one of many scattered all over this land and others, all of which have arisen as a result of the fact that the children are not taught what they should be taught in the orthodox Sunday Schools, and that they grow up in ignorance of the true condition of things and the reasons behind them.

We aim to inspire in the children class-consciousness, and a love for the working-class. We sing with them and teach them indirectly by story and play and festivals. We seek to make each exercise so interesting that they will desire to remain with us. And many of them are deeply in love with our school.

Have YOU visited the School? Are YOU doing all you can to help us to carry out our aim and purpose? Are YOU sending YOUR own children here? If not, why not? Ask yourself, and answer your own question.

If YOU all would help, we could have a wonderful school here, and we could do much more good than is at all possible without your support.

Will you help us now? Will you send your children at once? Will you come yourself as often as possible? Will you speak of the school to others? Will you support the work in every way possible to you, even to the point of self-sacrifice?

We are waiting for you and yours. When shall we have the please [*sic*] of seeing you?

Yours for the working-class,

There is no indication of the success of these recruitment efforts. In general, however, the need for additional students was less of a concern to SSS activists than the adequacy of facilities and funding of the school, the recruitment of qualified teachers, and the development of suitable curriculum materials.

Students

Children who attended the schools were almost exclusively from working-class backgrounds. One former student from Milwaukee, for example, insists that this was "absolutely" the case: There is "no question about it."[19] In fact, SSS activists never appealed to other segments of the population. The schools never tried to remove themselves from the political and material interests of working-class neighborhoods; they were intended to be of, by, and for American workers and their children.

Schools generally appealed to a range of ages, typically from five- or six-year-olds to thirteen- or fourteen-year-olds, with many schools including adult classes as well. The student bodies appear to have been comprised of an equal number of boys and girls. Although they were broadly viewed as fellow radicals (being referred to at times as "little comrades," "kiddie socialists," "good rebels," and the like), and most children came from radical homes, not all the parents of the students considered themselves socialists. Some of the children's parents were strong union supporters and allies of the socialist movement, but not Party members. One former student of the International SSS, for example, describes his father as "more-or-less a socialist." A former student at the East Side SSS in Manhattan similarly recalls her parents as "socialist-minded." Indeed, most SSS organizers stressed that the schools were quite willing to enroll children of "near socialists," other radicals, and even liberals.[20] They sought to extend an appreciation of radical tenets to segments of the labor community less committed to the socialist cause.

The Socialist Sunday schools tended to be neighborhood schools that drew their students from the surrounding area. Despite their general rejection of any specific ethnic identification, some schools were comprised of students from a certain ethnic or religious background because their neighborhood was largely populated by a particular group. In New York City, for example, the student bodies of the East Side SSS in Manhattan and the Brownsville SSS in Brooklyn were almost entirely Jewish in composition, even though not all the teachers were Jewish. Similarly, a school in Rockford, Illinois, included a large percentage of Swedish children. On the other hand, former students of the International SSS who lived in a Jewish ghetto of Milwaukee, remember the student body of that school as only about one-third Jewish because the school drew from a larger geographic area than just their neighborhood. Indeed, some schools proudly proclaimed the international character of their student body. In 1916, the Hartford SSS, for example, boasted that its students were the children of "American, Irish, German, English, Jewish, Finnish, Lithuanian, Polish and Russian members of the Socialist party."[21]

Virtually all of the former students interviewed for this study recall their Sunday school experience as being quite enjoyable. Going to the International SSS, for example, was described as "a heck of a lot of fun" and "a great time," with "very wonderful, decent people" involved. One woman who attended the East Side school in Manhattan remembers that she and her sisters "really looked forward to it." Another former student at a Bronx school recalls that she and her sister "looked forward eagerly to going on Sunday mornings." And a former student of the Children's Socialist Lyceum in Los Angeles recollects that she and her cousins "loved the sessions."[22]

Two former participants had less complimentary memories of the Socialist Sunday schools, although theirs is clearly a minority view. One former student of the Rochester school, for example, went with a group of friends but remembers not really caring about the school and attending for only a short while. He did admit, however, that other children were more actively involved in the school and seemed to enjoy going. And the daughter of the man who headed a small school at the Brooklyn Labor Lyceum, located in a non-socialist area of the borough, maintains that "it was hideous! . . . I was . . . grabbed, pushed into this horrible atmosphere. It was never fun." Meant as an uncomplimentary comparison, she likens this socialist educational setting to that of a traditional Catholic school and is quite bitter at having been "pushed" into socialism as a child.[23]

The somewhat varied recollections of the SSS experience can be explained in a number of ways. First, as with public schools, different students may have different reactions to the same school experience or have different experiences in the same school setting. Given individual personalities and interests, the variations in children's home backgrounds, and the differential treatment children receive from teachers and other children, any child in a school may experience what is offered in a quite different way than another student in the same school. Second, the schools differed from one another. Some sponsored an extensive number of singing, dancing, athletic, and dramatic activities, while others, for lack of staff, funding or facilities, or because of a different view of the character of socialist education, offered very few. Some schools may have attracted experienced and creative teachers, while others did not. And third, the intervening years may have resulted in an exaggeration of either the positive or negative qualities of a school, so that a fair evaluation of the overall experience is difficult to make. In fact, those individuals who think more positively about socialism in general and their past involvement in the radical movement may have a more charitable view of their Sunday school experience than those whose thoughts are more negative. For example, the former student of the Rochester school mentioned above remarked that later in life he wanted "no part" of socialist politics, maintaining that "it's for the birds." And the former student of the Brooklyn Labor Lyceum school regretted the years that she was involved in the socialist movement and believed that she got away from it "as soon as I began to *think* about the United States and its relationship to the world." She asserted that one "gets over" socialism when one "matures."[24] While they did not all identify themselves with socialism, most of the former participants with positive recollections of their SSS experience expressed a a great respect for what the American socialist movement had tried to accomplish.

It is difficult to ascertain the effects of the Socialist Sunday School experience on the lives of the students. There are few accounts from students at the time to indicate what was actually being learned. However, one student from Brooklyn no doubt expressed what SSS organizers were hoping for:[25]

> The Sunday school has taught me things I never learned in [public] school. I have learned the right feeling to have toward fellow-beings, learned the wrongs of the present day and the way it may be righted. I do not know if the knowledge I have obtained there has made me a Socialist. If Socialism means a feeling of kindred toward all humanity, a wish to help those who are unhappy, to find in the future a way to make them contented and joyful, then I am a Socialist. . . . Not one of us is supposed to drudge and only drudge all our lives. Of course, we will always work, for the desire to work is born in us and it is a noble desire, but as a respite and a source of knowledge, we should see and hear the beautiful things in the world. . . . I have learned to wish to see the world a better place for all of us, to wish that I may soon find my place at the wheel and do my little part in the great work which will help all humanity.

Regarding the schools' lasting effects on students, several former students pointed out that it is virtually impossible to separate the influence of attending the weekend school from other aspects of growing up in a radical working-class home and community. Attendance at the school was just one element of a larger, dynamic socialist culture. The schools did not introduce the children to socialist and working-class themes as much as they attempted to deepen students' understanding and, in most of the schools, provide them with an enjoyable Sunday morning experience as well. They also gave the children an opportunity to meet other children from similar backgrounds, and in some cases from different backgrounds as well. Thus, Peggy Dennis, who attended the Los Angeles school, believes that her SSS experience offered her "for the first time, at that early age, an extension of my family-instilled radicalism out into the 'world' beyond. This would have been my first contact with 'Gentile' radicals and the realization there were others beyond our radical Jewish community who held ideas similar to ours."[26]

Occasionally, as is the case for all schools, the lasting effects may have been unexpected. For one former student of the International SSS, for example, a visit by Dudley Watson, the director of the Milwaukee Art Institute at the time, is particularly memorable. Focusing on "Being Artists Together," Watson emphasized to the children that "everybody should be obliged to do a part of the 'dirty work' of civilization, but that everybody should also have a chance to enjoy artistic activity as well." Listening was ten-year-old Joseph Friebert, the youngest of three brothers attending the school (where their father led the chorus). Friebert went on to become a member of the art faculty at the University of Wisconsin at Milwaukee and was described by a local newspaper years later as "the best painter" in the Milwaukee area. Friebert vividly recalls Watson's visit to the Socialist Sunday School and maintains that it greatly influenced him to become a painter, that it touched a nerve within him that may otherwise have been left unrealized.[27]

Whether or not these former students became socialists (or, as in the case of Dennis, communists) when they reached adulthood probably did not turn on their Sunday morning educational experience. On its own terms, the SSS movement was ultimately unable to ensure a positive future for the socialist movement of the United States. On the other hand, that weekend schools could ever fulfill such a role is doubtful under the best of circumstances. Moreover, the Socialist Sunday schools were fatally hobbled by the fact that they were never given a fair and full opportunity to maximize their influence on the children of radical workers.

CHAPTER SIX

Socialist Sunday School Curriculum

Throughout the lifetime of the Socialist Sunday schools, the curriculum was limited by the nature and intention of the schools. After all, the schools met for only two hours a week; there was no time to cover a wide variety of topics or any one topic in great detail. And because of extensive family, school, and work commitments, as well as involvement in other Party activities, most SSS directors and teachers had little time to devote to the development of creative and detailed lesson materials and ideas. There was also no central organization to lend significant assistance to the construction of a curriculum over an extended period of time. And it was never expected that the Socialist Sunday schools would prepare the children for college or for an occupation, as was expected of the public schools. Indeed, the schools were never even charged with providing a complete socialist education for youth, only a more formal and systematic one than could be received at home and at Party-sponsored clubs, parades, and rallies.

Taken as a whole the American SSS movement provided numerous lesson materials and activities that challenged the messages being transmitted by the public schools and other mainstream social institutions. Narrowly conceived economic subjects and socialist tenets did not constitute the entire scope of this socialist curriculum, and lectures and recitations were often supplemented by group discussions, role-playing activities, games, songs, plays, and festivals. Although it is not always clear how these materials were used in the schools (and, of course, they were no doubt read by participants in differing ways), they represent a body of alternative knowledge un-familiar to most historians and educators. While only a representa-tive sample of this curriculum can be provided here, it can serve to illustrate the variety of ways that these schools directly contested the academic canon of the time, attempting to educate workers' children about the inadequacies of industrial capitalism, the nature of class struggle, and the potential benefits of socialism.

Lesson Outlines: Rochester and Milwaukee Schools

Lesson outlines provide the clearest indication of the specific topics that were taught in the Socialist Sunday schools and the ideo-logical perspective that was adopted. Detailed documentation is available only for the schools in Rochester and Milwaukee.

Kendrick Shedd developed lesson outlines and made a con-certed effort to publicize their availability to other schools. He in-cluded additional information with the outlines so that their in-tended use would be clear to teachers with whom he did not have regular and direct contact. For example, accompanying his Roches-ter SSS *Lesson Topics for January–March 1914* is the recommendation that while "there are many points or ideas suggested by the ques-tions and statements, . . . [it] is not intended that you should touch upon them all, for your time is too limited. Use what you need. Much is left to your own discretion." At the same time that Shedd urged teachers to "encourage intelligent questions . . . [so that] the little ones . . . [will] grow up with inquiring minds," he stressed the need "to help them to get the economic viewpoint, the viewpoint of the working class." Shedd was particularly adamant that SSS teachers not use his lesson outlines in a way that would be more appropriate for adult classes: "We must make everything clear and simple. Chil-dren do not understand stilted economics, and it would be a crime to get the poor things into a corner somewhere and shoot economic de-terminism, class struggle and such classic things at their young hearts."[1]

Shedd's lesson outlines were usually issued a few weeks or months at a time and were often printed in pamphlet form or on cards. He received numerous requests for copies of his lessons but he never sought to gain financial advantage from them, as all the money that was received for copies was used to cover printing costs. By 1916, however, he announced that his own stock of Rochester lessons "is exhausted. . . . I wish I had copies of my lessons, but have none at present."[2]

The main component of Shedd's outlines were suggested ques-tions about particular topics. (In this respect, his approach was simi-lar to that of Myles Horton of the Highlander School, who remarked many years later that "one of the best ways to educate is to ask questions. . . . You can get all your ideas across just by asking questions and at the same time you help people grow and not form a dependency on you.") For example, a focus on "Work" was to be guided by the following questions: "1. Who works? And who does not? Why? 2. Why do we work? 3. What is produced by work? 4. What are the various kinds of work? 5. How many hours should people work? 6. Should little children and mothers work in factories? 7. Do the workers get all they earn? Who gets most of it? 8. How can the workers get all they earn?" Shedd's lesson outline thus moves from the general nature of labor and the laboring force to a more specific emphasis on contemporary labor conditions and the inequality of earnings.[3]

Similarly, for another lesson on "Health," students were expected to come up with their own list of "enemies of Health," but Shedd offered several possibilities to assist teachers in the class discussion (for example, lack of food, clothing, and shelter; overeating and harried eating; overwork and lack of rest; lack of light and bad air; fear and worry; and lack of playgrounds). Emphasis was placed on the health problems fostered by industrial capitalism, rather than stressing particular socialist tenets. Subsequent lessons focused on such topics as "Success" and "Justice." Shedd's suggested questions help to reveal how his treatment of these concepts differed from how they might have been covered, if at all, in the public schools: "What is necessary for [success]; are the following: Possession of Money? High Position? Power? Was Abraham Lincoln Successful? Compare the Work of Abraham Lincoln and Karl Marx. Do successful persons always realize their success? Name some who did not. Can true success be gained at the expense of one's brothers? What is success?" and "Is competition just? Do the workers get justice? Have we political justice? Name some instances of political injustice. Are these things just: Child wage workers? Mothers employed outside of their homes? Use of militia to settle strikes? War? Capitalist courts? Capitalist Press? Suppression of Free Speech and Assemblage? What is justice?" Each of these outlines begins with a discussion that links the general topic to social conditions and then concludes with a definitional question. The children were encouraged to view these "commonsensical" notions critically and then, in the light of the unsatisfactory character of prevailing, "capitalist" views, to adopt an alternative perspective. In addition, a link was made between what could be considered abstract philosophical constructs with the social context in which they are experienced. Thus, success and justice only have meaning in relation to who benefits when certain individuals and groups in an unequal capitalist society are "successful" or "justly treated."

During the month of March 1913, Shedd's lessons dealt with "Striking and Scabbing," "Working and Shirking," and "Buying and Selling." Suggested questions for the first lesson include the following: "What is a strike? Who strikes? What do strikers expect to gain by it? Against whom are they striking? Against what are they striking? Is striking easy or hard? The right to strike—Is it really a right? Who denies it and why? The advantages and disadvantages of striking. Name all you can think of. The Scab. Who is he? What is meant by scabbing? What forces men to scab? Are Scabs bad men? How looked upon—by the employers? by the workers? Would YOU like to be a scab? Would YOU be a scab. Reasons." The relatively sympathetic treatment afforded scabs is in line with the general approach of American radicals at this time to blame "the system" for the misdeeds of misinformed workers. One socialist activist of this period later expressed the point this way: "You did not hate the capitalists as individuals, but you hated the system for which they stood, because you didn't think the interests of the people and of profit would be finally reconciled."[4] Of course, at the same time that scabs as individuals could be treated somewhat tolerantly, the children were explicitly taught that they themselves should never engage in anti-strike activity. Scabbing by others who did not know better could be understood, especially given the inhuman pressures of the capitalist system, but such practices were still anathema to anyone with an allegiance to the working class.

Shedd also prepared a series of lesson outlines entitled "Home Destroyers." The first lesson examines the problems of "Unemployment, Poverty and Drink" in the context of their effects on "home life." The point is made that the absence of drink by itself would not insure a significantly improved home life because capitalist relations is the core problem. Suggested questions include: "Remove 'drink' from the world but keep Capitalism: would all have real homes? Why not?" The next lesson deals with "Slums, Sweatshops, Sickness and Disease," with a concluding comment that maps out the general perspective being taken: "No true homes for workers while Capitalism robs them of health, time, comforts, life." The following lessons in this series focus on "No Home-makers; No Marriages; Race Suicide; Divorce," and "Why John Green Loses His 'Home.'" What is evident is that despite the accusations of opponents that socialism was antithetical to moral family life, Rochester SSS teachers sought to portray industrial capitalism as producing conditions that served to destroy healthy family relations. The maintenance of family values and ties could be fostered, not endangered, by a socialist society. A cartoon that was used in conjunction with these lessons helps to clarify Shedd's perspective. Drawn by Art Young, a well-known radical cartoonist, it pictures a long, slithering snake—identified as "Capitalism"—with dollar signs covering its skin. The snake is crawling up a tree to a nest of little birds, presumably to attack them. The title of the cartoon is "The Sanctity of the Home."

A series of lesson outlines that Shedd prepared for the 1914–1915 school year was in response to a suggestion by some of the school's older students that more attention be given to the specific natures of capitalism and socialism.[5] Although it is clear that Shedd intended to address this request in full, no evidence of detailed Rochester lesson outlines on the topic of "Socialism" has been located. Prior to his leaving for Milwaukee in the spring of 1915, however, Shedd prepared a "Capitalism Series." After an introductory section on the "very selfish . . . [and] unjust" nature of capitalism, twelve social issues are addressed: Poverty and Pauperism; The "Drink Curse" and Unemployment (Or Being Out of Work); The Wage-System; Work or Labor; Disease and Accidents; Rent and Interest; Profits—What Is Meant?; Waste and War; Education (or Teaching the People); Freedom and Justice; Criminals, In Prison and Out; and The Private Owners of the People's Life. Shedd hoped that students exposed to this curriculum, which was intended to include a similar series of lessons on socialism, would learn not only about "the evils which result from it [capitalism] under which people are daily suffering" but also "the real meaning and purpose of Socialism and be prepared to give intelligent answers, when asked questions concerning it." Evident in this series of lessons is a strong sense of the need to place working-class behavior, political and otherwise, within the larger social context (that is, capitalist society) from which it emanates. His list of questions pertaining to "Education" is illustrative: "Why don't the workers get more schooling? Don't they want it? Would they rather work hard? . . . Do all people have the same chance or opportunity to travel, to study music or art, to read the best books, and to see the grandest sights? Why? . . . Are the Newspapers good educators? Do they tell the truth? . . . Are School Teachers good educators? Do they always teach the truth? . . . Do the rich men, bankers and the brokers and the stockowners, and the politicians and the grafters and those who ride on the backs of the workers want the 'common people' or the workers to become highly educated? Why not? What would happen, if they should get their eyes open?"

Kendrick Shedd left Rochester for Milwaukee in the spring of 1915. Information on the curriculum of the Milwaukee schools in 1915–1916 and 1916–1917 is sketchy, although it appears that Walter Thomas Mills's text, *The Struggle for Existence*, was adopted for some of the lessons. (Mills's text focuses on the evolution of civilization from its beginnings to the capitalist stage of development and eventually to the more advanced stage of socialism, in the continuing "struggle for existence.") However, beginning with the 1917–1918 school year and continuing through the next half-dozen years, the *Milwaukee Leader* published descriptions of SSS lessons that were used in Milwaukee. The general theme of the 1917–1918 curriculum, for example, was "cooperation in everyday life." Each of the thirty lessons focuses on a social activity in which doing things together would help to resolve problems and difficulties. In order, the activities are singing, playing, keeping well, voting, learning, making money, owning, being world citizens, making war, governing, judging, railroading, investing, being policemen, house cleaning, owning theatres, being milkmen, owning books, campaigning, being artists, profiteering, writing stories, cooking, rejoicing, gardening, being readers, running a newspaper, building, dancing, and running industry. The lesson outlines highlight the need for SSS teachers to go beyond "finding fault with the existing order" and to help "make real Socialists out of the children." Each week's topic was intended to help structure the entire school session (assembly, classes, and re-assembly), as the description of the initial lesson on "Singing Together" makes clear:[6]

> 1. Let a number of children try to sing different songs at the same time. Then the same song starting at different times. Then the same song starting together but at different pitches. Then end with utter confusion and shouting and disorder.
> 2. Dismiss children to go to the classes. Class hints: What was the trouble? Shall we stop singing altogether? Why not? How shall we have good singing? What is needed to sing together? Why not have each sing alone?
> 3. School reassembles. Superintendent reminds school of disorder at beginning of lesson. Any suggestions for better way of doing things? Children will volunteer results of class period. A number of children will then try to sing together in orderly manner. More are added. Finally the whole school together gives everyone a chance to take part, each helping the other, and results in harmony and good feeling. Singing separately in competition gives only one or two a chance, while the majority must remain silent, or results in disorder and confusion and noise. Let us sing together.

Occasionally, adaptations of school lessons were performed as part of special school celebrations. Such was the case for the November 25, 1917, lesson on "Being World Citizens Together," which was used as "a specimen lesson" at the school's December 30 holiday program. The lesson plan begins with the superintendent giving out flags of various nations to the classes so that each class has the flag of one country. A child from each class rises and tells the assembly why the flag that she or he is holding is "better than the flags of any other countries." It is pointed out that every flag "has its boastful defenders," and consequently "the school threatens to become the scene of a miniature world war." The potential "conflict" is averted when the children are dismissed to go to their separate classes. In their classes, the teachers discuss "citizenship," with the following questions to guide them: "Why do we like to feel that we are the greatest country on earth? Why do the people of other countries feel the same way about themselves? Does this feeling make it easy for capitalists to stir up war between nations? Who benefits from war? Would there be so many wars if the people of different countries were less ignorant and less boastful? Can love of country be transformed into love of the world?" When the whole school reassembles, each child with a small national flag comes up to the front: "All stand harmoniously together, while the big flags of internationalism and peace are spread over them all." The message of this lesson, which initially took place seven months after the United States's entrance into World War I, is "When we are world citizens, all marching under the banner of international peaceful Socialism, our ignorant nationalistic boastfulness will give way to helpful and enlightened co-operation with other nations." When the lesson was performed for the holiday program, the displaying of "the International Flag" and "the end of national conflicts" reportedly brought cheers from those assembled.[7]

Several lessons in 1919 focused on the environment as a major influence in individuals' lives. First, a culture quite unlike "our own" was studied: for example, traditional Eskimo culture. The main point is that Eskimos actually have little time for play because "th[eir] time is all spent in getting the necessities of life, such as food, shelter, clothing." For the Eskimo, it is truly "a struggle for life or existence." Subsequent lessons are primarily concerned with a comparison of life in "the torrid zone," "the temperate zone," and "the frigid zone." It is emphasized that "if you want to be a fine, strong person, your environment must produce those qualities in you." It is important, then, for one to surround oneself with people and conditions that will allow one to live a "fine and worth while [*sic*] life." This series of lessons concludes with a story of twin brothers whose parents died when they were young and so they were put up for adoption. One of the boys, Charles, stayed in the small town where they were born, "had plenty of fresh air and room to play," was encouraged to be active and industrious, and because "he had never lacked what he needed or wanted—home, friends, clothing, school, food, play—it was easy for him to become honest." He eventually went to college, became a doctor, and moved to the city. Edward, on the other hand, was adopted by people who moved to the city. He grew up "in a wretched dirty tenement on a dirty street, with little fresh air, and very little schooling." As a result, "he had grown up rather weak and had never had a chance to learn a trade or good business." At the free health clinic where he worked one day a week, Charles saw one of his patients steal his watch. He "looked at the name on his record and saw to his amazement that the miserable, sick and dirty man who had pocketed his watch was his own twin brother, no longer recognizable." The story eventually concludes: "So we can see that had Edward stayed in the village he, too, might have been a great doctor, or had Charles gone to the city when 4 and lived in a crowded dirty tenement house, and been poor and hungry and weak, he might have been a thief." The story thus reveals "how surroundings or environment make people what they are to a great extent" and that we should "not . . . be too quick and harsh in judging people until we know what kind of surroundings made them what they are."[8]

From November 1920 to June 1921, the *Milwaukee Leader* published an entirely new SSS curriculum. Unlike previous ones published in the newspaper, these lesson outlines (and future ones as well) do not include how the materials were to be presented at the school. The materials were published as a serialized story that gives more attention to democratic management than to public ownership. For example, the third lesson on "Trade Unions" emphasizes, "Working people do not have much to say about managing the factory they work in. They are treated like children, instead of like grownup men and women. They are helpless even when they have trade unions. If all the working people formed one big union perhaps they would have more to say about the factory." The serialized story continues with workers forming such a union but meeting great obstacles in the way of the union's growth, in particular from the newspapers, banks, police, judges, federal government, and so on. In an optimistic conclusion (during an actual time of great tumult within the American radical movement), the struggle is won: "The workers in every country in the world now helped each other. They do not fight for profits and bring on world wars. The people of the world live in peace and plenty. Socialism rules."[9]

The 1921–1922 SSS curriculum in Milwaukee was guided by a new series of lessons that was intended as "a combined course of geography and Socialism," one that was perceived as particularly "suitable to [a] Socialist Sunday school where many nationalities are represented."[10] This course of study focuses on different countries, with an emphasis on the achievements of and prospects for the socialist movement in each nation. Source materials for classwork were to include the personal experiences of students and their family members, books such as the *American Labor Year Book*, and factual information presented in the lesson outlines themselves. From October 1921 to May 1922, twenty-six countries were studied: Finland, Sweden, Rumania, Poland, Turkey, Palestine, Mexico, Haiti, San Domingo, Spain, Portugal, Italy, Japan, Siberia, Switzerland, Australia, Belgium, Denmark, Holland, Norway, India, China, Ireland, Hungary, Bulgaria, and Canada. There is little indication, however, of the ways in which this curriculum was used in the classroom.

Lesson Outlines for Other Schools

Although extensive documentation is available only for the Rochester and Milwaukee schools, other lesson outlines appeared from time to time in the socialist press or were published in pamphlet or book form. Many of these materials were developed by New York City activists. One was Bertha Matthews Fraser's *Outlines of Lessons for Socialist Schools for Children*, published in 1910. Given her prominent place in the SSS movement in the New York City area, there is little doubt that Fraser's lesson ideas were adopted there (as well as in Rochester and Milwaukee). In addition, her course of study was recommended by the Woman's National Committee of the Party in their 1912 pamphlet, "How to Organize Socialist Schools."[11]

Fraser's curriculum consists in large part of 300-plus-word essays, with a few suggested actitivies and readings. She summarized her nineteen lessons as follows: "The first lesson deals with the earth; the three following lessons deal with food, clothing and shelter, and trace their connection with the earth. Next we show that, although nature provides everything in abundance, we can have none of the things necessary to support and protect life without the expenditure of labor. A lesson is then devoted to each of the three subjects mentioned above, showing the labor necessary to produce them. Three lessons are devoted to a comparison between the working class and the idle class; first, in connection with food; second, clothing; and the last the homes. A lesson is given upon the cause of this contrast—the unequal distribution of the products due to the exploitation of labor, and the consequent suffering of the working class. The last two lessons deal with the remedy and how it is to be applied." The "remedy" for existing inequities that SSS teachers were to share with their students entails "making the earth's resources and the machinery of production the collective property of the whole people." The rationale for this change is also provided: "Everything that is produced and sold to-day is a social product; that is, it requires a portion of the labor of all the workers to make it a finished product. Since this is true, the only way we can enjoy a share in the gifts of nature, finished and completed by social labor, is by making land and the machinery of production the collective property of the entire people." In case it is not already obvious, Fraser makes it clear that, "this, Socialism proposes to do."

Another important contribution to the SSS curriculum was authored by Edith Commander Breithut, who taught for a while in the public school system. Although she does not appear to have taught in the Socialist Sunday schools, she aided the SSS movement by teaching a course on Pedagogy at the Rand School and developing several series of SSS lessons that were reprinted in socialist publications. One six-lesson course in particular, entitled "Social Things and Individual Things," was used in New York City, Buffalo, Milwaukee, Rockford, and probably elsewhere as well.[12] It explores the differences between "individual things" (for example, a hat, a spoon, and a bed) and "social things," which are defined as "so large that they are quite useless to one person or one family" (for example, a subway, a steamship, a coal mine, and a shoe factory). The first lesson concludes with a list of items to arrange in two columns (individual things and social things) that includes the Brooklyn Bridge, a watch, a park, a telephone, a table, a railroad, a doll, and a merry-go-round. The children are then asked to contribute the names of three individual things that are not included on Breithut's list. The second lesson probes further into "Private Ownership," emphasizing that "THERE IS NOW AND THERE ALWAYS WILL BE PRIVATE OWNERSHIP OF ALL INDIVIDUAL THINGS." The following lesson focuses on "the great question which divides Socialists and non-Socialists": Who should own social things? Using coal mines, shoe factories, and the like as examples, the socialist answer to the question is given: "EVERYTHING USED BY THE PUBLIC AND NECESSARY TO THE PUBLIC SHOULD BE PUBLICLY OR SOCIALLY OWNED, and should be managed for the benefit of the public." The non-socialist rejoinder is also provided: "That is all nonsense. Individuals should own everything and manage it for their own benefit." In the final lessons, three specific examples are discussed: the school, the post office, and the fire department. The emphasis is placed on the evolution of these examples from privately owned and operated enterprises to public ones. The final message of the course of study reinforces its overall theme: "Public ownership is increasing" in many countries and it can be shown that "ALMOST ALWAYS A CHANGE FROM PRIVATE TO PUBLIC OWNERSHIP BENEFITS THE PEOPLE. THAT IS WHY SOCIALISTS ADVOCATE PUBLIC OWNERSHIP OF ALL SOCIAL THINGS."

Another SSS activist who wrote a course of study was David Greenberg, who taught for a time at the Brownsville school. His fifty-nine page *Socialist Sunday School Curriculum* was published in 1913, the result of a request by the Socialist School Union of Greater

New York for lesson materials.[13] Greenberg's effort is unique not only because it was sponsored and given approval by an official SSS committee but also because he outlined a broadly conceived course of study for as many as six different grade levels. The outline for the Primary class (six- and seven-year-olds) can serve as an example of this curriculum.

Greenberg suggested that historical lessons taught to the youngest children concentrate on "lead[ing] the children back to the sources of our laws and institutions, by reading about and acting (dramatically) the lives of the primitive people." Since younger children were involved, this was to be done "in a pleasant, simple manner." Formulas and definitions were to be avoided: "Real, living stories, vivid pictures, and relics" were to be utilized instead. The lives of the Tree-Dwellers, Cave-Dwellers, and Lake-Dwellers (see later discussion of the Katherine Dopp books), and the American Indians, were suggested as topics of study. Attention was to be drawn especially to their means of acquiring food, clothing, and shelter; the relation of the individual to the group; and relations between different groups, communities, or tribes. Reminiscent of Fraser's outlines, economics lessons for the Primary grade focused on helping children "to see that the source of all things is the earth which belongs to everybody and that it is labor that takes everything from the earth and turns it (1) into machinery and (2) the things that labor makes with the machine." Ethics and morals, in particular a "passionate love of right and justice," also were a part of Greenberg's course of study. Discussions and "strong stories," rather than proverbs and pledges, were to be used for this purpose. Specific traits to examine included obedience, honesty, courage, loyalty, comradeship, love, duty, patriotism, and humanity, with special attention given to the "wickedness and wastefulness" of war. In addition, the young children needed to learn that "good air and good food are necessary to life," that cleanliness affects health, and that the habits of the individual can affect the health of the many. Finally, Greenberg also recommended that marching, calisthenics, dancing, and singing be part of the SSS curriculum, and that "at all times, in some form, allow the pupil to express every impression made upon him."

Among the many other SSS lesson outlines that have been located, one series that received the official endorsement of the Socialist School Union of Greater New York was published in the *Young Socialists' Magazine*. It was developed by Helen Dunbar, who reportedly "worked it out practically in a little class she had during the year 1910–1911." Dunbar stressed that the overall aim of her lessons was not to "attempt to teach Socialism" directly but rather "to instruct and entertain the children with songs, stories, games and occupations which are chosen as being in line with the Socialist philosophy." She was addressing an important difference between teaching socialist tenets and teaching "in line with the Socialist philosophy." Especially for younger children, Dunbar argued, the latter was the more appropriate approach.[14]

Dunbar adopted the general theme of "Water" to teach "the Socialist philosophy" indirectly. Among the suggested activities are a short talk on "how the sea touches all hands and unites them," as a way of stressing the "unity of all people," and using pictures of "all kinds of boats or toy boats," in particular "a row boat and galley with many oars, to illustrate [the] added strength and power of concerted action." Finally, although Robert Louis Stevenson was not a socialist, his poem entitled "Where Go the Boats" was suggested, as a way of reinforcing a view of the interrelatedness of individuals in society:

> Dark brown is the river,
> Golden is the sand.
> It flows along for ever,
> With trees on either hand.
> Green leaves afloating,
> Castles in the foam,
> Boats of mine aboating—
> Where will all come home?
> On goes the river
> And out past the mill,
> Away down the valley,
> Away down the hill.
> Away down the river,
> A hundred miles or more.
> Other little children
> Shall bring my boats ashore.

Readers

Several textbooks and readers published between 1900 and 1920 were utilized by SSS teachers. Aside from those originally written for an adult audience that were adapted for use in the Sunday schools, such as Walter Thomas Mills's *The Struggle for Existence*, they were of two kinds: those that were written by non-radicals but were still used by SSS teachers; and those that were written specifically for use in the socialist children's schools and clubs.

Socialist Sunday School staff members, chronically short of time and money, and often untrained as well, had little choice but to use non-socialist materials like Robert Louis Stevenson's poem to help develop lessons.[15] One prominent example was the work of Katherine Elizabeth Dopp, who studied with John Dewey at the University of Chicago where she received her Ph.D. in 1902; later she was an instructor at Chicago for ten years and an author of several series of children's books. Her first series was the six-book "Industrial and Social History" series. Its first three books (*The Tree-Dwellers: The Age of Fear* [1903], *The Early Cave Men: The Age of Combat* [1904], and *The Later Cave Men: The Age of the Chase* [1906]) were used by SSS teachers in New York City, Milwaukee, Cleveland, Brockton, Pittsburgh, and Baltimore.[16] In fact, in 1920 William Kruse highlighted the use of Dopp's books by SSS teachers but warned that some teachers were going through the books too quickly in their classes, within a few months' time. He advised that "if properly used these books would be sufficient for years of S.S.S. exercises."[17] Of course, by the time Kruse's comments were published, many of the schools had closed.

Dopp described the subject matter of the "Industrial and Social History" series as including "the most significant steps in the early development of our industrial and social institutions, [and] is not only so closely related to [the] child's experience as to be readily appreciated and controlled by him, but it is of profound significance as a means of interpreting the complex of the present."[18] The first volume, *The Tree-Dwellers*, intended for children 6½ to 7 years old, illustrates her general approach. The book contains 120 pages of narrative, questions "to think about," and "things to do," and 25 pages of "Suggestions to Teachers" that include recommended reference materials for each section of the book. Dopp's intention was to provide a dramatization of various scenes (rather than trying to depict them realistically), to coincide with the child's interest in drama, and "to awaken the inquiring attitude" by the use of stimulating questions and activities. The narrative is divided into thirty-three 2- to 6-page "lessons," beginning with "A Story of Long Ago" that introduces the focus of the book: "This is the story of long ago. It will tell you of the first people we know anything about. It will tell you how they lived before they had fire. It will tell you how they worked before they had tools." Dopp intended to reveal how the animals "knew how to do one thing" but that "people could do a great many things." In particular, people "could remember, too, what had happened before." She thus sought to link animals to humans at the same time that the superiority of human behavior is stressed. Humans are also connected across generations, so that the young reader will understand that those who came after the Tree-Dwellers learned (or remembered) from their predecessors and thus represent the continuing progress of the human species. They "take advantage of what has been accomplished during many long ages." This link between generations is portrayed in another way as well, with regard to the early people being similar to twentieth-century people in their need for food, clothing, shelter, and means of protection.

The Tree-Dwellers story revolves around the adventures of Sharptooth and her family, who are portrayed as often swinging from branch to branch instead of always walking on the ground. The early family structure, the beginnings of a textile industry (that is, weaving), and the dangers of living at the time (for example, among wild animals) are discussed. Different geographic areas in which Tree-Dwellers lived are described, as are the early use of tools, the fear (and eventual use) of fire, and the need for the constructive use of leisure time even among these Tree-Dwellers. Finally, questions and suggested activities accompany each of the chapters (or lessons) of the book, for the purpose of helping readers explore their own understanding and emotional reactions to the story. Before a reading on "How the Tree-Dwellers Taught Their Children," for example, the following questions are asked: "Do you think that the Tree Dwellers had schools? What did their children need to know? How would they teach them? Have you ever seen a cat teaching her kittens? Have you ever tried to teach a baby? What can you teach a baby to do? What do you need to have done for you? What can you do to help yourself? What can you do to help others?" Among the suggestions for "Things to Do" are modeling in the sand, drawing pictures, cutting out shapes from papers, play-acting the story, and telling one's own story. Dopp's books provided SSS teachers not only with ideas for activities in which to engage children but also with interesting readings on the complex origins of human civilization, the prominence of issues relating to food, clothing, and shelter in the lives of the early people, the nature of progress, the need for cooperative relations in the struggle for existence, and other elements of what could be construed as a socialistic perspective.[19]

The most significant group of texts were those written specifically for use in the children's schools and clubs. One of the earliest was Nicholas Klein's *The Socialist Primer*, which was intended as "First Lessons in Socialism for Children." Published in 1908 and widely advertised in the socialist press, it is a fifty-two page social studies and language arts book that attempts to expose children to what Klein considered to be basic socialist tenets. It includes numerous illustrations by Ryan Walker, a well-known socialist cartoonist. One of the most common drawings is that of "The Capitalist," caricatured in rather typical fashion, resembling the unpleasant memory of one who grew up in a socialist home during this period: "an inflated villain dressed in dollar signs, puffing at a fat cigar, sitting on a heap of money bags."[20]

The main body of Klein's primer uses simple phrases (for example, "Man needs joy") to help teach morals to young readers. The ninth of his thirty-two lessons, for example, begins with a drawing of a capitalist passing by another man who is holding a cup and a sign that reads, "Please Help the Poor." The rest of the lesson is as follows:

Work	Man	He
Makes	Gets	Don't
Wealth	Fat	Work

Just look at these men! There are two men here. Are they both men? They are both men. One is Fat and Rich. One is Lean and Poor. Why is this? It must be that the Fat Man likes to work, and so by his toil gets all the good things; while the Thin Man will not work. It would seem so, but this is not the truth. No, my child; things are not as they seem. The Fat Man here does not work at all. The Thin Man would like to work for his food, but he can not get work, so he must beg. Is this not Queer? Yes, it is very queer! But it will all be plain to you, my child, when I tell you that the Fat Man owns the land, the shops and the mines and lives upon the wealth made by the man who toils. The Thin Man owns nought. Is it right for the Fat Man to own the means of life of the Thin Man? That is the Law now, but we must mend the law, so that all can be free.
I WANT TO BE FREE. I WANT ALL TO BE FREE.

The Socialist Primer also includes a "Theory Review," in which the concluding morals of the previous lessons are listed in order, emphasizing the right of individuals to have greater freedom and social equality and the consequent need to work for social change. Klein also provided readers with ten socialist "commandments" that are worth noting because very similar ones were adopted as recitations in several of the schools:[21]

THE TEN RULES OF LIFE

1. Love your school fellows, Who will be your fellow-workmen in life.
2. Love learning, which is the food of the mind: Be as grateful to your teacher as to your parents.
3. Make every day holy by good and useful deeds and kindly actions.
4. Do not hate or speak ill of anyone: Do not be revengeful, but stand up for your rights and resist oppression.

5. Honor good men and women: Be courteous to all: Bow down to none.

6. Do not be cowardly: Be a friend to the weak and love justice.

7. Remember that all the good things of the earth are produced by labor: Whoever enjoys them without working for them is taking what belongs to labor.

8. Observe and think in order to discover the truth: Do not believe that which is contrary to reason, and never deceive yourself or others.

9. Do not think that he who loves his own country must hate and despise other nations or wish for war, which is a remnant of barbarism.

10. Look forward to the day when all men will be free citizens of one fatherland and live together as brothers in peace and righteousness.

Another reader was John Spargo's *Socialist Readings for Children*, dedicated to "my children George and Mary and all their little Socialist comrades." Spargo's 132-page book consists of eleven chapters and a review section in the form of "A Short Catechism."[22] While Klein's primer is rather disjointed, simplistic, and full of caricatures and stilted language, Spargo's book attempts to weave an elementary version of the history and nature of the socialist movement into a continuing and generally well-written story for young readers. Intended for intermediate grades, the story takes place at the American home of Mr. and Mrs. Webb, whose two children are enjoying a visit from three English cousins. It begins with Mr. Webb explaining to the visiting children that epithets directed at socialists by a minister whom they heard speak are untrue. The story continues with a recounting of the life of Robert Owens, "not the first man in the world to have Socialist ideas, but . . . the first man to call himself a Socialist . . . in the year eighteen hundred and thirty-three." The discussion about Owens whets the children's appetite to learn more about socialism. The Webb family is actually quite well off but they believe that "there will never be true freedom for all the people until we have Socialism." They advocate the public ownership of land, mines, forests, factories, and so on, to be "used for the equal benefit of all instead of for a few." As the whole family takes a car ride around a river, they pass many poor areas. The Webbs' daughter "earnestly" cries out, "Oh, I do wish Socialism would come soon!"

The children then accompany Mr. Webb to a socialist meeting. The review questions that follow this "lesson" indicate its content: "What song did the people sing? What did Mr. Webb say about

Nature being kind to us? Ought there to be any poor people? What do Socialists mean when they say that all should be rich? What are the two sources from which wealth comes? Do Socialists mean that brain labor does not help to make wealth? What must we have before we can grow food or do anything? Do all the people own land? Do all the people own factories, mines, and machinery? When the people who work get wages, do they get more than they produce, or less? Under Socialism will women have the same rights as men?" The children next learn about a song that is sung at socialist meetings ("The Red Flag"), the concept of "evolution" (with an emphasis on change as "the law of life"), the May Day holiday, and the life of Karl Marx.

The story ends with a tale told by Mr. Webb's poor friend, Old Peter. He tells the children of a wonderful place that he has seen but about which "you never hear a word . . . in the schools, and there is no map of it anywhere." The land is intended to resemble a socialist utopia, where "no one ever saw a poor man or woman in the land, except a stray visitor from some other country." All people are able "to live in beautiful homes, surrounded by flowers, and to wear beautiful clothes." Because all people do their fair share of work, there is plenty of leisure time for all: "Some spent their leisure hours in the great public garden, listening to the band; others loved to climb the mountains or sail upon the great lakes. Then there were others who chose to paint pictures, or to write poems and operas, and books about important subjects." The newspapers "were not filled with horrible stories of crime and other evil things as our papers are. Instead of these things, there were records of good deeds and happy events." All of these things were possible, Old Peter tells the children, because all the people, through the government, "owned the land, the mines, the factories, and the railways." Their motto was "When all the citizens work together for the good of us all, there is joy and peace in the land."

In answer to a query in 1913 about the existence of "any Socialist books for children," the *Party Builder* recommended Spargo's *Socialist Readings for Children*. It was used in several children's schools, including ones in New York City, Milwaukee, and Newport, as well as by schools of the Party's Finnish federation.[23] Since Spargo was one of the Party's most well-known theorists before he left the radical movement in 1917, his book was probably adopted by other socialist schools as well.

Another reader intended for use in the schools and advertised in the socialist press was Caroline Nelson's *Nature Talks on Economics*, which was subtitled "A Manual for Children and Teachers in Socialist Schools." Nelson originally prepared this densely written fifty-nine-page book for the Young Socialist Sunday School in San

Francisco, where she taught for a brief period of time.[24] She took a different approach in her book by presenting socialism in a way that coincided with her view of Nature itself: "The organic structure in nature, built of the individual cell life, with the group divisions of different activity, furnishes a realistic illustration of what practically goes on in human society by the division of labor, with the differences that the cell groups work in perfect harmony with one another, and interchange their products according to their needs. The human group workers, on the other hand, make the fearful mistake of tolerating parasites in their system of division of labor. Parasites that are all the more deadly and dangerous because they are of their own species, and can therefore impress the minds of the group workers with the idea that they could not get along without them, while they steal their produce from them to pile it up to rot and decay while the workers die of starvation."

The book is divided into eleven chapters and is woven around the adventures of the two children of a carpenter and his wife. In the first chapter, for example, the children go with their father to the woods to saw a tree. While there, they see a nest of baby birds and ask how "the birds grow inside the eggs." The ensuing discussion leads to an analogy about capitalism: The shell of an egg is like capitalism and the workers need to grow strong together like the baby bird inside in order to break the shell. Evolution, then, is the growing and laboring within the shell. Breaking through the shell is comparable to revolution. Life is viewed as "always active and always changing." Nelson also used examples from nature to focus on the notion of class struggle. (She wrote, "You can't get away from your class. You will have to fight for it and win with it. . . . [It] is your only salvation in this life.") An explanation of the "inner workings of a tree," for instance, leads to a focus on relations between capitalists and workers. Step by step, the children are taught to understand the necessity for socialism through observing the cooperative forces that exist in nature itself. Focusing on such varied topics as crystals, seaweed, trees, measles, reproduction, the human family, and unions, the book emphasizes the benefits associated with making, managing, and owning things cooperatively instead of individually.

The *Appeal to Reason* referred to Nelson's reader as "urgently needed to counteract the poison that is daily being taught the child in the average school" and more specifically as "an excellent manual for teachers in Socialist Sunday schools."[25] In the preface to her book, Nelson claimed that the children at the San Francisco school were in fact "much interested [in the readings], especially in the objects used such as crystals, minerals, eggs, flowers and seaweeds." Of course, such self-reporting must be approached with caution.

Stories, Essays, Poems, and Recitations

Numerous essays, short stories, and poems published in a wide variety of sources were used by teachers in the socialist schools. One source was Emilie Poulsson's generally popular *Finger Plays for Nursery and Kindergarten.*[26] Her verses, such as "The Hen and Chickens" and "A Little Boy's Walk," could not be construed as having a clear radical message, and in all likelihood, SSS teachers of the youngest children used her book for general enjoyment and did not concern themselves with whether or not the finger plays contained socialist content.

A more explicitly radical poem was Thomas Hood's "The Song of the Shirt." Seventy years after she attended the East Side SSS in Manhattan, a former student recalled reciting the poem at the school. Its last eleven lines go like this:

> With fingers weary and worn,
> With eyelids heavy and red,
> A woman sat, in unwomanly rags,
> Plying her needle and thread—
> Stitch! stitch! stitch!
> In poverty, hunger, and dirt;
> And still, with a voice of colorous pitch,
> Would that its tone could reach the rich!
> She sang this "Song of the Shirt!"

Less serious poems were utilized in the schools as well, although many of them were viewed as embracing a socialistic message. Sometimes familiar verses would be altered for this purpose. One example comes from a series of "Socialist Mother Goose" poems that were recited at the East Side SSS May Day celebration in New York City in 1913. The first and last (fifth) stanzas of this alternative version of "Hickory, Dickory, Dock" go like this:

> Hickory, dickory, dock!
> The time-keeper looks at the clock.
> The clock strikes eight, the girl is late.
> 'To dock her pay, is the only way!'
> So hickory, dickory, dock! . . .
> Hickory, dickory, dock!
> Oh, girl, look up at the clock!
> And you strike, too; we'll see you through,
> For a shorter day and better pay!
> And no hickory, dickory, dock![27]

The *Young Socialists' Magazine* was a valuable resource for the SSS curriculum. It was published monthly and varied from twelve to sixteen pages in length. A general description of the magazine was offered in *Socialist Woman*: It helped children "to become Socialists . . . in a manner [not] likely to become obnoxious to children." It hoped to accomplish this by "cloth[ing] its teachings skillfully in small stories, fables, and historical sketches, so that children imbibe the Socialist spirit and conceptions almost unconsciously."[28] Its explicit purpose was to serve as a forum for points of view that were not being made available elsewhere to working-class children.

One representative story from the magazine was "The Selfish Little Woodpecker."[29] It tells the tale of a "little Lady Woodpecker . . . who lived in a hole in a big Pine Tree, which she called her Home, although it had been builded [*sic*] for her by other birds." Her house is "cozy and comfortable, all lined with moss and wool, and protected by a little brown bark door." And yet, despite her good fortune, "she was such a selfish little bird that she never asked any other birds to come and visit her, and she never gave them any of the nice things to eat that were brought to her by her friends, that came to help in her house in the Pine Tree." Contrasted to the Lady Woodpecker is a "Fluffy Sparrow," whose nest "was loosely built and untidy and it rested insecurely in a fork of a tree so that the wind blew it this way and that." He is always too busy helping others to fix his own home. One day, "an unusually heavy storm came" and the Fluffy Sparrow's nest is blown to the ground. As he stands out in the cold rain, he asks the Lady Woodpecker to "have pity on me and take me into your house." But she refuses, saying she is too busy collecting "the ingredients of juniper berry pies" from other birds. But, she adds, "Come again, some other time, and perhaps I may let you in." For four straight days a similar conversation takes place between them, while "the rain and the wind and the snow" make Fluffy Sparrow "very, very wet and cold." Finally, on the fifth day, he finds that when he comes again to ask Lady Woodpecker for shelter, she is not at home. She is away "trying to find a key with which to lock her door while she ate her juniper berry pies that had been baked for her with the berries and the flour that had been brought to her." So Fluffy Sparrow goes in and "calls all the other birds" who had helped to build the Lady Woodpecker's "warm and cozy and comfortable house." They eat the juniper berry pies and put a sign on the door that the Lady Woodpecker finds when she returns. It reads: "Those who will not work, may not enter. But all who will work may help and there will be comfortable houses and juniper berry pies enough for all and everybody."

The *Young Socialists' Magazine* also printed essays about famous radicals, often in celebration of their birthdays, such as Eugene Debs, Victor Berger, "Mother" Jones, Karl Marx, Frederick Engels, Rosa Luxemburg, William Morris, Peter Kropotkin, Edward Carpenter, Karl Liebknecht, August Bebel, and J. Kier Hardie. In addition, poetry and excerpts from the fictional and nonfictional writings of well-known socialists and non-socialists were published, including those of Walt Whitman, Charlotte Perkins Gilman, Percy Shelley, Charles Dickens, Jack London, Leo Tolstoy, Upton Sinclair, Maxim Gorky, Thomas Paine, Karl Kautsky, Morris Hillquit, Edward Bellamy, Abraham Lincoln, Karl Marx, and Frederick Engels.[30] Articles of current interest that covered a wide range of topics also were frequently included, focusing on such topics as mass entertainment, health and recreation, safety, nature, militarism, patriotism, capitalist exploitation of workers, child labor, education, class consciousness, and the prospects of the radical movement in the United States and elsewhere. And during its early years, important monthly historical events were also listed, with choices quite unlike those used in public schools. One example was for May:[31]

May 4, 1886:	Bomb thrown in Chicago at Haymarket meeting
May 5, 1818:	Karl Marx, Socialist philosopher, born
May 8, 1901:	Riots in Barcelona, Spain
May 15, 1525:	Thomas Muenzer, agitator, executed
May 16, 1901:	Militia shoots at strikers in Albany, N.Y.
May 23, 1906:	Henrik Ibsen died
May 28, 1871:	End of Paris Commune
May 31, 1906:	Bomb thrown at King and Queen of Spain

Perhaps the most ambitious series of articles to appear was the twenty-seven-chapter "History of Our Country for Boys and Girls." Intended as a "revisionist view of history," it was prepared by Frederick Krafft, who was active in the Newark Socialist Sunday School. In the eleventh and twelfth installments, for example, Krafft attempted to debunk the mythology surrounding George Washington. He described Washington as a man who did tell lies and who became friends with the Indians in large part so that he could use them to spy on the French for the English before the American Revolution. In fact, Krafft wrote, "We will learn the more we study history, that the so-called great patriots and statesmen always become great either by deception, brutality or some other evil propensity." In later chapters, Krafft presented Thomas Paine as a true, modest hero, contrasting him to the "ambitious and overbearing" Washington who, like Alexander Hamilton, was "an aristocrat of the deepest dye." Andrew Jackson was criticized for his introduction of the spoils system and for his tolerance of slavery while William Lloyd Garrison was praised in contrast. And when discussing the Civil War, Krafft concluded that "the saddest part of the whole war was that the common people believed that they were fighting for a good cause, and many noble, good men lost their lives, while political rogues remained at home and became wealthy thru [*sic*] the war."[32]

Ditties, short jokes, riddles, and sayings helped to lighten the spirit of the *Young Socialists' Magazine*. Although authors often were not identified, strong working-class and socialist sympathies were usually present. Examples of such sayings include: "Talk about equal opportunity! Capitalism ties a balloon to the shoulders of the rich child, a ball and chain to the feet of the poor child, and tells them that they have an equal opportunity to fly!"; "In the future society the private ownership of natural resources by individuals will be regarded with the same distaste with which we to-day regard the ownership of one man by another"; and "It would be easy for the workingmen to support their wives and children but for the fact that they have also to support the wives and children of their employers." While many jokes seem to have nothing to do with furthering the socialist cause but were intended simply to appeal to young readers, some of them did include a radical message of sorts, for example, " 'Why didn't you laugh at the boss's joke, Bill?' 'Don't have to; I quit Saturday.' "[33]

It is important as well to take note of the editorials that were published in the *Young Socialists' Magazine*. During its last several years, many of them dealt with the infighting that was taking place within the American radical movement. Earlier, however, staff members expressed their views on a wide range of issues. Excerpts from four editorials can serve to represent the variety of social messages that were presented: (1) With reference to a mine accident that took place in Illinois: "We hope the little boys and girls of these miners will never forget that their fathers lost their lives because the rich mine owners did not do everything to prevent such accidents. It costs money to do this and the more the mine owners would spend the less they would have, so they rather sacrifice the lives of the miners." (2) True patriotism is defined as "to make your country better; to die, not for your country, but for that which you know is right." (3) Concerning race relations, it is stressed that "every color of the rainbow is just as good as the other, is it not? There are flowers of different color, but all are pretty. There are people of different color, but all are good and useful." And (4) The end of summer vacation is noted and readers are urged to make the most of the chance to go to school, which is described as "the opportunity of preparing yourselves for your future life." At the same time, a critical outlook is encouraged: "But remember that the public school teaches only those things which our capitalist masters wish you to learn. Remember that not everything told you in the public school is true. You, as young Socialists, must never accept a fact as true unless your own reason accepts it. Never say it is so because my teacher said so, but think it out for yourself."[34]

Finally, there is ample evidence that children in many of the socialist schools were expected to recite (sometimes from memory) certain verses and sayings as part of their socialist education. Sometimes these recitations were simply part of the lessons while at other times they were rehearsed during school sessions for upcoming special events. At the Rochester school, for instance, a series of *Red Rebel Lessons* included students reciting one or more of the following passages: "I ought to be contented with those things which cannot be changed; but I must never be contented or satisfied with such conditions as can be made better"; "I shall always remain a Red-Rebel as long as there is one child in this world who cannot enjoy a sweet, wholesome, happy, healthy childhood filled full of sunshine, pure air and fun"; and "I shall always remain a Red-Rebel as long as there is any poverty in the world, and I will do all I can to abolish poverty and make this world a better place in which to live." Similarly, at the Brockton school a "Socialist Pledge" was recited. Written by Thomas Heath Flood, a local SSS activist, copies of the recitation were printed and made available to other schools at a small cost. It reads as follows:

As we leave Sunday School today
Each comrade brave and true,
We have before us one and all
A mighty task to do;
And all the strength we gather here
Of heart, and brain, and hand
We'll use to free the working class,
In this, and every land.
And so dear comrades, one and all,
Whatever else I do;
When comes a chance to strike a blow
I'll never let it pass,
But I will strike with all my might
To free the working-class.[35]

Many other recitations took place in the Socialist Sunday schools, some from materials already discussed and some with titles similar to those used by the Milwaukee Socialist Propaganda School: "The Old Red Ticket," "If Socialism Comes," "My Country," "I Don't Obey," "The Cry from the Ghetto," and "Mr. Workingman."[36] In addition, SSS children would sometimes chant verses as they participated in radical parades. At the Manhattan and Bronx SSS May Day parade in 1914, for example, the following chant could be heard:

Are we in it? well, I guess;
We're the children of the S.S.S.!
Are we in it? well, I guess;
Socialists, Socialists, yes, yes, yes!

The Rochester school even had its own "yell." To the tune of "Hail, Hail, the Gang's All Here," the children, no doubt under the inspired direction of Kendrick Shedd, would "yell" the following at parades and the like:

Hail, hail, the kids are here!
Better than the money,
Sweeter than the honey—
Hail, hail, the kids are here
From the Socialist Sunday School![37]

Tests and Student Essays

Test questions and students' own writings represent a direct statement of what students were expected to learn in these radical weekend schools. Although not commonly mentioned in school reports, an occasional quiz or exam was given. Children in Milwaukee, for example, took a quiz on the nationality of flags.[38] In Rochester, in the fifth year of the school (1914–1915) Shedd referred to "a little written test" that was given every several months. However, the students could choose not to take the tests, and evidently many students so chose. The second test was given in December and consisted of six short-answer questions. "(1) What ought the people to own and why? (2) Name some things that are public property and other things that are private property? What is the difference? (3) What does it mean when somebody says that Mr. Brown is competing with Mr. Green and others? (4) What does co-operated mean? Have you ever co-operated with anybody in anything? Tell about it. (5) Who said: 'Workers of the world, unite.' Was that all he said? What else? What did he mean? and (6) What is meant by a Labor Union? And why do they exist?" One student received a "99" grade for the following answers:[39]

1. They ought to own everything because they make everything.
2. a) South Park, Seneca Park, the public schools, etc. . . .
   b) A. Bausch and Lomb, Sibley's, Lindsey and Kerr Co., Schubert Theatre, Lyceum Theatre, etc. . . .
   c) Public property is property owned by the people; private

property is property owned by an individual or a few men.
3. It all means that Mr. Brown is going against Mr. Green and others.
4. a) Co-operation is working together.
   b) Yes, I co-operated with my club members to win a game in Arch Ball.
   c) We all worked together and tried to win the game, by trying to get the ball in the basket in the shortest time.
5. a) Karl Marx. He said, "Workers of the world, unite. You have nothing to lose but your chains. You have a world to gain." He meant the workers should unite and go against the masters, throw off their bonds and rule themselves.
6. a) A body of laborers or workers who unite and make certain plans. These plans are brought to the bosses who must agree to them or not [*sic*] the workers refuse to work for them. This union protects them when they refuse to work and helps them if the bosses do not agree to the plans.
   b) They exist because of the unfair conditions the bosses would have the people work by.

Another test was given at the Rochester school in February 1915, with six short-answer questions that asked about what is meant by a capitalist; the reasons for and consequences of poverty, unemployment, sickness, and accidents in workers' lives; and the nature of the wage system. In analyzing the results of this test, Shedd concluded that the children seemed to realize "that the existence of two classes is a wrong, and they also know that it gives rise to an everlasting struggle." However, he recognized that some of the nine- to twelve-year-olds who took the test were clearer on this point than others. For example, one student declared that there were three classes: the capitalists, the workers, and the socialists.[40]

The results of the teaching in the Socialist Sunday schools can also be seen in original compositions by the students, some of them published in the socialist press. The student essays that gained the most notoriety were the six published in a 1907 issue of *The Worker*. These essays, written by students in Anna Maley's class at the close of the initial year of the first SSS in New York City, were cited by anti-socialists at the time to illustrate the "rising tide of Socialism" that was threatening to destroy the fabric of American life.[41] An eleven year old's essay on "Why Men Are as They Are" can serve as an example:

In the capitalist system it cannot be different, because most children, instead of educating themselves, go to work and work all their lives from early morning till late at night. When they are married and have children they hardly have time to see their children, because they go to work while their children sleep, and when they come home it is the same. Some men work seven days out of a week to make some kind of poor living. When these men meet by some chance, with their friend, they are afraid to tell him the truth about their work, because their friend might go up to the boss and work for cheaper wages than his friend did. In this way people cannot be kind, true, or honest.

But in the Socialist system it will be different. The people won't have to work seven days out of the week from morning to night because every man will have the same right over the social use of property as any other man.

Finally, the theme of an essay contest at the Brockton school was "Why a Workingman Should Send His Child to a Socialist Sunday School." Twenty children entered the contest, writing for about an hour under test conditions. The winner's composition could stand as a representative statement from SSS advocates:[42]

The difference between our Socialist Sunday School and our daily school is: The daily or public school has more power because it is controlled by the ruling class, who try to train the mind of the child to be obedient and patriotic to our country, and they make us believe this country guarantees equal opportunity for the boy whose father works in the mill, . . . with the boy whose father owns the mill.

They also teach us to love the flag because it stands for high ideals and good principles. But the Socialist Sunday School develops the young mind to think. We are beginning to see, through the S.S.S. study, that not only is this equal opportunity of us children and the children of the rich untrue, but we learn that our fathers are not even guaranteed the right to work and earn a living for us. In our S.S.S. we discover that the "Stars and Stripes," which we are taught in our daily school to revere, does not at the present time represent what it did one hundred-odd years ago. But on the contrary, today it stands for oppression against free speech and free assembling. Every time our fathers go on a strike for more wages to support us and our mothers a little better, down comes the club of the man in uniform representing the Red, White and Blue.

Picture the Lawrence strike.

These are the reasons why the worker's child should go to the Socialist Sunday School. To do away with this capitalist system, and to make one class the world over (the working class) and each one to have the full value of the wealth he creates. They should learn to teach the workers how to do away with the capitalist system and the best place to do this is in a Socialist Sunday School.

Songs, Plays, and Festivals

It is the songs, plays, and festivals that former participants most clearly remember about their SSS experience. Whether they served as reviews of lessons or as part of fundraising ventures, in many of the socialist weekend schools for children these activities were extensively rehearsed during school time and were viewed as integral aspects of the curriculum.

In addition to using generally popular songbooks like Harvey Moyer's *Songs of Socialism* and Charles Kerr's *Socialist Songs with Music*, SSS activists produced several songbooks of their own. The most prominently advertised one, not surprisingly, was edited by Kendrick Shedd. Indeed, no one waxed more ecstatic about singing than Shedd. He believed, "You can't talk Marxian economics to a 'kid,' but you can make an excellent rebel out of him by the right use of song and story." He was never at a loss for words when describing the merits of "good singing": "A Sunday school without singing is like a child without joy, or a garden without flowers, or a nest without birds. By all means let there be singing and a good deal of it." Other SSS collections included Josephine Cole's *Socialist Songs, Dialogues and Recitations*; professionally printed song cards, containing the lyrics of forty-two songs, issued by the International SSS of Milwaukee; and songbooks compiled by the Brownsville and Buffalo schools.[43]

SSS songs such as "The Red Flag" were popular in the radical movement as a whole. The chorus illustrates its general tenor:

Then raise the scarlet standard high!
Within its shade we'll live and die.
Tho' cowards flinch and traitors sneer,
We'll keep the red flag flying here.

Other similar "adult" songs sung by SSS children were "The Marxian Call," "The Internationale," "The People's Hymn," "Humanity's Call," and "We're Comrades Ever." Of more interest are songs that were more closely linked to the SSS movement. They can be grouped into three (sometimes overlapping) categories: First, those whose lyrics, and sometimes music, were written by Kendrick Shedd; second, those that adopt the music of popular traditional songs but substitute radical lyrics; and third, those whose content relates directly to the role of children in general or to the work of the

Socialist Sunday schools in specific. One example of each follows.

Schools, including those in Rochester, Milwaukee, Buffalo, Hartford, Washington, D.C., and New York City, made extensive use of Shedd's songbook.[44] One popular song in it was "A Rebel I Will Be," for which Shedd wrote both the lyrics and the tune:

> A Socialist I am indeed, the name I'm proud to own.
> I've got rebellion in my heart, It's bred in flesh and bone.
> If you would know what I rebel, just open your eyes and see,
> My countless brothers suffering the ills that need not be.
> *(Chorus):*
> A rebel I will be, a rebel I will be,
> As long as men shall men exploit, on either side of the sea.
> While right upon the scaffold lies, and wrong upon the throne,
> I'll be a blooming rebel, sir, a rebel to the bone.
>
> The workers by the billion toil this great, wide world around,
> In slavery to the ruling class to whom they are fast bound.
> They're fighting for their human rights, for life and liberty,
> And I am fighting by their side in solidarity.
> *(Chorus)*
>
> Oh, can't you hear the children moan? They're crying for the crumbs.
> Oh, can't you hear the mothers groan? They're sweating in the slums;
> While on the heights o'er yonder there, the lolling idlers dwell—
> Oh, who can blame the workers, sir, if they rise and rebel?
> *(Chorus)*

Another group of songs used in the schools borrowed the tunes of well-known traditional songs and replaced their lyrics with ones with a more radical perspective. One popular song, whose lyrics were written by Harvey Moyer, was referred to both as "Bring Back My Money" and "My Money Lies over the Ocean." It was sung to the tune of "My Bonnie Lies over the Ocean":[45]

> The Capit'lists over the ocean,
> The Capit'lists this side the sea,
> The Capit'lists in ev'ry nation
> Are taking my money from me.
> *(Chorus):*
> Bring back, bring back,
> Bring back my money to me, to me,
> Bring back, bring back,
> Oh! bring back my money to me.

The Socialists over the ocean,
The Socialists this side the sea,
The Socialists in ev'ry nation
Will bring back my money to me.
(Chorus)

Last night as I lay on my pillow,
Last night as I lay on my bed,
Bright visions of plenty enwrapt me,
I dreamed that the Capit'lists were dead.
(Chorus)

Vote right, my friends, over the ocean,
Vote right, my friends, this side the sea,
Vote comfort and wealth to all people,
So vote back my money to me.
(Last Chorus):
Vote back, vote back,
Vote back my money to me, to me,
Vote back, vote back,
Oh! vote back my money to me.

The third category of songs focused on the role of children and the Socialist Sunday schools in the larger radical movement. One example, "Kid Comrade," was written by Shedd and was intended as a rousing anthem:

We'll sing you a song, we'll not make it long,
We sing of the kids in our dear Sunday school.
They're young and they're bright, they're surely all right;
And they're learning to kick like a mule! Ho! ho!
(Chorus):
Ching-a-ling-a-ling, ching-a-ling-a-ling, ho, ho, ho, ho;
We are yet kiddies, but some day we'll grow,
Ching-a-ling-a-ling, ching-a-ling-a-ling, ho, ho, ho, ho;
Kid comrades we are, don't you know? Ho! ho!

I've heard it said, too; I believe it is true,
A kid is the most precious thing you can find;
If kids weren't born, this earth to adorn,
Then where would you get mankind? Ho! ho!
(Chorus)

A kid is no shirk if trained to do work,
He'll work for the party, for Truth he will fight,
He'll make a comrade as good as his dad,

And the way that he sticks is a sight. Ho! ho!
(*Chorus*)

They call us young rebs, they say we're like Debs,
We hope it is true, sir, for that is our aim.
We like to be seen in line with Eugene,
For his name is a name of good Fame. Ho! ho!
(*Chorus*)

Some schools no doubt displayed great reverence toward the singing of radical songs. However, the example of "In Competition's Way" and the reminiscences of a student of the International SSS help to provide a more balanced picture of the extent to which a serious or solemn atmosphere prevailed. The song was acted out by the children at a Milwaukee school celebration, with the following lyrics:

The earth was made for brother men
To live in peace, they say;
But men have turned it into hell
In competition's way.
(*Chorus*):
For it is so fine to cuss and swear,
To rend, and tear, to pull the hair;
Oh it is so sweet to threat and scare
In competition's way!
You hit, you hurt; you laugh ha, ha
You shout, ha ha, you do them dirt
In competition's way!
Tra la la, tra la la, tra la la, tra la la,
Tra la la, tra la la, tra la la.

Slap bang! Hit them hard again,
Dig them in the chin, Rip them through the skin,
Slap bang! Do them if you kin
In competition's way!
(*Chorus*)

"Do unto others as ye would—"
You know the rest, you say;
But wolfish men have altered that
In competition's way.
(*Chorus*)

More than sixty years after her participation, a student remembered several lines from the song and that the lyrics represented "what you do when you compete." She also recalled that one time during the singing at a school assembly, she and a friend "got the giggles and couldn't help laughing." The girls' mothers, who were in the audience, were "furious" at their behavior and wanted them to apologize to Shedd. However, Shedd saw no reason for them to apologize, responding instead that "they were great and it was the best thing they could have done."[46] This outlook was in keeping with Shedd's general approach to the schools. They were to be enjoyable as well as educational. He believed that of all the activities of the schools, certainly singing should be fun for the children.

An emphasis on drama in the Sunday schools was in keeping with the use of theater for entertainment, educational, and agitational purposes by the American radical movement in general (as well as with a similar use of theatrical activity among workers' children in Britain, dating back to the Owenite and Chartist movements of the 1830s and 1840s). As Emma Goldman suggested, drama was "particularly suited to the radical purpose . . . in that its emotional impact on large audiences could inspire individuals to see their lives differently."[47] The schools utilized drama in an attempt to illustrate political themes in an entertaining format that allowed for participation by students in the school. A student of the East Side SSS in Manhattan, remembers that "there were always plays being put on . . . by the kids." A student of the Bronx school on Claremont Parkway similarly recollects that the children of the school often sang, danced, and acted in plays, "things not done in the public schools" at the time. And a student from Milwaukee recalls a good deal of school (and after-school) time being spent on rehearsals: "We had so many plays and things like that going on all the time. It seemed we . . . got through with one [and] we'd be involved in another one."[48]

The SSS dramatic scripts that have been located vary in length, number of characters, need for scenery and costumes, and complexity of plot. While their story lines are quite diverse, they all include an underlying concern with working-class interests, social and economic inequities, and the prospects of a socialist victory. One three-act play, for example, was written by Shedd and performed at least in Rochester and Milwaukee.[49] Variously entitled "Mister Profits," "Mister Greed," and "Fat Mr. Greed," it begins with a dialogue between two children whose fathers are both workers. Leo's father has told him that "the Socialists are the worst people in the world. They want to steal away all that other people have. He says that if the Socialists should ever win, they would put everything in a big pile— all houses and lands and banks and stores and money—and then they would give everybody a share, no matter whether he deserved it or not." Sally argues, "Your father is wrong. That is not what the Socialists stand for at all." She reassures him that his parents are good people but "they have been told lots of things that aren't true, and so they believe them, for most people believe what is told them by their newspapers and their priests and professors." She urges Leo to do his own thinking, adding, "That's what the Socialists do."

Sally then tells Leo to watch carefully "while I show you how the masters and bosses rob the working class every day of their lives." The next scene consists of children, each with big potatoes in their hands, happily talking to each other and singing "My Country 'Tis of Thee." Eventually, two figures (Mister Greed and Mister Profits) enter, holding a big sack between them. They praise the children's patriotism, telling them that it is, indeed, the "Sweet Land of Liberty." But the potatoes that they possess are not really meant for them. "Those belong to us. We are the masters and you and your fathers are only our slaves. So hand those big things over to us at once." The children hesitate, step back, and begin to whimper. But the evil Misters Greed and Profits eventually take all of the big potatoes and throw them into their sack. Then, as the children are sent out to bring all their potatoes, even the smallest ones, Mister Greed says to his partner: "It's a joke the way we can rob those poor working Dubbs.[50] Good thing they are as blind as bats in the daytime, or else they wouldn't stand for it. We must keep them blind, Profits. We must dope them everyday with Church dope and Patriotism dope and newspaper dope, and especially baseball and tango dope. We must keep them doped up to their ears. Then they won't realize they are being robbed." When the children reenter with the smallest potatoes, Mister Greed laughs and remarks that "a fly would starve eating those." So he lets the children keep them, because after all, "they are good enough for the working class. Any old thing is good enough for those boobs." At first it appears that the children will begin to cry again. But instead, they begin to sing several songs, such as "A Rebel I Will Be," shaking their fists at appropriate places. They then walk off the stage together.

The final scene is very brief, allowing just enough time for Sally to be sure that Leo has gotten the message of the scenario they have just witnessed. Leo now says: "I feel sorry for the workers. They ought to have all they make and produce and not just a little bit. (Shaking his fist) I guess I'll be a rebel too, for I feel just like those children felt." When he inquires as to where the children learned the songs, Sally tells him that it was at "our Socialist Sunday School that meets at the Labor Lyceum." She invites him to come to the school, and he replies, "I want to, and I'll ask my parents whether I can go next Sunday and maybe they'll come along, too."

The didactic approach of "Mister Greed" is matched by another SSS production with a rather unusual theme, "The Strike of Santa Claus." This play was presented at the New York City SSS "Children's Day" celebration in 1915 and at the International SSS, and as the script was published in the *Young Socialists' Magazine* (although with no author indicated), probably elsewhere as well.[51] The location of this one-act playlet is "any worker's home" and the time is "just before Christmas, early Twentieth Century." Three girls and a boy are looking for Santa, who rumor has it has "gone on a strike." When they find him, he tells them that "big business and the Trusts have got it fixed so that none but the rich can help me at all. The poor are so busy working long and hard to get enough to eat and wear that they have no time left to do a single thing about Christmas." Consequently, only rich children are able to enjoy Christmas and, Santa exclaims, "I will not give to any child till I can give to all!" The children eventually figure out that the only way to end Santa's strike is for people (including the audience) to "vote the Socialist ticket." Thus, rather than adopting an anti-religious stance, "The Strike of Santa Claus" suggests that it is only the triumph of socialism that can ensure that a true holiday spirit can prevail for all.

Another dramatic script performed by the schools was "When the Cry Was Stilled," written by Ethel Whitehead, who taught at schools in Pasadena and Los Angeles. It was not only published in the *Young Socialists' Magazine* (spread out over seven consecutive issues) but also made available in booklet form by the Young People's Department. There is also evidence that it was presented by Chicago's Douglas Park SSS in 1919.[52]

"When the Cry Was Stilled" contains several songs and dances composed especially for it, fourteen major characters and a host of minor ones (such as fairy guards, elves, and so on), and costumes and scenery on a grand scale. The opening of the play reveals that despite attempts by fairies to make the world beautiful, a sorrowful sound can be heard throughout the land. It is "the cry of the little children who suffer." One fairy, Narcissa, tells of following the sound of the cry to the city and discovering that it comes from the horrid conditions under which the children there must be living. Philip, a mortal, is brought in to be questioned about what Narcissa has reported. He tells of various problems related to illness, housing, hunger, the cold, and so forth. When he leaves, the Queen of the Fairies, Olanthe, asks Narcissa if what Philip has told them is true. She responds: "True and more than true. I went to city after city. I saw storehouses full of things, beautiful houses, plenty all around and yet thousands in poverty and squalor." Despite the "cold and pain and suffering" that she may face while there, Narcissa volunteers to take mortal form and go to the city to try to help improve the situation there.

The second act takes place at the palace of King Winter (who is "known to every poor family"). He is being tormented by the snow fairies, who march slowly by in twosomes, chanting in solemn tones: "Little children perish, Dying in the snow, Children that we cherish, Go cruel Winter, go." Jack Frost is also blamed for the mournful cry of the children as the snow fairies chant: "Who froze the children? Cruel Jack Frost. Cruel Jack Frost." Even Santa Claus does not escape unscathed, as he is accused of being "mean and selfish" for bringing joy to people only once a year. But Philip and Narcissa return from the city and defend Winter and the rest, "for you might just as well blame Summer. Ever so many people are killed by the heat." They in fact have found the real culprit and they drag forward Business, who is big and fat and wears a frock coat and a high hat. Seeming very self-assured, he carries a big bag of money and a bottle of wine in his coattail pocket. Claiming that the charges against him are "absurd" and that the world "could not get along without" him, he suggests that the crying is simply "ingratitude" for all the "nice, easy employment" that he provides. Narcissa then describes such "easy employment" in an animated voice: "I suppose you call it easy to work all day long in a dark coal mine or stand in a stuffy factory all day tying knots in threads." North Wind begins to shake his fist and Jack Frost nips the fingers of Business. Business begins to feel more uncomfortable as more accusations are thrown at him. Finally, following on Santa's suggestion that they "put the spirit of love into business," the others decide to give Business a heart, "a heart with the love of all." After a struggle, a ceremony takes place to mark the successful "transplant," with Business running off the stage and yelling, "Oh! I see it all now! That cry! That children's cry—I can't stand it!"

But the play does not end there, for in the final scene a new character, Labor, emerges to explain to all assembled that giving Business a heart only kills him: "Business cannot afford to have a heart, if he does then Business is no longer Business." Labor announces that he will take the place of Business, for "All thru [sic] the ages I have really done all the work. I have fed the world and clothed the world. I have made all the wheels turn. I have done the work . . . [while] Business would strut around, . . . [and] claim all the credit, and take away everything that I produced for his own benefit." Finally, Philip realizes that he has heard this person before, that he is "the fellow who used to stand out on the soap box and talk to the people about getting together." He realizes that his name is "Socialism," and Labor replies, "Yes, one of my names is Socialism, that's my political name. Labor is another name that I am known by, Education is another, Freedom is still another. But whatever I am called does not matter. I shall free the working class from its slavery and the cry shall never be heard again."

Among the many other SSS plays, some were adapted from familiar story lines. What the socialists did here was similar to what has occurred over several centuries to folk tales such as "Little Red Riding Hood." Like other social groups before and after them, they imbued traditional story lines with different ideological content.[53] Four in particular were written by Carl Haessler and staged as end-of-the-year productions by the International SSS in Milwaukee from 1918 to 1921: "The Triumph of Socialism," a retelling of "Sleeping Beauty"; and socialist versions of "Cinderella," "Jack and the Beanstalk," and "Aladdin and the Wonderful Lamp." Each one garnered the school considerable attention in the local press, comprised a significant part of the school's curriculum in the months leading up to the performance, and was a lavish entertainment for the children, parents, and friends of the school.

Haessler's version of "Cinderella," for example, which was written while he was in prison, featured elaborate scenery by a local artist and costumes that women of the school organization, with help from some of the children, had worked on for weeks before the performance. The cast was unusually large, about one hundred in all, because of the considerable number of dancers in the production. The June 8, 1919, performance was seen by six hundred people, with so many people reportedly turned away that a repeat performance was added for the following Sunday.[54] A listing of the characters' names in this six-scene play provides an indication of its general theme and how it appropriated a well-known story line for more radical purposes. The prince is Prince Brotherhood, the stepmother is Baroness Capitalisma, and her daughters (the step-sisters) are Lady Idylrich and Lady Profiteeria. The fairy is called Fairy Solidarity, and Cinderella is Cinderella, except when she is transformed by the fairy for the grand ball and when she is finally reunited with the prince at the end, at which time she is then known as Princess Commonwealth. The play thus represents the victory of Brotherhood, Solidarity, and Common Wealth (Public Ownership) over Capitalism, the Idle Rich (the Capitalist Class), and Profiteering.

The following year witnessed another elaborate end-of-the-year production at Milwaukee's International SSS. The May 30, 1920, celebration featured Haessler's socialist version of "Jack and the Beanstalk," directed by his wife, with over one hundred children and adults taking part.[55] The six-scene play begins with a dying Trade Union John appealing to his son Jack to continue his fight against the giant Capital. He tells his son: "We sweat blood. He laughs and robs us of almost all we make. In the factory he takes the profits. In the field he takes the rent. In the bank he takes the interest and then the mortgage too. We tried to smash him with our trade unions but he has smashed us first." Now Trade Union John realizes that only one big union can succeed, that narrow interests need to be put aside. Help can be gotten from some magic beans and from the Giant's wife, Lady Charity, who the Giant forced to marry him. The first scene ends ominously, with a voice in the background calling out: "Fee! Fa! Fo! Fum! I smell the blood of a workingman. Be he alive or be he dead, I'll grind his bones and make war bread."

The play continues with Slippery Samuel, Jack's uncle and master of the village Harvest Festival, telling Jack's mother that her son should be careful about entertaining some radical ideas. (Slippery Samuel was given his nickname by Trade Union John because of Samuel's claim that the Giant had his good points and that labor and capital have a common interest.) Mother Meta calls Slippery Samuel "a stool pigeon of the bloodthirsty giant" and tells him to leave Jack alone. Eventually, Jack plants the magic beans and, ignoring Slippery Samuel's protests about the Giant being too powerful and unforgiving to be challenged, ascends the beanstalk. When he arrives at the Giant's kingdom, he meets Lady Charity and introduces himself as Wobbly Jack. She agrees to help him but urges Jack not to kill the Giant if he ever has the chance. Their plans call for Lady Charity to hide Jack and, when the Giant is asleep, they will take all of his secret papers and run off. As Lady Charity explains: "His whole system is a secret based on paper and when we have that we'll have everything."

While Jack hides, the Giant convenes his monthly meeting with his servants. One by one they report. The Honorable Overman Flunkey, a senator, does a somersault for the Giant, and tells of his efforts to "smash all labor unions, labor papers, labor institutions, and labor leaders." The Reverend Jenkinson Bellhop offers a prayer to the Giant, for which the Giant tosses a few coins to him, and talks about the need to "suppress almost all discontent." Mr. Henry Rattlesnake, a journalist and editor, whose leading advertiser is the Giant, reminds his keeper of his journalistic motto: "We cannot tell a lie unless we're paid to do it." Professor I. Blabber Bunk, who occupies the chair of Applied Sociology and Patriotic Economics at the University of Chokethetruth, discusses his new book, "The Newest Freedom," whose central premise is that one should trust "one's betters" as the faithful guardians of happiness and welfare. Finally, Kennesaw Mountain Lynchem, a judge, calls the Giant "your honor" and advocates death by torture for all who criticize the Giant and his system. He reveals that he has made a deal with Slippery Samuel "to deport all youngsters who talk about one big union," and starts to tell about Wobbly Jack. Upon hearing this, Jack begins to stir. The Giant starts his "Fee! Fa! Fo! Fum!" chant but Lady Charity soothes him with a song and a dance, and the Giant falls asleep.

With Lady Charity's help, Jack secures the secret papers and heads down the beanstalk. The Giant awakens and chases them, whereupon Jack yells: "Capital Bloodsucker, the old Giant, is actually coming down the beanstalk after us. Now we've got him! I'm sorry Lady, but your husband is done for." While Lady Charity implores Jack not to kill the Giant, Jack wields his ax and replies: "Can't help it. It's his life or ours. Humanitarianism is out of the question here. So long, old Bloodsucker." The Giant and the beanstalk crash down, and Jack exclaims: "I've smashed the Giant. . . . And I've got the secret of this system. We'll bury his carcass and burn the papers and run the world our own way for the benefit of everybody." A celebratory Harvest Festival then takes place, at which Jack and the others gain the support of the Spirit of Plenty. Lady Charity, cheered for her help, announces that she wants to give up her old name and old life to become a fellow worker. The play concludes with a "world community" dance and song, and the singing of "The Marseillaise," as everyone on stage dons red caps. Whether or not the play is great art is debatable, but it was no doubt great fun for the children to perform and it got the intended message across.

Several of the previously described dramatic productions were prominent parts of larger school festivals or pageants. But they were truly plays, with plots, scenery, characters, and dialogue. Other theatrical productions offered by the schools were less unified than plays and constituted a mixture of different activities (such as, recitations, flag drills, piano solos, dances, songs, and slide shows) related to a particular theme. These festivals and pageants often were staged to celebrate holidays. Three in particular were given attention: May Day, Yuletide (or Christmas), and Harvest time (or Thanksgiving).

May Day festivals were particularly common within the SSS movement. For example, at the 1914 May Day Festival of the Rochester school, the students presented a slide show (plates) of famous radicals. Children were given the responsibility of coming forward on stage to make brief remarks about each of the persons whose portraits were shown. Twenty heroes and heroines, comprising diverse radical viewpoints, were honored, including August Bebel, William Morris, J. Kier Hardie, George Bernard Shaw, Francisco Ferrer, Daniel DeLeon, Emil Seidel, George Lunn, Helen Keller, and Eugene Debs. One student delivered the following comments about "Mother" Jones: "The face of our old Comrade 'Mother' Jones. But recently she was lying in prison in Colorado and West Virginia for the crime of—what? Of believing in the working-class, and speaking for the rights of the working-class, Think of it! Comrade Debs says of her: 'Mother Jones is not one of the "summer soldiers" or "sunshine patriots." Her pulses burn with true patriotic fervor, and wherever the battle waxes hottest there she surely will be found upon the firing line. . . . She has won her way into the hearts of the nation's toilers, and her name is revered at the altars of their humble firesides and will be lovingly remembered by their children and their children's children forever.' Hurrah for Comrade 'Mother' Jones!!" The slide show was modified and presented several more times at the Rochester school.[56]

Yuletide or Christmas celebrations were also held at many schools. The Socialist School Union of Greater New York directly addressed the question of whether socialist schools should sponsor festivals during Christmas time. Its members sympathetically concluded that "children live in a land of their own, with its codes and ostracisms, and a sense of isolation comes to those who are out of the focus of enjoyment because a holiday is alien to the ideas of its parents." Thus, "rational celebrations," for "the religion of humanity" and to "blend harmoniously the joyous recognition of natural phenomena with the progressive teachings of the Socialist schools," should be promoted. In that way, the children who attended the socialist schools would be able to feel a part of the joy of the season, but more in celebration of the approach of spring, longer days, and "the increasing light of knowledge."[57] The perspective of the Socialist School Union of Greater New York was probably a middle ground within the American SSS movement. Some schools unabashedly sponsored Christmas festivals, others referred to theirs as Yuletide celebrations or Festivals of Light, and others waited until the new year to sponsor their special holiday entertainments.

Harvest festivals also were sponsored by Socialist Sunday schools. In one instance, 120 children actively participated in the 1912 Harvest Festival in Rochester, including 40 who sang in the children's choir. A dramatic presentation was included that emphasized the viewpoint that only the wealthy have reason to give thanks during this holiday season. Most others do so only by custom, without thinking, and for the wrong reasons; they should really be thankful that socialists are striving to advance their interests. Included in this presentation was a long compilation of "reasons to be 'glad'" counterposed by "reasons to be 'sad'," recited by children from the school: for example, "I am glad because President Taft says that the country is very prosperous. I am sad because this wondrous prosperity is not for all but only for a few. . . . I am glad that the grains and fruits are so full of good nourishment. I am sad because for the sake of profits so much of the food of the workers is falsified and adulterated or even poisoned."[58]

The Rochester school's yearly "Red Flag Day" was an elaborate affair that was always planned with great fanfare. In February 1912, it attracted an audience of six hundred children and adults. The hall was decorated in red, with banners, streamers, crepe paper, and rosettes. At the beginning of the program, the younger children unfurled a new eight-by-five-foot silken crimson banner while parading around and singing "The Flag of Brotherhood" and other songs. A dramatic presentation followed. Its main features were entitled "The Cleansing of the Stars and Stripes" and "The Cleansing of the Red Flag." The first dealt with the soiling of the American flag by injustice, the profit motive, corruption, and graft, and its need to be cleansed by representatives of the working class. Seventeen specific incidents of recent American history and contemporary American life were highlighted as staining the American flag. Among them were chattel slavery, the hanging of anarchists in Chicago in 1887, the imprisoning of Eugene Debs in 1894, strikebreaking in Lawrence in 1912, unjust wars (for example, the war with Mexico), wage slavery, and capital punishment. After all seventeen statements were presented, a student dressed to represent a worker and bearing the name "The People" came on stage and took down the soiled flag. He pretended to wash it in a tub (that had a new American flag hidden underneath red crepe paper) and then pulled out a clean flag. After fixing it upon a pole and raising it aloft, the children sang "Let the Stars and Stripes Be Clean!" In the next scene, eighteen workers paraded on stage, representing such aspects of American society as child worker, slum dweller, sweatshop, needless disease and death, poverty, prostitution, women's rights, and freedom of speech. After eighteen statements were read, the children sang "We Claim Right to Fight 'Neath the Red." Shedd explained the general perspective taken in the festival this way: "Not that we love Old Glory less, but the crimson banner the more because of its wider extension of those things of which the national flag is the emblem; and because it must in the nature of things stand for revolution against injustice."[59]

Games, Role Playing, and Other Activities

The curriculum of some schools also included occasional activities such as games and role playing. Indeed, the *Young Socialists' Magazine* strongly recommended that the children's schools engage in play as well as more serious work. One activity suggested in the magazine was "The Boss Was Here." Children are instructed to form a ring, with one child playing the "boss." The boss tells the first person in the circle to "get to work," which is symbolized by the child shaking her right hand. After doing so, the first "worker" turns to the player on the right and says, "The boss was just here." The other asks, "What did he make you do?" "He made me shake my right hand," the first child might respond while doing so. The next player then copies the same action and the same interaction and response continues throughout the group (of "workers"). The boss then comes in again and tells the first student to, for example, shake his left hand. The game goes on, with similar instructions given to shake one's foot, head, and so forth. The "silliness" continues, apparently with great fun for the participants, until "the workers go on strike and the game comes to an end."[60]

At the West Hoboken SSS, a role-playing exercise allowed the children to learn about "a panic" without being lectured about it directly. The boys in the class were instructed to make paper hats. The teacher played the role of the "boss" and the girls became the "buyers." Each boy was told to make three hats, with the teacher keeping two of them and giving one back to the boy. Each girl proceeded to buy one hat, so that the teacher (boss) had one left over. The teacher then declared that there was "overproduction" and he turned the boys out of work. A discussion followed that made the connection between this situation and the "logic" of the capitalist system.[61]

Guest speakers, field trips, hikes, parades, and flag drills were also included in the curriculum of most Socialist Sunday schools. But perhaps the most radical curricular recommendation was made by a student of the East Side SSS in Manhattan. Morris Gebelow suggested that what the students needed most of all was training for "future citizenship." What Gebelow had in mind went well beyond the usual lecturing, discussions, and reading, however, and extended to the administration of the schools: "The best way of getting this necessary training is by establishing a miniature Socialist government in the schools. Each school should represent a city. A mayor should be elected by the whole school to take charge of that particular class; while a certain number of children can meet together and make laws for the school."[62] As discussed earlier, some schools did encourage student input into school decision making. But there is no evidence to indicate that the East Side school or any other Socialist Sunday School allowed for the kind of student reorganization of governance and curriculum proposed by young Gebelow.

CHAPTER SEVEN

The Socialist Alternative

Perspectives on Teaching and Curriculum

Socialist Sunday School instruction was shaped by the period and length of time that the schools were in existence, the political movement with which teachers were allied, and the everyday problems with which teachers had to contend. It was also influenced by the character of the children who attended the schools. In other words, the SSS movement never had to develop a coherent educational theory that could accommodate the diversity and lack of political progressivism prevalent among the general community of school children. While not all SSS children came from socialist families, their backgrounds were skewed to the radical end of the political spectrum. What was offered to them in the Sunday schools was not a comprehensive radical or critical pedagogy that was fully cognizant of the nature of childhood learning and that had to reckon with the fact that some children might be initially antagonistic to socialist tenets. It was instead an education specifically for the children of radical working-class families that would, it was hoped, fortify their understanding of and commitment to socialist principles and goals. Furthermore, because the children attended public schools, there was no need to wrestle with the concerns of parents who did not want to jeopardize unduly their children's chances of doing well in high school, going to college, and getting a decent job when older. This is in contrast to the experience of anarchist and progressive educators who initiated weekday schools that were intended to substitute for, rather than supplement, the public school experience.[1]

Not only, then, was SSS instruction limited by time constraints and by the schools' struggle to stay afloat, but its very nature was circumscribed by the narrow range of children from which the schools drew and by the perception of this instruction as a supplement rather than a substitute for the education provided by the state. This is not meant to find fault with or excuse the Socialist Sunday schools for the teaching and curriculum that was offered. It is rather to clarify the context of the development of curriculum materials discussed in Chapter Six. The limitations inherent in these weekend educational experiments of over seventy years ago should be kept in mind when considering more closely the answers that SSS teachers provided to two basic educational questions: "What should be taught?" and "How should it be taught?"

Perspectives on Teaching

While there were practical conditions (such as the lack of suitable texts, insufficient staff training, severe budget constraints, and so on) that directly affected the nature of SSS instruction, there were pedagogical choices (based on educational assumptions) made as well. Practical conditions have been discussed; the pedagogical choices made by SSS activists are the focus here.

The generally stated aims offered by proponents of the Socialist Sunday schools centered on the idea of teaching the children of working-class families to be "good rebels" and "intelligent defenders" of the socialist cause. Children were encouraged to prepare for participation as adults in the struggle for a more egalitarian and just social order. However, the specific form that this education would take varied considerably, as Bertha Mailly admitted in 1911.[2] SSS activists were caught between the two driving forces of radical educational theory of their time. The first placed primary emphasis on the creative development and self-expression of the child, on freeing the child intellectually, emotionally, and culturally at a time when anti-progressive social institutions seemed to be fostering a climate of conformity and passivity. This view was summarized by the Swedish libertarian and feminist Ellen Key, whose writings on child rearing and education were occasionally cited by SSS organizers. She referred to the oft-quoted saying, "As the twig is bent the tree inclineth," but instead argued against "bending" anyone. Rather, children should be encouraged to follow their own paths, or at least prevented from being "deformed" or weakened emotionally and intellectually. The other side of the radical fence was illustrated by the comments of Milwaukee activist Frank Cherdron. In a glowing account of the newly opened Sunday schools, Cherdron proudly

referred to the children as "being molded into class-conscious Socialist kiddies. We are filling them with a spirit of rebellion against the
system that robs the laborers of the fruits of their toil." Given the
conditions of working-class life in capitalist America, the direct
teaching of a socialist vision to children was not only necessary but
desirable.[3]

These differing views were well-represented in a heated debate
that took place in the pages of the *New York Call* in the fall of 1911
between "Nesor," who had taught in a Socialist Sunday School in
New York City for three years, and Jeanette Pearl, who at the time
was teaching at the Progressive Sunday School of Brownsville.[4]
Nesor opened the published controversy by lambasting the Socialist
Sunday schools for trying to convert the children to the socialist
cause, "with the object of ultimately getting them into the party, just
as the religious Sunday schools aim to lead their lambkins into the
fold." He claimed that it was an impossible task because the children
were not old enough to accept and understand any "ism" readily,
and it was an undesirable task anyway because children should be
allowed to be children, with all their "fancies and frolics." Nesor
believed that "to confront them with an analysis of social injustice
would be an act of satanic disillusionment." Capitalism destroys
childhood enough; should socialists assist in the process? The socialist schools were only succeeding in "cramming the childish head
with a lot of nonsense about the 'boss,' the 'workingman,' the 'capitalist,' the 'poor' and 'society.' We take advantage of the helpless-
ness of the child mind by imposing upon it our opinions, our
dogmas, our sympathies and our antipathies. It is doing violence
and injustice to the young to so direct its developing brain that
when it grows up it will function in some predetermined way."
Nesor suggested that the schools instead stress freedom from re-
straint, both physical and mental, and sponsor numerous games,
gymnastics activities, hikes, picnics and parties.[5]

Pearl's response came two weeks later. While recognizing that
the Socialist Sunday schools deserved "much criticism," she dis-
agreed with Nesor's educational views: "As long as our children are
being taught by the church and the public schools to be loyal to their
country—the plute's country—we must teach them loyalty to
class—the working class." Nesor's criticisms were only appropriate
to "a slim minority" of SSS teachers. Most were not trying to make
"party converts." But, Pearl continued, "make no mistake, children
of 10 and over know much of the sadness and sorrow of life which
this system of capitalist exploitation inflicts upon them. Our children
are the workers' children; and they have imbibed the suffering and
privations of the working class with their mothers' milk." Pearl objected to Nesor's contention that it was possible in a capitalist nation

for working-class children to live "in a mental world of fancies and frolics." The social problems discussed in the schools were not far removed from the everyday concerns of the children, as Nesor had implied. In fact, it was because the children "cannot frolic" that the schools were initiated, as well as to counter the "lies, false economics, false history, false morals, false ethics" and the "docile and submissive mentality" that marked the public schools.[6]

Nesor countered that Pearl had missed his main argument. He was not primarily concerned with children's minds being molded "into conformity with the requirements of the present iniquitous social system" but with "the process of molding itself." Whatever such molding would be "for," it would still be "mental coercion, and not education. And mental coercion, no matter from what noble motive it springs, is a crime against the child." The Socialist Sunday schools, he claimed, were simply substituting one kind of conformity for another.[7]

Pearl's final comments were published a month later. She stressed the Socialist Sunday schools' efforts to "break through" the very "molding" of children into "automatic machines, docile and submissive," that Nesor railed against. In her arguments, she revealed the basic differences in their outlooks. Nesor was focusing primarily on the individual child and how the "free" child was in keeping with the ideals of industrial democracy. Pearl, however, was mainly concerned with the labor movement and especially with "how best [to] educate for the overthrow of a rotten ripe industrial autocracy." For Pearl, the ideal educated person was an impossibility in "this capitalist mire . . . where, in order to live at all, we must first sell ourselves into bondage-wage slavery." All that could be realistically hoped for at this time was to "point out the desirability and grandeur of free self-expression." But free self-expression itself would not necessarily help the plight of workers and was thus insufficient. As for the teaching of "isms," Pearl responded: "If giving facts their true interpretation be classed as an ism, we have a new definition of the term. I confess to the guilt of holding up to the children a high ideal and often telling them that the acquisition of a job is not the ultimate aim of life. If drawing sketches of the dawn of a new era, where poverty and suffering will be no more, where dreams are to be realized and ambitions fulfilled, be classed as an ism, I stand condemned."[8]

The curriculum materials described in Chapter Six demonstrate that methods varied a great deal and to some extent incorporated both Nesor's and Pearl's concerns. Indeed, prominent SSS activists, who were cognizant of progressive educational ideas linking school knowledge and activities to the interests and abilities of children and allowing for spontaneity and creative self-expression, attempted to develop a middle ground between the "hands off" approach of Key and the "filling and molding" approach of Cherdron. It is unclear whether this middle ground was ever clearly formulated or demonstrated in any school, perhaps in part because of the brief life of this educational movement. Also, progressive educational ideas themselves were only beginning to be fully articulated at this time. It was not until 1918, for example, that William Kilpatrick's "The Project Method" was published, and the Progressive Education Association was not founded until the following spring.[9] Within a year of the formation of the PEA, most Socialist Sunday schools had closed.

Unlike most progressive and anarchist educators, the approach put forth by Key and Nesor seems to have had less impact on the practice of the Socialist Sunday schools than that of Cherdron and Pearl. The position adopted by most SSS teachers was similar to Charlotte Perkins Gilman's, whose writings were often on SSS book lists. Gilman wrote, "There is no question as to whether we should or should not teach ethics to very little children. We do, we must, whether we will or not. The real question is what to teach, and how." May Reinhardt Schocken, a teacher at Socialist Sunday schools in New York City and Yonkers, extended Gilman's argument when she observed that "no child grows to maturity without being influenced and biased in some way or another."[10] In a world dominated by capitalist social institutions, a hands off approach encouraging self-reliant individualism was against the best interests of socialists and, it was assumed, the vast majority of skilled and unskilled laborers. It represented a naive response to the realities of the dominant culture and the material conditions of working-class childhood.

From all indications, most SSS activists agreed that it was appropriate for the weekend schools to adopt what could be construed as a propagandistic purpose. Many of the recitations, tests, lesson outlines, and readers certainly confirm this. Comments from staff members are also revealing, such as those by teachers from the Children's Socialist Lyceum of Los Angeles, who expressed the school's purpose as in part "to fortify [the children] with the knowledge that will help them to carry their sense of duty into deeds, [and] . . . to instill in them a correct knowledge of history and economics." For like-minded socialist educators, the teaching of a particular body of knowledge and ways of viewing the world was wholly defensible. A truly "progressive" education had to be infused with a theory of social formation, that is, a socialistic perspective. Anything else constituted at best a form of sentimental and watery reformism. Esther Sussman of the Hartford SSS remarked that it was only by teaching the children "the fundamentals of scientific Socialism . . . that when they grow up they may be able to face and overcome the social problems of the day with intelligence and broadmindedness."[11]

As the Party's National Education Committee warned in 1913, this kind of emphasis could lead to the propensity to teach "stilted economics and dogmatic exercises to children."[12] In schools where teachers had little or no prior experience in teaching, had undergone little or no teacher training, and were unfamiliar with progressive educational ideas, this clearly occurred. That is why more informed educators such as Kendrick Shedd urged the national office of the Party to take more of a role in coordinating the schools' efforts, specifically by funding and disseminating appropriate position papers and suitable lesson materials. In fact, Shedd and other prominent SSS activists attempted to blend pedagogical assumptions that might otherwise seem in conflict. Shedd wrote often about the need to encourage "inquiring minds" at the same time that he stressed the need to transmit "the [socialist] economic viewpoint, the viewpoint of the working class." In an introductory statement to his *Lesson Topics for May 1913*, for example, Shedd explained the overall aim of his lessons as "to study the principles and ethics of Socialism, . . . to correct . . . false ideals by a thorough analysis and study of the true International principles of Socialism." On other occasions, he argued that the schools should not strive to teach "Marxian economics" directly to children. In his *Lesson Topics for September–October 1913*, he stressed that teachers should "open the eyes of the children . . . [and] get them to asking WHY" by using more indirect teaching methods like stories, songs, and plays.[13] One can view such contrasting emphases—on the teaching of a particular body of knowledge on the one hand, and encouraging a generally critical attitude toward social problems and independent thinking on the other—as a sign of ambivalence and an inconsistent educational philosophy, or as a sincere attempt at balancing and blending contrasting aims.

William Kruse echoed similar sentiments in 1917. While believing that a socialist vision was appropriate to teach to children, he emphasized that the purpose of the Sunday schools was not the simple inculcation of socialist dogma. He advised against the overly didactic teaching of some SSS instructors that robbed children of any opportunity to "think clearly and freely for themselves." In a strongly worded appeal, he warned, "Nothing can be worse than to attempt a Prussian school-mastering over the youngsters." He worried that "some well-intentioned 'educators' have thought that they were helping the cause of freedom by crushing out the individuality of their young ones" and argued that "teaching children to say, parrot-like, 'I hate the boss and I love the workers' . . . and to stamp their little feet and clench their little fists at an imaginary foe" would only succeed in "driving the children away from the movement." To Kruse, such tactics were "the very opposite of Socialist education; it teaches blind hatred instead of an effort to understand opposing conditions. There is enough blind hatred among the workers as it is; intelligence is their need."[14]

No evidence indicates that many SSS students were driven away by Prussian-style instruction and it is doubtful that Kruse would have been satisfied with children who, in thinking for themselves, rejected the socialist alternative. But it is clear from many of the curriculum materials and the descriptions of school activities that there was cause for Kruse's concern. "Golden texts of the day" were memorized and recited by children at the Haverhill school and a Milwaukee school taught lessons on "The ABC's of Socialism." Nicholas Klein's *Primer* and John Spargo's *Socialist Readings* both included catechism-like suggested exercises. Indeed, the regimented classroom learning of traditional public school education was adopted by some of the socialist schools; only the content of the messages being transmitted, recited, and memorized was changed.

But it would be incorrect to emphasize too strongly that traditional methods predominated in the socialist schools. The curriculum materials detailed in Chapter Six make clear that by no means was all teaching dull, drab, humorless, and regimented. May Wood Simons, Bertha Mailly, David Greenberg, and several others who helped to develop SSS curriculum materials were influenced by the work of John Dewey and Katherine Dopp. Prominent SSS activists such as Shedd and Kruse often stressed that an overly didactic approach to Sunday school instruction was no cure for the overly romanticized approach of more libertarian-minded radicals. Many schools attempted to incorporate more creative educational experiences and student activities as part of their curriculum. While it is clear from Shedd's lesson outlines that he did not eschew the teaching of facts and the reciting of slogans, he strongly recommended an instructional approach based on discussion questions and often stressed that some of the best teaching took place indirectly, through enjoyable games, plays, and songs. Frances Gill sounded current when she wrote of the need to develop "inquiry on the part of the child," that "we do not intend to dogmatize on anything whatever, neither Socialism nor anything else." Schools in Cleveland and Buffalo included democratic decision-making activities for students as part of the curriculum.[15] The trips taken by children to museums, zoos, and parks provide further evidence that SSS instructors were not locked in to an educational vision that emphasized only the transmission of socialist tenets and the dreary "molding and filling" of young minds.

Of course, while Gill and others objected to the perception of the schools as merely "teaching dogma," they were certainly providing a particular ideological slant to their students. There was never any intention to do otherwise. The schools were established explicitly to challenge the dominant messages of capitalist America, not to enhance the creative abilities or self-esteem of children. A New Jersey activist put the rationale for and nature of the Sunday schools in perspective when he wrote: "We Socialists do not believe in forcing our faith—so to speak—on anyone. We do not wish our children to be Socialists because we are. The true Socialist wants his children to do their own thinking, and of course form their own conclusions. But we have been so busy with other matters that we have failed to inform our children about our movement as they should be informed if they are to form intelligent opinions regarding it."[16]

In their attempt to deny their dogmatic tendencies, SSS proponents would sometimes seek to have it both ways. Their comments would occasionally exhibit a self-deluding quality, as if they did not comprehend the contradictions inherent in their own arguments. Perhaps this can best be seen in the remarks of staff members at the Newark school, who claimed that the children were taught "to think without bias" at the same time that they were being taught "to act so that all people shall respect, admire and join the Socialists."[17] At other times, they adopted a naively optimistic view, such as Samuel Meyerson of New York City, who commented that perhaps all that could be hoped for was not that all children would immediately "become Socialists" but that "they all think more or less, which is vastly more important," and then expressed his belief that such thinking would in fact "eventually lead them into the Socialist ranks."[18]

If the perspectives of these radical educators from 1900 to 1920 seem somewhat confused and amorphous, it is because they were wrestling with difficult pedagogical questions that remain largely unanswered. Their lack of agreement and clarity resulted from differing concepts of childhood learning, the role of teachers, the purpose of schooling, and strategies for social change that continue to be hotly debated by political allies and opponents alike. In addition, SSS teachers were primarily political activists first and educators second. Their lives were dedicated to instilling an allegiance to the socialist movement; what form an educational process with children should take was never fully outlined. They were struggling to develop and clarify their educational assumptions and practices, and planning a national federation of schools, when the SSS movement collapsed. It would appear that prominent SSS activists were becoming increasingly influenced by the ideas of child-centered progressive educators. Socialist educators would never have abandoned their radical theory of social formation and their belief in an emancipating social vision. But with additional time and resources, they may have come up with an interesting and unique blend (praxis) of radical political theory, progressive educational practice, and curriculum, from which later educators such as the social reconstructionists of the 1930s and the critical theorists of the 1980s and 1990s could have drawn. Instead, their ideas never became clearly formulated and never gained a serious audience outside their own circle of socialist youth activists.

A sympathetic view of SSS teaching was provided years later by two students of the International SSS in Milwaukee. They remember well the "moralizing" that took place. However, at the same time that they recognize that "it was propaganda," they insist that "it was taught at a very nice level. . . . It certainly wasn't offensive and it wasn't hammered down into your throat or anything like that."[19] Perhaps this was the socialist educational alternative at its best in the early 1900s.

Curricular Themes

The SSS movement in part represented a reactive effort to contest the capitalist ideological messages of the public schools and other mainstream social institutions. In the Rochester public schools, for example, workers' children were taught daily about the sanctity of private property; the dismissal of class as a viable social category in American history; an emphasis on traditional military and political heroes (for example, Benjamin Franklin and George Washington); a denigrating view of the poor; the portrayal of organized labor primarily in terms of strikes, violence, and the loss of life and property; and a dismissal of reform as part of the nation's progressive heritage. Even such characteristics as cooperation, goodness, and honesty were presented as promoting a law-abiding, efficient capitalist social order and not, for example, in terms of social change.[20] Socialist youth activists believed that some kind of formal education was needed to oppose these messages. The SSS movement was thus also a proactive attempt to acquaint young, potential Party members with an alternative, socialist perspective. But establishing weekend schools meant that some kind of new organization of subject matter had to take shape. Socialist directors and teachers struggled to solve the age-old educational question—what knowledge should be taught?—as it applied to their weekend schools for children. They created a curriculum that comprised an alternative body of school knowledge, one that presented a version of people, events, and ideas that challenged the dominant, selective tradition of ideological values, beliefs, and meanings being promoted in the public schools and other social institutions.

While the SSS movement was marked by disagreement over the specific form that the teaching would take, there was little doubt in the minds of proponents that some kind of socialist message was to be the hallmark of their curriculum, whether directly or indirectly taught. The methods may vary, Bertha Mailly contended, but the schools had a common aim: "to teach the children *what* is not just and true and beautiful in things as they are, *why* there is no justice, truth or beauty in people's lives, and *how* to bring justice, truth and beauty into the world." Children needed to be freed "from the many prejudices" and introduced to "a new social ethic founded upon the conception of society in which profit and wage slavery are to be removed."[21] In other words, it was not just the negation of dominant ideas and practices that was to be taught to working-class children but an alternative body of knowledge and values to question and contest existing education.

The Socialist Sunday schools were closely allied with a political movement that in large part defined issues affecting the quality of life and the possibilities of change in terms of the processes and structure of the social system. It is hardly surprising that much of the curriculum of the Socialist Sunday schools would be called social studies in the 1990s. As Kendrick Shedd stressed, "Anything that concerns the conditions under which human beings live is of interest to us." The schools focused in general on the development of children's social awareness and, as William Kruse noted, on the will and desire to "work as well as talk for their ideal."[22] Ethics and morals were to be taught, in particular, David Greenberg suggested, "a passionate love for right and justice."

Similar to a point made by Carol Poore concerning immigrant socialist workers' theater, the importance of the SSS curriculum in its own time as well as for my own rediscovery of it perhaps lies not so much in the curriculum itself as in "its place within the multifaceted effort to create alternative possibilities for cultural expression involving the restructuring of daily life and political participation."[23] Nevertheless, it might prove interesting and helpful to educators to highlight some of the specific themes that predominated in the curriculum of the Socialist Sunday schools as a whole. While some recurrent themes were emphasized to a greater extent or taught more directly than others, they each represented a significant element of this radical curriculum. Although not always easily differentiated from each other, thirteen major curricular themes can be highlighted.

The first theme involved a reaction to the concept of "the abstract individual." Michael Apple has described this individualism as related to the fact that "our sense of community is withered at its roots. We find ways of making the concrete individual into an abstraction and, at the same time, we divorce the individual from larger social movements which might give meaning to 'individual' wants, needs, and visions of justice."[24] The life of the individual, as an economic and social being, is not situated within the structural relations that play an influential role in determining, for example, the level of comfort that one does or does not enjoy. In contrast, the SSS curriculum was strongly infused by a perspective of the place of the individual in the social world, and in particular of the interdependence and indebtedness of the individual to countless others, especially workers. Such was the emphasis for instance, when Helen Dunbar used Robert Louis Stevenson's poem, "Where Go the Boats," and when many of the schools used the books by Katherine Dopp. It was also the focus when teachers and students from Omaha, Nebraska, took school trips to local manufacturing plants and Bertha Mailly, a teacher at the school, discussed with the children how a guide at a shoe factory proudly told the children about the work of the machines without any reference to the laborers in the plant. Mailly made a point of stressing the social character of products and the children's debt to unknown workers for the shoes that they wore.[25] With tongue firmly in cheek, Oscar Ameringer succinctly summarized this alternative vision of the interdependence of the individual with others when he commented: "Except that I inherited certain characteristics from an unknown number of ancestors, was deeply influenced by persons most of whom were dead before I was born, and shaped by circumstances over which I had no control, I am a self-made man."[26]

A second curricular theme that was prominent in all the schools entailed an emphasis on being conscious and proud of belonging to the working-class community. The dignity of labor (if not all laborers) was stressed and virtually every social issue or problem was viewed primarily from its effect on workers. The necessities and luxuries people were able to enjoy were viewed as owing primarily to workers (for example, "Labor produces wealth," as Bertha Fraser put it), and yet workers did not enjoy the full fruits of their efforts. Class relations in American society were highlighted by the exploitation of the labor of the working class by elite groups, as Nicholas Klein, Caroline Nelson, and others stressed. It followed, then, that class struggle rather than class compromise was the most effective political strategy to follow. Two former students from Milwaukee recall that many school lessons highlighted the important role to be played by workers in general, and labor unions in specific, in the lengthy, nonviolent struggle to overthrow the capitalist system.[27]

Economic relations that were cooperative and collectivist rather than intensely competitive and privatized made up a third theme of the SSS curriculum. Lessons such as those developed by Edith

Breithut focused on the nature and advantages of social ownership and management of industry at a time when public ownership of utilities was considered a radical demand. This sense of cooperation and collectivism was extended to social relations in general, so that working together in a variety of ways (for example, the Milwaukee lessons on "Singing Together" and "Running Industry Together") was viewed not only as a key to working-class success in contesting the capitalist system but also to more equitable and congenial personal relationships. Selfishness was deplored, such as in the "Little Woodpecker" story and the "In Competition's Way" song. John Spargo illustrated this theme in his book, *Modern Socialism*. Spargo wrote about a wise teacher who placed a beautiful rose in the classroom "to brighten the day for her children." Before long, "the boys and girls began to clamor for the rose, each begging the teacher for the sole possession of it." The teacher explained that to give it to any child "would be unjust to all the others. . . . Besides, it would be unwise, for whoever obtained it could not get more of its beauty than now." The teacher went on to explain that she could not divide it, "for if I do the rose will be destroyed and each child will have a worthless petal only; there will be no rose. Together, we can enjoy it; in a real sense each of us owns the rose."[28]

A fourth curricular theme was internationalism, the sense of viewing oneself as inextricably linked to the interests of workers in other nations. Correspondence with schools and youth clubs in Canada, England, and Scotland was not only to gather information but also to encourage a connectedness with youth and radical political movements abroad. The *Young Socialists' Magazine* frequently published information about groups, people, and events in other countries. International songs (for example, "The Marseillaise") and flags were a part of the lessons at all schools, including Milwaukee's course of study on "geography and socialism" and in a "parade of nations" performed at the Rochester school that included socialist vote tallies from different countries written on the front of cards that the children carried.[29] Rather than discouraging this emphasis, World War I intensified the schools' focus on the international character of a successful socialist movement. Future workers in the United States needed to realize that workers in other countries shared a common enemy, the capitalist system, and a common aim, its overthrow.

A fifth and related theme was anti-militarism, especially during the middle years of the second decade when the European conflict started and the United States massed troops along the Mexican border. The "wickedness and wastefulness" of war, as David Greenberg put it, was associated with what he referred to as "anti-sham patriotism." Military adventures were viewed as primarily hurting the lives of workers (who had to fight in such endeavors), breaking down a feeling of internationalism, and taking attention and funding away from pressing domestic needs. Of course, this theme became more prominent when the United States entered World War I and numerous radical activists faced military service, prison, and various forms of harassment. Socialist Sunday School children sang songs like "War What For?" and some schools participated in protest rallies and the Party's Prison Comfort Clubs to provide the children with more active involvement in anti-militarist efforts.

A sixth curricular theme can be explained as a revisionist interpretation of history and sociology. Socialist Sunday School children were taught lessons that transformed the typical school's teaching so that the laboring class was perceived as an instrument for social progress. Heroes and heroines whose birthdays were celebrated in the pages of the *Young Socialists' Magazine* and during school sessions included William Lloyd Garrison, Susan B. Anthony, "Mother" Jones, Eugene Debs, William Morris, Karl Marx, and other national and international social critics and activists whose contributions typically were ignored, at best, in the public school classroom. Radical agitators were portrayed not as a lunatic fringe of bombthrowers but rather as important allies in the workers' struggle to improve their lot significantly. Moreover, the traditional glorified account of the American past was counterposed with a consideration of other factors, for example, in Frederick Krafft's portrayal of many of the Founding Fathers as owning slaves and in the seventeen incidents of American history presented at the Rochester school's Red Flag Day celebration. The plight of the poor was viewed not as the result of defective skills or character on the part of individuals but rather as caused primarily by the capitalist organization of society, as was indicated in Shedd's lesson outlines and in the student essay on "Why Men Are as They Are." In essence, as an educational critic of 1971 put it, the students revisited American history to find out "what they [the public schools] didn't tell us."[30]

A seventh and related theme involved the study of anthropology and in particular the evolution of the human race, with an emphasis on the progress of people from the Stone Age to the Iron Age, from feudalism to capitalism, with the logical next step in "the struggle for existence" being socialism. It was an optimistic message, and one that embraced a liberal notion of progress, but it subverted conventional teaching by assuming the necessity and inevitability of a next, socialistic stage of human civilization. Anthropological accounts were further guided not so much by a sense of how "primitive" early people were but by the cooperative and collective spirit that had stood them well, a spirit that was portrayed as "natural" to humans but that had been distorted and suppressed by capitalist social relations. In addition, as expressed by one school participant, the goals of such lessons were "to show the child that change and adaptation are ever universal," and to foster "the general principle to go from old to new, from simple to complex, from concrete to abstract, to appeal to the imagination." It has been argued more recently, in fact, that "the recognition of change is inherently radical. To know that things have changed is to know that the present is not eternal. To know how change has occurred is to know how to direct it."[31] The teaching of anthropology and evolution, even the specific focus on Tree- and Cave-Dwellers, has been vividly recalled by a number of former students interviewed for this study, all taught "of course on a ten year old level."[32]

Social equality and justice was an eighth theme of the SSS curriculum, with the differences between the few "haves" (with great wealth) and the many "have nots" (with needless suffering) a consistent focus. Because American socialists at this time embraced a political vision that held class struggle to be pre-eminent, that is, that racial and sexual inequities could not be fully addressed until the capitalist organization of society was eradicated, this conception of equality tended to concentrate primarily (one might say narrowly) on materialist issues. Economic disparities were viewed as decisive throughout history and true equality of opportunity could only be attained when workers had the same advantages in life as managers and owners, when wage slavery was eliminated. Adequate levels of food, clothing, and shelter were highlighted time and again as the most vital elements of human life, from the beginning of civilization to the present, with only a socialist society able to guarantee them to all individuals. In a sense, this emphasis on adequate levels of food, clothing, and shelter for everyone amounted to "the basics" of the SSS curriculum.

This does not mean that race and gender issues were never addressed, for prejudicial attitudes were sometimes directly attacked. According to Edward Friebert, who had been a staff member at Milwaukee's International SSS, "tolerance was strongly stressed." During the general assembly time of one lesson, for example, about a dozen children were summoned to the hall platform, with a sign placed around the neck of each one. The signs were labeled "American," "English," "German," "French," "Russian," "Negro," and so on. Kendrick Shedd, the director of the school, asked the children what would happen if he cut the veins of the American child: "What would flow?" The children answered that "blood" would come out. Shedd then asked its color, and the students answered, "Red." He continued to do this for each child except the one designated "Negro." After he addressed that child, he cried out, "You mean to tell me that the same red blood would abound from this negro [sic] child as from these white children?!"[33] What happened next is not known, but the lesson serves as an example of how one school dealt with the issue of race relations.

A ninth theme revolved around an awareness of serious social problems and the need to agitate for their alleviation. Some of the lesson outlines, like Shedd's, represent a social-problems approach more than the teaching of socialist principles. What differentiated the social-problems approach of these socialist teachers from other educators was their consistent emphasis on poverty, unemployment, unhealthy and unsafe work conditions, child labor, alcoholism, poor housing and sanitary facilities, the destruction of nature, and disease as endemic to industrial capitalism. In other words, social ills (for example, "Home Destroyers") could not be fully comprehended or eliminated without taking into consideration the oppressive nature of the capitalist system. They were viewed not as isolated phenomena that could be attacked and resolved by well-meaning reformers but rather as integral features of capitalist America. Thus, the aim of the staff of the Third Assembly District SSS in the Bronx "to develop the children into useful citizens" did not refer merely to voting and participating in uncontroversial social service activities. It meant assisting in the long struggle to eradicate serious social problems in the only way that could be effective, by agitating for the end of capitalist control of economic and social life.[34] And it meant *Red Rebel* recitations at the Rochester SSS, emphasizing the need for students to do everything possible "to abolish poverty and make this world a better place in which to live." The SSS movement never assumed the structures of domination to be so pervasive or so powerful as to preclude individual initiatives on the part of the working class.

A tenth theme of the SSS curriculum also focused attention on the everyday conditions of working-class life, beyond those that were directly economic in nature. Thus, teachers sought to expand the children's awareness of and appreciation for the need for good hygiene, healthy diets, proper exercise, safety, and nature outings. Significantly, these aspects of one's lifestyle were perceived as benefitting not only the individual but the community at large as well. After all, sickness can spread to others, and nature can be enjoyed by others. It was the responsibility of everyone to learn to take care of these matters. An emphasis on health could be linked to the community in another way as well, as in the suggestion made by educator Eliot Wigginton that health be thought of as "a total package that . . . includes a lack of greed and encompasses Socrates' statement, 'I love to walk through the market place and see all the things I can live without.'"[35] Indeed, the everyday conditions of working-class life were often related to more political concerns, as shown when students in Buffalo and Rochester recited "We Want," linking desires for "more of sunshine and air" and "to be well and to know" with "each mortal his share" and the need to gain "all the value we're worth."[36]

An eleventh theme involved the presentation of the Cooperative Commonwealth as embracing the ideal conditions of human life. This was the "remedy" in Bertha Fraser's lesson outlines and the land depicted by Old Peter in John Spargo's *Socialist Readings for Children*. In other words, a utopian society was presented as a goal toward which all progressive people, including children, should and could strive to make a reality. The socialist vision was not left as a vague rendering of some future world, however. It would specifically be marked by public ownership and management of industry and social property, the end of wage slavery, and the elimination of the class structure. Associated with this focus was the notion that socialism should in fact be identified with happiness. This was used as an argument for augmenting the curriculum with games, trips, concerts, pageants, and picnics. While some of these activities were utilized for fund-raising purposes, SSS advocates stressed that as a by-product the children would be having fun and would think of being part of a socialist community as an enjoyable experience. This view was articulated by Eleanor Marx Aveling, the daughter of Karl Marx, when she urged the Council of the Socialist League in Britain to have a Christmas tree because "we cannot too soon make children understand that Socialism means happiness."[37]

Education (and self-education) was the twelfth important theme of the SSS curriculum. It was not just college-educated participants like Shedd and Haessler who repeatedly urged the children to become better educated about the problems of capitalist America and the nature of the coming socialist society. In addition, as one of the *Young Socialists' Magazine* editorials illustrated, working-class children needed to take full advantage of the opportunity of a public school education, while remaining critical of its messages. Education was viewed, however, as only part of the overall program to transform the fundamental organization of social life. This outlook is in some contrast to that of the later social reconstructionists, who believed that schooling by itself could propel significant social change.[38] Socialist educators did not adopt this perspective. They always included the necessity of political work outside the educational arena as crucial to the realization of the new social order.

Finally, the thirteenth theme of the SSS curriculum sought to instill a generally critical approach toward everyday social life, dominated as it was by capitalist institutions. Thus, Gill stressed that the schools should develop "inquiry on the part of the child" and Shedd urged SSS teachers to "get them [the children] to asking WHY?" Public schooling, for example, was not portrayed as a neutral site and

SSS students were discouraged from accepting at face value what their public school teachers taught them. While no one recommended that the children outrightly reject the messages and practices of the public schools, the entire content of this oppositional curriculum was intended to reveal that if truths existed, and they certainly did for these socialists, they would not necessarily be found in the weekday schools, the mainstream press, mass entertainment, the church, and so on. It was not just a matter of focusing on different heroes and different interpretations of important historical events. Even alternative notions of everyday concepts were considered, so that success and justice were viewed critically from a more socially-informed perspective. In this way, the SSS curriculum perhaps resembles late twentieth-century critical and feminist theory, in that a concept like justice "is not organized around an appeal to abstract principles but is rooted in a substantive project of transforming those concrete social and political structures that deny dignity, hope, and power to vast numbers of people."[39]

The Socialist Difference

Nowhere in the reports issued by the schools or by prominent activists was the SSS curriculum described as coherently and comprehensively as in this account. The movement was never able to analyze closely the lesson materials and activities of its different schools. Nevertheless, this examination highlights the specific ways that the practices of the Socialist Sunday schools were substantially different from instruction in the state schools. Perhaps the central difference of this socialist education was summarized succinctly in 1910 by a student from a school in Brooklyn. She described what she was learning this way:[40]

Not alone has it broadened my outlook on all questions connected with life in general, but it has also caused me to view with kindred feeling the sufferings of all less fortunate than myself.

The Social [sic] school has taught me to distinguish more clearly the difference between government as it is and as it should be. It has taught me to be useful to all people, to be a useful member of the community, taking an absorbing interest in all things that concern the welfare of all its members. Thus you see that the Social school has taken me from the drift, as it were, and educated me to feel the impulses of affectionate interest in all things pertaining to the welfare and good of all people.

SSS teachers sought to enlist the children of workers in the transformation of dominant economic and social relations. While their teaching may have been propagandistic, they claimed that ultimately so was all teaching. They argued that their teaching was intended to reveal rather than to conceal, to enlighten children about the true conditions and possibilities of working-class life rather than to mystify or misrepresent them, as in the public schools. They sought to prepare children for the realities of the lives they would face as workers and for the struggles that needed to take place so that their lives and the lives of their fellow workers could be substantially improved. They did not conceive of the possibility that some of the very children of the working class they were teaching would not be won over by capitalist tenets as much as they would become successful in rising out of the working class and in enjoying the fruits of American middle-class life.

Former teachers at Commonwealth College, an adult residential labor college in Mena, Arkansas, in the 1920s and 1930s, observed that the basic premise, "and you may call it a dogma if you will," of workers' education was "the acceptance of social revision as axiomatic." While such education may turn out individuals with widely differing views regarding the exact nature and means of such revision, "it will turn out no strikebreakers."[41] This is essentially what SSS proponents sought. Not that the children would become mindless followers of socialist doctrine when they reached adulthood but that they would comprehend the need for, and seek to enlist in, the battle against exploitation, prejudice, and social inequality—in effect, that they would become "good rebels." Whatever the results or lack of results that can be claimed for the educational activities of American socialists during the Progressive era, they should not serve to obscure or eliminate from our collective memory the reasons for and nature of the efforts that were made.

CONCLUSION

Our Socialist Past, Our Curriculum Future

Part of our difficulty with constructing alternative ideas and practices is that we have lost a sense of past efforts in this direction. Indeed, the people, activities, and materials described in this study essentially stand outside the selective tradition that has such a powerful impact on the way that we think and act. This is the case in several significant ways.

The educational (as well as political) ideas and activities of American socialists during the early 1900s are "outside" in the sense that educators and others in the 1990s are hardly aware of their existence. One reason for this is indicated by an analysis of the ideological nature of school textbooks. Jean Anyon found, for example, that of seventeen widely used textbooks two decades ago, twelve did not describe the Socialist Party of America or its platform, nor did they mention the existence of other radical groups. Of the five books that did discuss the Socialist Party, all but one contained disparaging comments about the socialists' intentions, and four of the five minimized the extent to which workers were attracted to radical ideas.[1] In our schools and elsewhere, then, a strong sense of a respectable American socialist political tradition has largely been eradicated from our history. It is hardly surprising that an awareness of socialist educational perspectives and experiments has also been lost. As one of the characters in the film *Northern Lights* observes, there are parts of our history that have been forgotten or rewritten, leaving us ignorant of our own "rebel roots."

It is not only our awareness of history that is at issue but also the very reasons, in the past and present, for adopting a radical approach that are in danger of being eradicated. For example, a study of the very popular Curriculum Foundation Readers (more commonly known as the "Dick and Jane" readers), which were published by Scott Foresman from 1935 to 1966, revealed that they embodied a vision of literacy that aimed for "more efficient adaptation to existing social knowledges and organization." Social adaptation to capitalist culture without "a parallel concern with social transformation" were the norms in these widely used school texts.[2] In another analysis of forty-seven social studies, reading and language arts, science, and mathematics textbooks used in grades one through eight, it was found that the image conveyed is that "the United States is not stratified on the basis of social class, that almost everyone is middle-class, that there is no poverty and no great wealth." It is simply the case that "social class and poverty . . . do not appear on the curricular agenda."[3]

Besides the homogenizing nature of school materials, another way that the mechanism of the selective tradition operates involves the suppression of efforts to introduce a more critical perspective into our social institutions. This suppression is most overtly manifested during what Gramsci called a "crisis of authority," for example during World War I and its aftermath, but it can occur at other times and in more subtle ways as well. One example involved a former student of the East Side Socialist Sunday School in Manhattan, who graduated from elementary school in 1915, and then attended Washington Irving High School. In her third year of high school, she and her classmates were given an assignment by their English teacher who asked them to read the lead editorial in their favorite newspaper at home and then bring in "a little resume of what you read." Her family received the *New York Times, New York World*, and her favorite, the socialist *New York Call*. She used the *Call* editorial, which dealt with the war, to complete her homework assignment. When she brought in her resume, the teacher was furious at the views presented and reported her to the principal. Although sympathetic, the principal warned her about getting into trouble with the teacher.[4] Another example involves Michael Moore's difficulties in having his film *Roger and Me* shown and discussed in certain communities, in certain schools, and on television and radio interview programs.[5] In such ways throughout our history, multiplied many times over, a more critical perspective of society has been to a large extent selected out of our public discourse. A comprehension of the effects of the selective tradition therefore needs to take into account the historical dimension of its development. The past does not determine present practice, but it indeed weighs heavily upon it.[6]

At the same time, while we should guard against a romanticization of their efforts—after all, they were hardly successful in creating a strong allegiance to the socialist vision—the efforts of American socialist activists during the early 1900s represent the active questioning and contestation of hegemonic culture. Inside and outside the public schools, these radicals opposed the dominant messages and practices of the public school curriculum and attempted to foster an understanding of and allegiance to alternative, more socially responsible knowledge and values. The particular curriculum that Kendrick Shedd and others developed, for example the thirteen curricular themes discussed in Chapter Seven, in large part also stand outside the selective tradition. Their lessons represent a version of reality and a commitment to fostering "good rebellion" that has in large part been selected out of the instruction that we offer to children. Indeed, it represents our most concrete indication of the views of American socialists toward the education of children, of the specific ideological messages that they believed were not but should be included in public school classrooms.

The primary intent of this historical study has been to illuminate the very existence of this past contestation. The reasons why the groups and individuals discussed are among the "losers" in the struggle for the American curriculum can be primarily explained by the demise of the political movement to which they were strongly attached. But perhaps we should not be too certain of their defeat. While we cannot reasonably predict some future triumph of their educational ideas and practices, things might have looked quite different if their efforts had never taken place.

In addition, for someone like me, who has been a nursery school teacher, a high school social studies teacher, an instructor in teacher education programs, and a parent during the last dozen years, the question arises of whether this examination is relevant to late twentieth-century curriculum theory and practice. Clearly, the educational perspectives and lesson materials of these socialist educators should not be adopted as a critical pedagogy in the 1990s. It would be ridiculous to expect otherwise, as this work took place more than seventy years ago, when social conditions were far different, the prospects of an American socialist movement seemed much brighter, and progressive educational ideas were first being widely discussed. Moreover, the schools were severely limited with regard to meeting time, only two hours a week; availability of resources and staff; the nature of the student population, only children from working-class backgrounds; and so forth.

More important, the character of the SSS curriculum itself was deficient. For one thing, SSS teachers were more concerned with socialist content than with instructional process. Consequently, although the social vision embedded in the SSS curriculum stressed critique, cooperation, and collectivism, the activities planned for the children were often lacking in opportunities for creative self-expression, self-criticism, and collaboration. Too often Socialist Sunday School instruction resembled the kind of didactic "banking approach" to education that Paulo Freire and others have criticized.[7] Relatedly, despite, or because of, the fact that the radical movement was wracked with disputes, the socialists' educational strategies rarely included a critical perspective toward their own ideas and practices. Socialist knowledge itself was often presented authoritatively. Indeed, the SSS curriculum perhaps represented more of an education for socialist children than a socialist curriculum for children. A comprehensive effort was never made to formulate an educational theory that was fully aware of the nature of childhood learning, and it was never necessary to develop instructional strategies that took into account the diversity and lack of progressive politics that mark the general community of school children. In the attempt to construct a pedagogy that balanced political radicalism with a vision of personal liberation, it is clear that the SSS curriculum gave insufficient attention to the latter.

Even with regard to the content of the SSS curriculum, there are serious problems for efforts to develop critical pedagogies. In particular, there is a clear de-valuing of other social categories besides class, most notably race and gender. This is not entirely unexpected, given the Socialist Party's general adherence to scientific socialism during the first decades of the twentieth century. Ethnic, racial, and gender issues were viewed by most Party officials and members as secondary to class concerns, both theoretically and politically. In contrast, as historian Linda Gordon argues, "a gender analysis is *always* necessary—nothing, no social relations are free of gender." Similarly, as Michael Omi and Howard Winant suggest, race "will *always* be at the center of the American experience" and cannot be reduced "to a mere manifestation of other supposedly fundamental social and political relationships such as ethnicity or class."[8] The focus of the SSS curriculum was overly economistic, although it can be congratulated for emphasizing the significance of material relations in people's lives.

Despite these serious weaknesses, the efforts of these early socialist educators can assist us in two related ways. First, the SSS curriculum can help to provide the stark contrast sometimes needed to clarify the political nature of school curriculum making. Political nature is meant here not in the important but more narrow sense of how specific participants in the local selection process have more power to decide matters than others (for example, which programs to fund), but in the broader sense of how social institutions legitimize particular identities and knowledge.[9] Indeed, if the messages of this curriculum seem overly propagandistic or political in tone, perhaps it is primarily because they are not the ones we expect from schools. For instance, learning in a public school how to invest in the stock market is as much an act of advocacy as learning in a socialist school to pool one's resources in cooperative and socially responsible ventures. And while our public schools do not sing about "The Red Flag" or portray corporate capitalists as inhumane individuals motivated primarily by greed, they do have ultra-patriotic essay contests sponsored by the Daughters of the American Revolution, the singing of the militaristic "Star Spangled Banner," the staging of plays about the first Thanksgiving that offer little mention of how the colonists treated Native Americans, and many other instances of lessons that are steeped in propagandistic overtones. There have also emerged "Adopt-a-School" programs that encourage local businesses (such as banks, real estate firms, energy companies) to supply supplementary materials and support for local public schools. One kit provided to schools by the Chamber of Commerce has been described by a labor organizer as "preach[ing] the wonders of 'free enterprise' with no mention of plant closings, layoffs, unemployment, or pollution caused by the profits-at-any-cost thinking of 'free-enterprise' economics. The only 'monopolies' mentioned are labor unions; the multinational companies that exercise control over much of the economy are left alone."[10] While it is clear that the current fiscal crisis in school funding is the immediate impetus for such "Adopt-a-School" programs, what may be less clear to school participants is the ideological nature of such programs. To what extent, for example, might product advertising be taught as nutrition education, the benefits of nuclear energy as energy education, industry public relations as environmental education, and corporate promotion as economics education?[11]

It is clear that the question in teaching is not whether to advocate or not but rather the nature and the extent of one's advocacy. In that light, perhaps the socialist educational critiques and experiments of decades ago are worth reflecting about in the 1990s. Whether in agreement with the thrust of the SSS curriculum or not, an examination of such alternative knowledge and understandings that actually existed, even ones clearly outdated, can help to make the familiar strange, thus "heightening our critical sensibilities" and helping us to "reformulate our problems in fresh and constructive ways."[12] As Henry Giroux suggests, along with that of women, blacks, and ethnic minorities, "the disqualified knowledges of working-class communities . . . [can be] the starting point for understanding how curriculum and schooling have been constructed around particular silences and omissions."[13]

The SSS curriculum can also help in the difficult task of thinking of what could be otherwise. More specifically, socialist curricula can perhaps offer a concrete model of "really [or critically] useful knowledge" for children. This idea of "really useful knowledge" has a long history in radical circles, dating back to the efforts of working-class educational associations in early nineteenth-century England. Drawing on the work of Richard Johnson, the alternative lessons discussed in this study can be briefly viewed as having addressed six related aspects of this conception of educational knowledge.[14] First, as a body of work they encouraged the children to take pride in the role of labor in society and in their own working-class backgrounds. This was in direct contrast to the predominant division and hierarchy of mental and manual labor that tended to minimize and even denigrate the contributions of laborers to American progress.[15] A similar encouragement of taking pride in one's background and a focus on the significant contributions of other social groups would constitute an important aspect of a critical pedagogy today, not just for reasons of self-esteem but also with regard to a more honest depiction of past and current social relations. Indeed, as Maxine Greene has pointed out, "if the voices of participants or near-participants (front-line soldiers, factory workers, slaves, crusaders) could be heard, whole dimensions of new understanding (and perplexity and uncertainty) would be disclosed."[16]

Second, SSS teachers believed in the subordinate status of workers as shared and systematic, rather than individualistic and idiosyncratic, and encouraged a sense of solidarity with other oppressed groups. While gender and race issues were viewed as secondary to class ones, a perspective that equally considers and integrates these and other social categories could be advantageously adopted. This perspective could be based on a "nonsynchronous parallelism" that emphasizes the complex intersections between class, racial, and gender dynamics.[17] An emphasis on the issues of race and gender, and issues of disability, sexual orientation, ecology, and so forth, however, should not obscure the fact that class as a category will remain crucial in capitalist America, that where people are placed within the socioeconomic structure continues to have immense importance for both individual lives and society as a whole, both for the construction of personal identity and our visions of social change. Indeed, class was and remains "not only so ubiquitous and material a fact of life . . . that nobody can understand what is going on without some picture of class, but more that the effects of class . . . have wounded and poisoned so many lives [for so long a time] in such irrevocable ways."[18]

Third, there exists in the SSS curriculum a strong vision of social interdependence and collectivism: that we rely on countless others for many necessities in life, and that it is in our best interests to be socially concerned with and responsible for each other. Indeed, although he may have overstated the case, Lucien Goldmann did explicate a crucial point about understanding and commitment when he emphasized the concept of the "collective subject": "the affirmation that, historically, effective action is never taken by isolated individuals but by social groups, and that it is only in relation to these that one can understand events, modes of behavior, and institutions."[19] Moreover, it does not take a socialist to consider the kind of social concern and responsibility seen in the writings of several of the SSS students to be worthy educational goals for students in the 1990s.

Fourth, a focus on the everyday concerns of working-class life was used to highlight the relationship between current social problems and the general nature of dominant economic and political relations. While these radical educators may have been mistaken in seeing the evil hand of the corporate capitalist behind every social ill, they were free of the myopic vision of many of their contemporary observers. They sought to critique the concretely lived experiences of workers' lives, which most of the children could personally relate to, not as isolated and individual social problems but rather as the products of an inherently uncaring and unequal social order. They were able to do this because, although perhaps politically naive, reductionist, or "incorrect" by the standards of the early 1990s leftist culture, they nevertheless had a comprehensive social vision and commitment to guide them in connecting everyday life and the political sphere. To be sure, a socialist commitment in the 1990s must be more sophisticated than that of the 1900s. It would need to extend itself to a much wider range of the population, including ethnic and racial minorities and women. It would need to emphasize the end result of fairness and democracy rather than just the means of public ownership. And it would need to teach not a simplistic economic determinism but, for example, "that the struggles of ordinary people matter in history; that work in a capitalist society tends to be not only underpaid, but also fragmented and meaningless; and that by treating people like commodities, capitalism degrades humanity and obstructs human development."[20]

Fifth, there was an emphasis on the need for fundamental social change. Only large-scale cooperative (rather than short-term and individualistic) strategies could effectively overcome the hardships and sense of powerlessness that the working class (and other subordinate groups) experienced. While they certainly did not forgo more immediate strategies (such as, running for local political office), SSS advocates did not allow the possibilities for short-run success to deflect them from advocating the need for more comprehensive changes. This should not mean subscribing to the often paralyzing notion that "changing the world" is worth pursuing only on a grand scale, but rather that smaller-scale strategies must be viewed within the context of the larger movement for democratization of the public sphere.

And sixth, the socialist curricula adopted a generally critical view of the nature and consequences of contemporary arrangements of social and economic power and the common sense understandings of everyday life (such as, the nature of justice and success). Indeed, critical thinking here meant an informed and vigilant posture toward the complex and inequitable nature of capitalist relations, not step-by-step procedures for solving problems. While the socialist schools may not have adequately engaged children in problem-solving and decision-making activities, or attended to the development of personal identities, they did not confuse the need for critical social understandings with the mental gymnastics of solving "puzzles." The point here is that while the lessons discussed in this study are outdated and wrongheaded in some ways, they attempted to instill a critical understanding of the social world, as well as a commitment "to make this world a better place in which to live," and they may help to inform similar educational efforts in the 1990s.

It seems overly pessimistic to claim that "alternatives are as scarce as hen's teeth, and, for the moment at least, hope is at a low ebb."[21] But for those struggling to resist dominant ideologies in the classroom, there is a critical need for concrete suggestions of alternative cultural symbols, meanings, and educational activities. An alternative identity guided by "the common good" cannot be based on criticism and rejection alone. But neither can effective social reconstruction be based only on utopian or abstract visions of hope. It requires specific programs and specific answers to the questions of "what (and whose) knowledge is of most worth" that people can consider, argue about, revise, and perhaps attempt to implement.[22] Historical examples can play a role in their development. The point is not, as Howard Zinn has perceptively written, "to invent victories for people's movements." But history can "emphasize new possibilities by disclosing those hidden episodes of the past when, even if in brief flashes, people showed their ability to resist, to join together, occasionally to win."[23] The efforts of American socialists should be viewed from a similar vantage point, as hidden episodes of the past that may help to indicate possibilities for the future— possibilities of understandings, of activities, and, perhaps most important, of the human spirit.

Notes

Introduction

1. John Spargo, *Socialist Readings for Children* (New York: Woman's National Progressive League, 1909).

2. This study focuses primarily on the English-speaking children's schools organized by members of the Socialist Party. The foreign-language federations of the Party also established schools, and they are discussed briefly in Chapter Two. However, this study is monolingual for two main reasons: the scant documentation located about these other schools and the limited foreign-language proficiency of the author.

3. See, for example, Svi Shapiro, *Between Capitalism and Democracy: Educational Policy and the Crisis of the Welfare State* (New York: Bergin and Garvey, 1990); Michael W. Apple, *Teachers and Texts: A Political Economy of Class and Gender Relations in Education* (New York: Routledge and Kegan Paul, 1986); Ira Shor, *Culture Wars: School and Society in the Conservative Restoration, 1969–1984* (Boston: Routledge and Kegan Paul, 1986); Martin Carnoy and Henry M. Levin, *Schooling and Work in the Democratic State* (Stanford, Calif.: Stanford University Press, 1985); and Stanley Aronowitz and Henry A. Giroux, *Education under Siege: The Conservative, Liberal, and Radical Debate over Schooling* (South Hadley, Mass.: Bergin and Garvey, 1985).

4. See, for example, William J. Reese, *Power and the Promise of School Reform: Grass-Roots Movements during the Progressive Era* (Boston: Routledge and Kegan Paul, 1986); Julia Wrigley, *Class Politics and Public Schools: Chicago, 1900–1950* (New Brunswick, N.J.: Rutgers University Press, 1982); and David Hogan, "Education and Class Formation: The Peculiarities of the Americans," in *Cultural and Economic Reproduction in Education*, ed. Michael W. Apple (London: Routledge and Kegan Paul, 1982), pp. 32–78.

5. John Dewey, *School and Society* (Chicago: University of Chicago Press, 1899), and Edward A. Ross, *Social Control: A Survey of the Foundations of Order* (New York: Macmillan, 1901). See also Herbert M. Kliebard, *The Struggle for the American Curriculum, 1893–1958* (Boston: Routledge and Kegan Paul, 1986).

6. Joseph Femia, "Hegemony and Consciousness in the Thought of Antonio Gramsci," *Political Studies* 23 (March 1975): 31. See also Roger Dale, "Education and the Capitalist State: Contributions and Contradictions," in *Cultural and Economic Reproduction in Education*, ed. Apple, pp. 127–61, and Femia's more recent position, in "Gramsci: Marxism's Saviour or False Prophet?" *Political Studies* 37 (June 1989): 282–89.

7. Raymond Williams, *Marxism and Literature* (Oxford, Eng.: Oxford University Press, 1977), p. 110.

8. Herbert G. Gutman, *Work, Culture, and Society in Industrializing America* (New York: Vintage, 1976), p. 67. Of course, not all working-class "contestation" should be interpreted as a conscious rejection of capitalist relations. It may instead be a reaction to change in general. This is essentially an empirical question, although there is absolutely no doubt in the case of the Socialist Sunday schools. See Donald T. Critchlow, "Introduction," in his edited book, *Socialism in the Heartland: The Midwestern Experience, 1900–1925* (Notre Dame, Ind.: University of Notre Dame Press, 1986), p. 3; and John Patrick Diggins, "Comrades and Citizens: New Mythologies in American Historiography," *American Historical Review* 90 (June 1985): 614–38.

9. Carl Boggs, *Gramsci's Marxism* (London: Pluto, 1976), p. 86.

10. Martin Carnoy, "Education, Economy and the State," in *Cultural and Economic Reproduction in Education*, ed. Apple, p. 89.

11. Boggs, *Gramsci's Marxism*, p. 77.

12. Ibid. and Carnoy, "Education, Economy and the State," pp. 89–91.

13. Joseph Femia, *Gramsci's Political Thought: Hegemony, Consciousness, and the Revolutionary Process* (Oxford, Eng.: Clarendon, 1981), p. 53.

14. Harold Entwistle, *Antonio Gramsci: Conservative Schooling for Radical Politics* (London: Routledge and Kegan Paul, 1979).

15. David Montgomery, *The Fall of the House of Labor: The Workplace, the State, and American Labor Activism, 1865–1925* (Cambridge, Eng.: Cambridge University Press, 1987).

16. Fred Inglis, *The Management of Ignorance: A Political Theory of the Curriculum* (Oxford, Eng.: Basil Blackwell, 1985), p. 31.

17. Ibid., pp. 63 and 69.

18. Michael W Apple, *Ideology and Curriculum* (London: Routledge and Kegan Paul, 1979), p. 166.

19. Benjamin DeMott, *The Imperial Middle: Why Americans Can't Think Straight about Class* (New York: William Morrow, 1990), p. 37; and, for example, Michael W. Apple and Linda K. Christian-Smith, eds., *The Politics of the Textbook* (New York: Routledge, Chapman and Hall, 1991); Thomas S. Popkewitz, ed., *The Formation of School Subjects: The Struggle for Creating an American Institution* (New York: Falmer, 1987); Michael W. Apple and Lois Weis, eds., *Ideology and Practice in Schooling* (Philadelphia: Temple University Press, 1983); Raphaela Best, *We've All Got Scars: What Boys and Girls Learn in*

Elementary School (Bloomington: Indiana University Press, 1982); Jean Anyon, "Social Class and School Knowledge," *Curriculum Inquiry* 11 (Spring 1981): 3–42; Frances Fitzgerald, *America Revised: History Schoolbooks in the Twentieth Century* (Boston: Little, Brown, 1979); Sheila Harty, *Hucksters in the Classroom: A Review of Industry Propaganda in Schools* (Washington, D.C.: Center for Study of Responsive Law, 1979); and Apple, *Ideology and Curriculum*.

20. Philip Wexler, "Structure, Text, and Subject: A Critical Sociology of School Knowledge," in *Cultural and Economic Reproduction in Education*, ed. Apple, p. 279. See also Raymond Williams, *The Long Revolution* (Harmondsworth, Eng.: Penguin, 1961).

21. Williams, *Marxism and Literature*, p. 116. See also Henry Abelove et al., eds., *Visions of History* (New York: Pantheon, 1984).

22. E. P. Thompson, "The Politics of Theory," in *People's History and Socialist Theory*, ed. Raphael Samuel (London: Routledge and Kegan Paul, 1981), pp. 407–8.

Chapter One

1. *Progressive Woman* 4 (November 1910): 10; and "From the History of the Rochester Socialist Sunday School" and "Our Various 'Homes'," in a folder of miscellaneous materials, and letter from Kendrick Shedd to "Comrade Kreusi," dated January 14, 1914, in "Rochester Socialist Sunday School Scrapbooks, vol. 2," contained in the Kendrick Philander Shedd Papers, located at the University of Rochester, Rush Rhees Library, Rare Books Department, Special Collections, Rochester, N.Y. (Henceforth in this chapter this collection will be referred to as the Shedd Papers.)

2. For overviews of this transformation, see Howard Zinn, *A People's History of the United States* (New York: Harper and Row, 1980), pp. 247–78; Lawrence Goodwyn, *The Populist Movement: A Short History of the Agrarian Revolt in America* (Oxford, Eng.: Oxford University Press, 1978); James Weinstein, *The Corporate Ideal in the Liberal State, 1900–1918* (Boston: Beacon, 1968); Robert Wiebe, *The Search for Order, 1877–1920* (New York: Hill and Wang, 1967); Gabriel Kolko, *The Triumph of Conservatism: A Reinterpretation of American History, 1900–1916* (Chicago: Quadrangle, 1967); and Harold U. Faulkner, *Politics, Reform and Expansion, 1890–1900* (New York: Harper and Row, 1959).

3. Caroline Golab, "The Impact of the Industrial Experience on the Immigrant Family: The Huddled Masses Reconsidered," in *Immigrants in Industrial America, 1850–1920*, ed. Richard L. Ehrlich (Charlottesville: University Press of Virginia, 1977); and Abraham Menes, "The East Side and the Jewish Labor Movement," in *Voices from Yiddish: Essays, Memoirs, Diaries*, ed. Irving Howe and Eliezer Greenberg (Ann Arbor: University of Michigan Press, 1972), p. 202.

4. Will and Ariel Durant, *A Dual Autobiography* (New York: Simon and Schuster, 1977), p. 16; and John F. McClymer, "The Pittsburgh Survey, 1907–1914: Forging an Ideology in the Steel District," *Pennsylvania History* 41 (April 1974): 169–86.

5. See, for example, David Montgomery, *The Fall of the House of Labor: The Workplace, The State, and American Labor Activism, 1865–1925* (Cambridge, Eng.: Cambridge University Press, 1987); Sidney Lens, *The Labor Wars: From the Molly Maguires to the Sitdowns* (Garden City, N.Y.: Anchor, 1974); Jeremy Brecher, *Strike!* (Boston: South End, 1972); Richard O. Boyer and Herbert M. Morais, *Labor's Untold Story* (New York: United Electrical, Radio and Machine Workers of America, 1955); John Dutko, "Socialism in Rochester, 1900–1917," M.A. thesis, University of Rochester, 1953, p. 16; and Zinn, *A People's History of the United States*, pp. 314–22.

6. Jerome Karabel, "The Failure of American Socialism Reconsidered," in *The Socialist Register, 1979*, ed. Ralph Miliband and John Saville (London: Merlin, 1979), p. 217; and Aileen S. Kraditor, *The Radical Persuasion, 1890–1917: Aspects of the Intellectual History and the Historiography of Three American Radical Organizations* (Baton Rouge: Louisiana State University Press, 1981), pp. 50–52 and 305–15. See also David Hogan, "Education and Class Formation: The Peculiarities of the Americans," in *Cultural and Economic Reproduction: Essays on Class, Ideology and the State*, ed. Michael W. Apple (London: Routledge and Kegan Paul, 1982), pp. 32–78. Hogan suggests that "working-class educational aspirations can be best understood . . . not as imitations of middle-class behavior, but as a product of the structural contingencies that working-class families faced and the strategies of survival and the 'pursuit of dignity' pursued by working-class individuals" (p. 50).

7. Peggy Dennis, *The Autobiography of an American Communist: A Personal View of a Political Life, 1924–1975* (Westport, Conn.: Lawrence Hill, 1977), p. 19.

8. David M. Kennedy, "Overview: The Progressive Era," *The Historian* 37 (May 1975): 453–68.

9. Full-length historical treatments of American socialism include: Paul Buhle, *Marxism in the United States: Remapping the History of the American Left* (London: Verso, 1987); Mari Jo Buhle, *Women and American Socialism, 1870–1920* (Urbana: University of Illinois Press, 1981); Bernard K. Johnpoll, *The Impossible Dream: The Rise and Demise of the American Left* (Westport, Conn.: Greenwood, 1981); James R. Green, *Grass-Roots Socialism: Radical Movements in the Southwest, 1895–1943* (Baton Rouge: Louisiana State University Press, 1978); James Weinstein, *The Decline of Socialism in America, 1912–1925* (New York: Vintage, 1969); Daniel Bell, *Marxian Socialism in the United States* (Princeton, N.J.: Princeton University Press, 1967); David A. Shannon, *The Socialist Party of America* (Chicago: Quadrangle, 1955); Howard H. Quint, *The Forging of American Socialism: Origins of the Modern Movement* (Indianapolis, Ind.: Bobbs-Merrill, 1953); and Ira Kipnis, *The American Socialist Movement, 1817–1912* (New York: Columbia University Press, 1952). Edited collections include John H. M. Laslett and Seymour Martin Lipset, eds., *Failure of a Dream?: Essays in the History of American Socialism* (Berkeley: University of California Press, 1984); Bruce M. Stave, ed., *Socialism and the Cities* (Port Washington, N.Y.: Kennikat, 1975); Albert Fried, ed., *Socialism in America: From the Shakers to the Third International* (Garden City, N.Y.: Doubleday, 1970); H. Wayne Morgan, ed., *American Socialism, 1900–1960* (Englewood Cliffs, N.J.: Prentice-Hall, 1964); and Donald Drew Egbert and Stow Persons, eds., *Socialism and American Life*, vols. 1 and 2 (Princeton,

N.J.: Princeton University Press, 1952). See also Mari Jo Buhle, Paul Buhle, and Dan Georgakas, eds., *Encyclopedia of the American Left* (New York: Garland, 1990).

10. For example, see Gerald Sorin, "Tradition and Change: American Jewish Socialists as Agents of Acculturation," *American Jewish History* 74 (Autumn 1989): 37–54; Jerry W. Calvert, *The Gibraltar: Socialism and Labor in Butte, Montana* (Helena: Montana Historical Society Press, 1988); Donald T. Critchlow, ed., *Socialism in the Heartland: The Midwestern Experience, 1900–1925* (Notre Dame, Ind.: University of Notre Dame Press, 1986); William J. Reese, *Power and the Promise of School Reform: Grass-Roots Movements during the Progressive Era* (Boston: Routledge and Kegan Paul, 1986); Peter Kivisto, *Immigrant Socialists in the United States: The Case of Finns and the Left* (Rutherford, N.J.: Fairleigh Dickinson University Press, 1984); Chad Gaffield, "Big Business, the Working-Class, and Socialism in Schenectady, 1911–1916," *Labor History* 19 (Summer 1978): 350–72; Sirkka Tuomi Lee, "The Finns," *Cultural Correspondence* 6–7 (Spring 1978): 41–49; Carol Poore, "German-American Socialist Culture," *Cultural Correspondence* 6–7 (Spring 1978): 13–20; Maurice Isserman, "Inheritance Lost: Socialism in Rochester, 1917–1919," *Rochester History* 39 (October 1977): 1–24; Irving Howe, *World of Our Fathers* (New York: Harcourt Brace Jovanovich, 1976); Sally M. Miller, *Victor Berger and the Promise of Constructive Socialism, 1910–1920* (Westport, Conn.: Greenwood, 1973); Melvin Dubofsky, "Success and Failure of Socialism in New York City, 1900–1918: A Case Study," *Labor History* 9 (Fall 1968): 361–75; Henry F. Bedford, *Socialism and the Workers in Massachusetts, 1886–1912* (Amherst: University of Massachusetts Press, 1966); Arthur Gorenstein, "A Portrait of Ethnic Politics: The Socialists and the 1908 and 1910 Congressional Elections on the East Side," *American Jewish Historical Quarterly* 50 (March 1961): 202–38; and Henry G. Stetler, *The Socialist Movement in Reading, Pennsylvania, 1896–1936* (Storrs, Conn.: Henry G. Stetler, 1943). See also the sources listed in note 9 above.

11. Kent and Gretchen Kreuter, *An American Dissenter: The Life of Algie Martin Simons, 1870–1950* (Lexington: University of Kentucky Press, 1969), p. 83.

12. While the divisions were very real, the differences among individuals and sub-groups were relatively ambiguous and fluid. See James Weinstein, "Socialism's Hidden Heritage: Scholarship Reinforces Political Mythology," in *For a New America: Essays in History and Politics from "Studies on the Left," 1959–1967*, ed. James Weinstein and David W. Eakins (New York: Random House, 1970), pp. 221–52. This was certainly the case with regard to the Socialist Sunday schools, which attracted support and opposition from different factions (e.g., "sewer socialists" and "impossibilists"). On the Party's "recovery," see Weinstein, *The Decline of Socialism in America, 1912–1925*, and Buhle, *Women and American Socialism, 1870–1920*.

13. Robert K. Murray, *Red Scare: A Study in National Hysteria, 1919–1920* (New York: McGraw-Hill, 1955), p. 13.

14. Stanley Coben, "Postwar Upheaval: The Red Scare," in *The Impact of World War I*, ed. Arthur S. Link (New York: Harper and Row, 1969), pp. 107–8. See also Lillian Symes and Travers Clement, *Rebel America: The Story of Social Revolt in the United States* (New York: Harper and Bros., 1934), p.

298, and Edwin J. Gross, "Public Hysteria: First World War Variety," *Historical Messenger* 17 (June 1961): 4.

15. Telephone interview with Louis Hay, New York City, September 1, 1981.

16. Dennis, *The Autobiography of an American Communist*, p. 20.

17. Ida Crouch Hazlett is quoted in Frederic Cornell, "A History of the Rand School of Social Science—1906 to 1956," Ph.D. dissertation, Columbia University, 1976, p. 112. See also Shannon, *The Socialist Party of America*, p. 163; Theodore Draper, *The Roots of American Communism* (New York: Viking, 1957), p. 451; and "What's the Matter with the Socialist Movement Today?" *Appeal to Reason*, September 3, 1921. In his *Autobiographical Novel* (Santa Barbara, Calif.: Ross-Erikson, 1978), the poet and essayist Kenneth Rexroth remembered later in his life that during the early 1920s he met many former members of the Socialist Party, Socialist Labor Party, and Industrial Workers of the World, who had become "all free-lancers, completely disillusioned with the organized radical movements" (p. 138).

18. Quoted in Betty Yorburg, *Utopia and Reality: A Collective Portrait of American Socialists* (New York: Columbia University Press, 1969), p. 33; and Leslie Cross, "The *Milwaukee Leader*, an Unusual Newspaper," *Historical Messenger* 17 (December 1961): 11. This optimism gave the radical movement important sustenance in bad times and good times alike. But it also could be "paralyzing and debilitating," in the sense that radical activists would then make sweeping conclusions from single electoral victories and view every strike as a revolution-in-embryo. Simplistic rhetoric abounded, for example that the "ideal school" would be attained "as soon as enough men and women vote the Socialist ticket" and with headlines that proclaimed "CAPITALISM TOTTERING." This perspective may have mitigated against the development of long-term strategies involving the recruitment and education of workers (and their children). Gabriel Kolko, "The Decline of American Radicalism in the Twentieth Century," in *For a New America*, ed. Weinstein and Eakins, p. 198; Kraditor, *The Radical Persuasion, 1890–1917*, pp. 209–19; *Milwaukee Leader*, November 19, 1917; and Weinstein, *The Decline of Socialism in America*, p. 93.

19. William Mailly, "Undermining New York for Socialism," *Coming Nation*, October 8, 1910.

20. Stephen Yeo, "A New Life: The Religion of Socialism in Britain, 1883–1896," *History Workshop Journal* 4 (Autumn 1977): 5–56; Paul Buhle, "Interview with Ernie Reymer on the I.W.O.," *Cultural Correspondence* 6–7 (Spring 1978): 98; Will Herberg, "The Jewish Labor Movement in the United States," *American Jewish Year Book*, vol. 53 (New York: American Jewish Committee, 1952), pp. 65–66; and Kraditor, *The Radical Persuasion, 1890–1917*, pp. 363–64.

21. Charles Leinenweber, "Socialists in the Streets: The New York City Socialist Party in Working Class Neighborhoods, 1908–1918," *Science and Society* 41 (Summer 1977): 155–62.

22. John Graham, ed., *"Yours for the Revolution": The Appeal to Reason, 1895–1922* (Lincoln: University of Nebraska Press, 1990), pp. 186–90; *International Socialist Review* 9 (November 1908): 902–3; and Rexroth, *An Autobiographical Novel*, p. 139.

23. Leinenweber, "Socialists in the Streets," pp. 162–68.

24. Ibid., p. 153.

25. From photograph, in *Guide to the Manuscript Collection of the Tamiment Library* (New York: Garland, 1977), p. 57.

26. Joseph R. Conlin, "Introduction," in his edited volume, *The American Radical Press, 1880–1960*, vol. 1 (Westport, Conn.: Greenwood, 1974), p. 8.

27. *International Socialist Review* 9 (November 1908): 321–27; and *Appeal to Reason*, September 3, 1912, September 18, 1915, October 2, 1915, October 23, 1915, and September 30, 1916. "Textbooks" included Morris Hillquit, *History of Socialism in the United States* (New York: Funk and Wagnalls, 1903); Walter Thomas Mills, *The Struggle for Existence* (Chicago: International School of Social Economy, 1904); Mary E. Marcy, *Shop Talks on Economics* (Chicago: Charles H. Kerr, 1911); Jessie Wallace Hughan, *American Socialism of the Present Day* (New York: John Lane, 1911); John Spargo, *Applied Socialism* (New York: B. W. Huebsch, 1912); John Spargo and George Louis Arner, *Elements of Socialism: A Textbook* (New York: Macmillan, 1912); and William English Walling, *The Larger Aspects of Socialism* (New York: Macmillan, 1913). Series of articles that more directly focused on educational issues included a "Public Education Column" and later an "Education and Life" column in the *New York Call*; an analysis of "Education" in the *Young Socialists' Magazine*; a seven-part series, initiated by a column on "No Solution of Education Problem Short of Socialism," in *American Socialist*; and a "School and Home" column in the *Milwaukee Leader*. For example, see *New York Call*, January 23, 1909, and March 14, 1919; *Young Socialists' Magazine* 4 (December 1911): 7; *American Socialist*, May 20, 1916; and *Milwaukee Leader*, October 12, 1922.

28. John Dewey, "Education, Direct and Indirect," *Progressive Journal of Education* 2 (October 1909): 31–38; and Charles F. Dight, "Economic Wrongs of Capitalism" *Progressive Journal of Education* 1 (January 1909): 9–13. A series of articles by Algie Simons published in the *Progressive Journal of Education* was prominently cited in a scathing attack on socialist educational activities that appeared in the pages of the *National Civic Federation Review*. The socialist periodical was accused of posing "under the grandmotherly guise of 'Progressive Education'" in an attempt at having the minds of teachers and children "drugged by the deadly materialism and spiritual hopelessness of Socialism." Ada C. Sweet, "Socialists Active in the American Educational Field," *National Civic Federation Review* 3 (March 1909): 18–19.

29. Quoted in Cornell, "A History of the Rand School of Social Science—1906 to 1956," p. 8.

30. Buhle, *Women and American Socialism, 1870–1920*, pp. 103–75.

31. Cornell, "A History of the Rand School of Social Science—1906 to 1956."

32. For information on Ruskin College, see "Diary of May Wood Simons," July 1, 1903, and April 30, 1904 entries, Algie M. and May Wood Simons Papers, 1901–1951, located at the State Historical Society of Wisconsin, Archives and Manuscripts Division, Madison, Wisconsin; Kreuter and Kreuter, *An American Dissenter*, pp. 69–72; *International Socialist Review* 4

(September 1903): 192; Cornell, "A History of the Rand School of Social Science—1906 to 1956," p. 9; and *Milwaukee Leader*, March 27, 1917. For the International School of Social Economy, see Green, *Grass-Roots Socialism*, pp. 41 and 49; Graham, ed., *"Yours for the Revolution,"* pp. 178–81; and Mari Jo Buhle, "Feminism and Socialism in the United States, 1820–1920," Ph.D. dissertation, University of Wisconsin–Madison, 1974, p. 127.

For the Finnish Work People's College, see "National Convention Proceedings, 1912 Convention, Appendix O—Reports of the Foreign Speaking Organizations," *Socialist Party of America Papers*, microfilm edition (Glen Rock, N.J.: Microfilming Corporation of America, 1975), reel 76, located at the State Historical Society of Wisconsin, Madison; George Sirola, "The Finnish Working People's College," *International Socialist Review* 14 (August 1913): 102–4; *International Socialist Review* 15 (November 1914): 316; *New York Call*, November 16, 1909; *American Labor Year Book, 1930* (New York: Rand School of Social Science, 1930), pp. 188–89; *American Labor Year Book, 1932*, pp. 172–73; Cornell, "A History of the Rand School of Social Science—1906 to 1956," pp. 9–10 and 208–9; Timothy L. Smith, "Religious Denominations as Ethnic Communities: A Regional Case Study," *Church History* 35 (June 1966): 214; A. William Hoglund, *Finnish Immigrants in America, 1880–1920* (New York: Arno, 1979), pp. 15–20; and Kivisto, *Immigrant Socialists in the United States*. See also Richard J. Altenbaugh, *Education for Struggle: The American Labor Colleges of the 1920s and 1930s* (Philadelphia: Temple University Press, 1990).

For People's College, see *Appeal to Reason*, June 27, 1914, July 4, 1914, July 11, 1914, December 15, 1917, and March 2, 1918; *Christian Socialist* 5 (September 1915): 8; *Milwaukee Leader*, September 4, 1915; *Young Socialists' Magazine* 9 (August 1915): 12; *Debs Magazine* 1 (September 1921): 2; *Coming Nation* (July 1914): 2; *International Socialist Review* 16 (April 1915): 612–13; *New York Call*, October 10, 1915; and Meridel LeSueur, *Crusaders: The Radical Legacy of Marian and Arthur LeSueur* (St. Paul: Minnesota Historical Society Press, 1984), pp. xviii–xxiii and 44–46. See also J. Robert Constantine, ed., *Letters of Eugene V. Debs*, vol. 2 *(1913–1919)* (Urbana: University of Illinois Press, 1990), pp. 103, 111–12, and 118–20; Harold W. Currie, *Eugene V. Debs* (Boston: G. K. Hall, 1976), pp. 123–24; and Green, *Grass-Roots Socialism*, pp. 134 and 350. A few copies of *The People's College News* can be found in the Shedd Papers.

The Intercollegiate Socialist Society is given full-length treatment in Max Horn, *The Intercollegiate Socialist Society, 1905–1921: Origins of the Modern American Student Movement* (Boulder, Colo.: Westview, 1979).

See also Clyde W. Barrow, "Pedagogy, Politics, and Social Reform: The Philosophy of the Workers' Education Movement," *Strategies: A Journal of Theory, Culture and Politics* 2 (1989): 45–66; and Richard E. Dwyer, *Labor Education in the U.S.: An Annotated Bibliography* (Metuchen, N.J.: Scarecrow, 1977).

33. *American Labor Year Book, 1916*, p. 151.

34. "Socialist Education Platform," in *Socialist Party of America Papers*, reel 5.

35. Among the helpful discussions of public schooling during this period are Stephen F. Brumberg, *Going to America, Going to School: The Jewish*

Immigrant Public School Encounter in Turn-of-the-Century New York City (New York: Praeger, 1986); David Nasaw, *Schooled to Order: A Social History of Public Schooling in the United States* (Oxford, Eng.: Oxford University Press, 1979); David B. Tyack, *The One Best System: A History of American Urban Education* (Cambridge, Mass.: Harvard University Press, 1976); Joel H. Spring, *Education and the Rise of the Corporate State* (Boston: Beacon Press, 1972); and Raymond E. Callahan, *Education and the Cult of Efficiency* (Chicago: University of Chicago Press, 1962). A critical approach toward American public education emerged well before the 1900s. As early as 1829, for example, the Workingmen's Party of New York stressed the need for the expansion of the common school system at the same time that it critically assessed the quality of education being offered to the children of the working class. The Workingmen's Party complained about narrow pedagogy, strict discipline, and abstract lessons unrelated to current laws of the country. See Buhle, "Feminism and Socialism in the United States," pp. 6–7. See also Jay M. Pawa, "Workingmen and Free Schools in the Nineteenth Century: A Comment on the Labor-Education Thesis," *History of Education Quarterly* 11 (Fall 1971): 287–302; and Nasaw, *Schooled to Order*, pp. 48–50.

36. Joseleyne Slade Tien, "The Educational Theories of American Socialists, 1900–1920," Ph.D. dissertation, Michigan State University, 1972; and, for example, Lawrence Cremin, *The Transformation of the School: Progressivism in American Education, 1876–1956* (New York: Random House, 1961).

37. *The Worker*, August 4, 1901.

38. *Milwaukee Leader*, March 19, 1915, September 13, 1915, and March 31, 1917.

39. Tien, "The Educational Theories of American Socialists, 1900–1920," pp. 131–32; and Scott Nearing, *A Nation Divided (or Plutocracy versus Democracy)* (Chicago: Socialist Party of the United States, 1920), p. 25.

40. *Appeal to Reason*, August 8, 1914.

41. *Milwaukee Leader*, March 19, 1923.

42. May Wood Simons, "Vocational Education," *Progressive Journal of Education* 1 (November 1908): 7.

43. "Socialist Education Platform," in *Socialist Party of America Papers*, reel 5. Despite these public platforms, an educational committee during the same year reported, "Socialists in many instances are ignorant of the usual position taken by the Socialist party in educational matters. Thus, during school campaigns, some Socialists take positions directly opposite the usual attitude of the party." *New York Call*, March 17, 1913, and September 3, 1913.

44. "Social Elective Officials—United States," in *Socialist Party of America Papers*, reel 6; *Socialist Party Congressional Campaign Book of 1914* (Chicago: Socialist Party of America, 1914), p. 311; and *Milwaukee Leader*, July 7, 1915.

45. *Socialist Party of America Papers*, reel 76; and letter from Winnie L. Branstetter to "Socialist Teachers and School Officials," dated February 8, 1913, in *Socialist Party of America Papers*, reel 4.

46. *Party Builder*, June 28, 1913, and October 11, 1913; and "Report of the Woman's Department," in Socialist Party of U.S. Materials, 1915 Folder, located at the Tamiment Institute, Elmer Holmes Bobst Library, New York University, New York. No charge was levied and no guarantees for those

involved were offered. A list of either teachers or positions was sent, with participants being responsible for initiating correspondence. Particular mention was made that the lists would not fall into the wrong hands, that is, "capitalistic employment agencies." *Socialist Party of America Papers,* reel 76.

47. *Appeal to Reason,* May 10, 1913, and June 6, 1914. See also Zinn, *A People's History of the United States,* pp. 324–27.

48. *Milwaukee Leader,* October 13, 1922, and December 13, 1922.

49. Philip R. V. Curoe, *Educational Attitudes and Policies of Organized Labor* (New York: Arno, 1969 [originally published in 1926 by Teachers College Press]), pp. 112–13; and "Report of the Committee on State and Municipal Program," reprinted in *International Socialist Review* 4 (May 1904): 680.

50. Robert Joseph Schaefer, "Educational Activities of the Garment Unions, 1890–1948: A Study in Workers' Education in the International Ladies' Garment Union and the Amalgamated Clothing Workers of America in New York City," Ph.D. dissertation, Columbia University, 1951, pp. 5–9; and *Milwaukee Leader,* November 8, 1922.

51. *New York Call,* August 19, 1917.

52. *The Worker,* October 6, 1901, and January 12, 1902; *Party Builder,* April 4, 1914; *Appeal to Reason,* February 12, 1910; and *New York Call,* December 28, 1919.

53. *Milwaukee Leader,* November 19, 1919, and December 27, 1919.

54. *Milwaukee Leader,* January 23, 1920.

55. *Milwaukee Leader,* May 27, 1920, and June 2, 1920; and *New York Call,* October 28, 1919.

56. Bruce Calvert, "Public Schools and Socialist Propaganda," *New York Call,* August 19, 1917.

57. While perhaps not wholly incorrect, it is misleading for historian Ira Kipnis to argue that the "Socialist Party gave far more attention to winning the support of Protestant ministers than it gave . . . to youth." Kipnis, *The American Socialist Movement, 1817–1912,* p. 266.

58. *Party Builder,* March 14, 1914; Edwin F. Bowers, "The Infamy of the 'Boy Scout' Movement," *Young Socialists' Magazine* 4 (October 1911): 4–5; "The Struggle For the American Youth," *Young Socialists' Magazine* 9 (December 1915): 1; *Appeal to Reason,* March 9, 1912; and Mary O'Reilly, "Boy Scouts and the War," *Christian Socialist* 4 (October 1914): 5. See also Patti M. Peterson, "The Young Socialist Movement in America from 1905 to 1940: A Study of the Young People's Socialist League," Ph.D. dissertation, University of Wisconsin–Madison, 1974, pp. 40–42.

59. Arthur G. McDowell, "The Socialist Youth Movement," *American Socialist Quarterly* 3 (Summer 1934): 43–44; *Young Socialists' Magazine* 7 (January 1914): 12; Ernest Erber, "History of Young Socialists," in *Socialist Party of America Papers,* reel 140; and Peterson, "The Young Socialist Movement in America from 1905 to 1940," pp. 33–34.

60. Philip G. Altbach, *Student Politics in America: A Historical Analysis* (New York: McGraw-Hill, 1974), p. 44; and Peterson, "The Young Socialist Movement in America from 1905 to 1940," pp. 3 and 36–38.

61. *American Labor Year Book, 1917–1918,* p. 361; McDowell, "The Socialist Youth Movement," pp. 43–44; and Peterson, "The Young Socialist Movement in America from 1905 to 1940," p. 7.

62. Peterson, "The Young Socialist Movement in America from 1905 to 1940," pp. 43–44. Peterson asserts that older Party comrades generally remained wedded to the original skepticism of Marx and Engels toward young people's ability to adhere to "revolutionary discipline" (p. 240). On the other hand, these same arguments could be and were used by some Party activists to support the establishment of formal youth organizations. Such groups could help to insure that socialist youth would not "run wild" or unduly challenge the leadership (p. 23).

63. Maurice L. Malkin, *Return to My Father's House* (New Rochelle, N.Y.: Arlington House, 1972), pp. 48–57.

64. *Young Socialists' Magazine* 13 (May 1919): 10; and "Report of the YPSL," December 1932, in *Socialist Party of America Papers*, reel 81.

65. "Report of the YPSL," in *Socialist Party of America Papers*, reel 81.

66. *Appeal to Reason*, March 12, 1910; Alexander Gittes, "Socialism in the High Schools," *Progressive Woman* 4 (December 1910): 5; and *Coming Nation*, November 9, 1910.

67. "Report of the Director of Young People's Department," in Socialist Party of U.S. Materials, 1914 Folder; *Party Builder*, May 23, 1914; and *American Socialist*, March 20, 1915, and July 24, 1915.

Chapter Two

1. On balance, this is a conservative estimate. Some of the related schools discussed in this chapter may have been reported as though they were English-speaking, Party-affiliated Sunday schools and not all schools noted in the press or in correspondence may have made it past the planning stages. On the other hand, other English-speaking Socialist Sunday schools for children were probably initiated but failed to achieve notice in the radical press, perhaps because they lasted for so short a time or simply because they remained as unpublicized local endeavors. Relatedly, fourteen schools in New York City are listed below for one year, although there is no doubt that more than fourteen began (and closed) during this twenty-year period. Finally, some of the radical ethnic schools were sponsored by the foreign-language federations of the Socialist Party. Some of them were at least in part conducted in English and used SSS curriculum materials, yet they may not always have been listed as Socialist Sunday schools. It thus seems fair to claim that at least one hundred Party-affiliated Socialist Sunday schools were established in the United States during the first two decades of this century.

Socialist Sunday schools were organized in at least the following locations: California (Los Angeles, Pasadena, Prather, San Francisco, San Jose); Connecticut (Bristol, Hartford, Meriden, Mystic, New Britain, New Haven, Stamford, Stonington); Delaware (Wilmington); Illinois (Chicago, Oak Park, Rockford); Indiana (Mishawaka); Kentucky (Newport); Maryland (Baltimore); Massachusetts (Boston, Brockton, Fitchburg, Haverill, Lynn, Malden, Montello, New Bedford, Ware); Michigan (Detroit, South Haven); Minnesota (Minneapolis); Missouri (Bolivar, St. Louis); Nebraska (Omaha); New Jersey (Garfield, Jersey City, Newark, Passaic, Paterson, Stelton, Trenton, West Hoboken); New York (Auburn, Buffalo, Jamestown, New York City,

Rochester, Schenectady, Syracuse, Troy, Yonkers); Ohio (Bellaire, Cincinnati, Cleveland); Oklahoma (unidentified [Ada?]); Oregon (Portland); Pennsylvania (Philadelphia, Pittsburgh, Pottstown); Rhode Island (Providence); Wisconsin (Kenosha, Milwaukee, Racine); and Washington, D.C. More than one school existed in some cities, with the maximum number in a year indicated: Boston (3 in 1918); Buffalo (2 in 1918); Chicago (10 in 1919); Cleveland (3 in 1912); Milwaukee (3 in 1915); New York City (14 in 1912); Philadelphia (2 in 1912); Pittsburgh (3 in 1918); Providence (3 in 1920); and Washington, D.C. (2 in 1912).

2. See, for example, Anne M. Boylan, *Sunday School: The Formation of an American Institution* (New Haven, Conn.: Yale University Press, 1988); and Thomas Walter Laqueur, *Religion and Respectability: Sunday Schools and English Working Class Culture* (New Haven, Conn.: Yale University Press, 1976). Interestingly, the use of the "Sunday school" name led to the inclusion of a full-page description of "Socialist Sunday Schools" (submitted by the Socialist School Union of Greater New York) in a three-volume encyclopedia compiled in 1915 by religious figures in the United States, Canada, and Europe. See John T. McFarland, et al., eds., *The Encyclopedia of Sunday Schools and Religious Education*, vol. 3 (New York: Thomas Nelson and Sons, 1915), pp. 973–74.

3. George S. Counts, *Dare the School Build a New Social Order?* (Carbondale: Southern Illinois University Press, 1978 [originally published in 1932]). For a critique of the overly individualistic orientation of radical educational proposals in the 1960s and early 1970s, see Elizabeth Cagan, "Individualism, Collectivism, and Radical Educational Reform," *Harvard Educational Review* 48 (May 1978): 227–66.

Within the progressive education movement, some participants did identify themselves more closely with socialism. See, for example, Robert H. Hutchinson and Delia D. Hutchinson, "The Stony Ford School," in *Bureau of Educational Experiments, Bulletin* 5 (1917): 9.

4. Bertha H. Mailly, *How to Organize Socialist Schools* (New York: Rand School of Social Science, n.d. [1911?]), a copy of which is contained in "Rochester Socialist Sunday School Scrapbooks, vol. 1," in the Kendrick Philander Shedd Papers, located at the University of Rochester, Rush Rhees Library, Rare Books Department, Special Collections, Rochester, N.Y. (henceforth in this chapter referred to as the Shedd Papers); and William F. Kruse, *How to Organize, Maintain and Conduct the 'S.S.S.'* (Chicago: Socialist Party Young People's Department, n.d. [1918]?), a copy of which is included in the *Socialist Party of America Papers*, microfilm edition (Glen Rock, N.J.: Microfilming Corporation of America, 1975), reel 137.

5. Jane Addams, *Twenty Years at Hull-House* (New York: Macmillan, 1938), p. 91. For a discussion of the difficulty in identifying radical groups of the late nineteenth century as "anarchist" or "socialist," see Bruce C. Nelson, *Beyond the Martyrs: A Social History of Chicago's Anarchists, 1870–1900* (New Brunswick N.J.: Rutgers University Press, 1988), esp. pp. 5–6 and 153–73.

6. Michael J. Schaack, *Anarchy and Anarchists: A History of the Red Terror and the Social Revolution in America and Europe* (Chicago: F. J. Schulte, 1889), pp. 668–74.

7. For more on Ferrer's life and work, see Francisco Ferrer y Guardia, *The Origins and Ideals of the Modern School*, trans. by John McCabe (London: Watts, 1913); William Archer, *The Life, Trial, and Death of Francisco Ferrer* (New York: Moffat, Yard, 1911); Leonard D. Abbott, ed., *Francisco Ferrer: His Life, Work and Martyrdom* (New York: Francisco Ferrer Association, 1910); and Joseph McCabe, *The Martyrdom of Ferrer* (London: Watts, 1909).

8. Paul Avrich, *The Modern School Movement: Anarchism and Education in the United States* (Princeton, N.J.: Princeton University Press, 1980); and Joseph J. Cohen and Alexis C. Ferm, *The Modern School of Stelton: A Sketch* (Stelton, N.J.: The Modern School Association of North America, 1925). According to historian Laurence Veysey, Elizabeth and Alexis Ferm, who headed the Modern School in Stelton, N.J. for many years, were probably "most elated when they could report that a particular boy or girl, with no external prompting, had spent the day completely self-absorbed in a constant flow of purposeful activity—of what precise kind it did not really matter." Laurence Veysey, *The Communal Experience: Anarchists and Mystical Counter-Cultures in America* (New York: Harper and Row, 1973), p. 145. Another researcher believes that the Ferms personify individualism in American education. See Arthur Mark, "Two Libertarian Educators: Elizabeth Byrne Ferm and Alexis Constantine Ferm," *Teachers College Record* 78 (December 1976): 263–74. See also Elizabeth Ferm, *The Spirit of Freedom in Education* (Stelton, N.J.: The Modern School, 1919).

9. Fred Reid, "Socialist Sunday Schools in Britain, 1892–1939," *International Review of Social History* 11 (1966): 18–47; Hilda Kean, *Challenging the State? The Socialist and Feminist Educational Experience 1900–1930* (London: Falmer, 1990); and David Prynn, "The Clarion Clubs, Rambling and the Holiday Associations in Britain since the 1890s," *Journal of Contemporary History* 11 (July 1976): 65–77. See also Stanley Pierson, *British Socialists: The Journey from Fantasy to Politics* (Cambridge, Mass.: Harvard University Press, 1979), p. 154; and Brian Simon, *Education and the Labour Movement, 1870–1920* (London: Lawrence and Wishart, 1974), pp. 48–52. A London newspaper at the time described the schools' instruction as "strictly ethical and humanitarian" and a former student of the Patrick SSS in Glasgow recalls learning a combination of "the principles of socialism" and "a simple moral attitude." *New York Call*, March 28, 1913; and "Annie Davison," in *Dutiful Daughters: Women Talk about their Lives*, ed. Jean McCrindle and Sheila Rowbotham (London: Penguin, 1977), pp. 62–66.

10. *Little Socialist Magazine for Boys and Girls* 3 (April 1910): 12; *Young Socialists' Magazine* 4 (July 1911): 11, 5 (June 1912): 14, 6 (March 1913): 1, and 9 (December 1915): 3–4; *New York Call*, October 30, 1910; *Socialist Woman* 1 (November 1907): 8; and letter from Gladys Dobson of Jamestown to Bertha Vossler, dated February 14, 1916, and other materials in "Rochester Socialist Sunday School Scrapbooks, vol. 4," the Shedd Papers.

11. *The Worker*, August 17, 1907; *New York Call*, April 16, 1909; *Coming Nation*, November 30, 1912; *Little Socialist Magazine for Boys and Girls* 3 (January 1910): 13 and 3 (February 1910): 13; *Young Socialists' Magazine* 5 (February 1912): 1, 5 (June 1912): 15, and 13 (August–September 1919): 14; *International Socialist Review* 12 (June 1912): 884; and "Rochester Socialist Sunday School

Scrapbooks, vol. 1," the Shedd Papers. The New Zealand SSS movement is briefly discussed in Roger Openshaw, "Lilliput under Siege: New Zealand Society and Its Schools during the 'Red Scare,' 1919–1922," *History of Education Quarterly* 20 (Winter 1980): 403–24.

12. Sirkka Tuomi Lee, "The Finns," *Cultural Correspondence* 6–7 (Spring 1978): 43; and *Party Builder*, June 28, 1913. See also Kathleen M. Blee and Al Gedicks, "The Emergence of Socialist Political Culture among Finnish Immigrants in Minnesota Mining Communities," in *Class Conflict and the State*, ed. Maurice Zeitlin (Cambridge, Mass.: Winthrop, 1980), p. 180.

13. Maria Woroby, "Ukraninan Radicals and Women," *Cultural Correspondence* 6–7 (Spring 1978): 50–56; *New York Call*, October 12, 1911, May 1, 1914, and May 2, 1919; and "Rochester Socialist Sunday School Scrapbooks, vol. 4," the Shedd Papers.

14. Carol Poore, "German-American Socialist Culture," *Cultural Correspondence* 6–7 (Spring 1978): 19.

15. Mari Jo Buhle, *Women and American Socialism, 1870–1920* (Urbana: University of Illinois Press, 1981), pp. 1–48; and Poore, "German-American Socialist Culture," p. 20.

16. *Young Socialists' Magazine* 12 (December 1918): 2; and, for example, *New York Call*, May 28, 1911, and April 28, 1913.

17. Maximilian Hurwitz, *The Workmen's Circle: Its History, Ideals, Organization and Institutions* (New York: Workmen's Circle, 1936), pp. 13–17 and 155–56; Arthur Liebman, "The Ties that Bind: The Jewish Support for the Left in the United States," *American Jewish Historical Quarterly* 66 (December 1976): 294–95; Workmen's Circle, *Forty Years Workmen's Circle: A History in Pictures* (New York: Workmen's Circle, 1940); Will Herberg, "The Jewish Labor Movement in the United States," *American Jewish Year Book 53* (1952): 26; *American Labor Year Book, 1925* (New York: Rand School of Social Science, 1925), p. 218; and Jeffrey S. Gurock, *When Harlem Was Jewish, 1870–1930* (New York: Columbia University Press, 1979), p. 64.

18. This was especially the case in northeastern cities that had significant populations of Jewish radical workers. See, for example, *Young Socialists' Magazine* 5 (December 1912): 12; and *International Socialist Review*, 12 (May 1912): 794.

19. Samuel Niger, *In a Struggle for a New Education: The Arbeiter Ring Schools, Their Origins, Development, Growth and Current Position (1919–1939)* (New York: Arbeiter Ring Education Committee, 1940), pp. 41–42. I am grateful to Raphael Finkel for translating portions of this Yiddish manuscript for me.

20. *New York Call*, May 7, 1911, and May 14, 1911.

21. *New York Call*, July 30, 1911; and Bertha H. Mailly, "The Socialist Schools of Greater New York," *Little Socialist Magazine for Boys and Girls* 4 (May 1911): 6.

22. During the second decade, Workmen's Circle initiatives in the area of supplementary schooling for workers' children became increasingly more distinct from those of Socialist Party activists. This was due largely to internal changes taking place within the Workmen's Circle itself. In particular, the organization's expanded membership included many workers who were more cosmopolitan and nationalistic in outlook, more forthrightly Jew-

ish in identity, and less assimilationist. They still identified strongly with radicalism, but many of them and their children were encountering the prejudices of American society and were adamant that Jewish workers maintain and celebrate their own language and culture. One of the key issues between 1911 and 1917 centered on the establishment of Yiddish schools for members' children. By 1918, sentiment within the Workmen's Circle had shifted enough so that such schools were initiated. By 1924, the Workmen's Circle claimed to have schools in forty cities. See C. Bezalel Sherman, "Nationalism, Secularism and Religion in the Jewish Labor Movement," in *Voices From Yiddish: Essays, Memoirs, Diaries*, ed. Irving Howe and Eliezer Greenberg (Ann Arbor: University of Michigan Press, 1972), p. 229; Niger, *In a Struggle for a New Education*, pp. 41–50; Hurwitz, *The Workmen's Circle*, pp. 36–38; Herberg, "The Jewish Labor Movement in the United States," p. 27; Gurock, *When Harlem Was Jewish, 1870–1930*, pp. 63–64; *New York Call*, May 8, 1916, April 28, 1919, and July 27, 1919; and *American Labor Year Book, 1925*, p. 219.

23. Nelson, *Beyond the Martyrs*, p. 112; and Buhle, *Women and American Socialism*, pp. 16 and 32.

24. *The Worker*, July 13, 1902, and January 8, 1905. For more on Josephine Cole, who was elected president of the Woman's Socialist Union of California in 1905, see *Socialist Woman* 1 (November 1907): 3, 2 (June 1908): 3–4, and 2 (July 1908): 11; and Buhle, *Women and American Socialism, 1870–1920*, p. 221.

25. *The Worker*, August 9, 1903. May Wood Simons's personal papers give only passing reference to her attending meetings of "socialist teachers to plan lessons for the new schools" and her development of such lessons in 1903. "Diary of May Wood Simons," June 29, 1903, and July 14, 1903, entries, Algie M. and May Wood Simons Papers, 1901–1951, Box 5 Folder 6, located at the State Historical Society of Wisconsin, Archives and Manuscripts Division, Madison. For more on May Wood Simons, see Kent and Gretchen Kreuter, *An American Dissenter: The Life of Algie Martin Simons, 1870–1950* (Lexington: University of Kentucky Press, 1969); Buhle, *Women and American Socialism, 1870–1920*, pp. 166–69; and *Socialist Woman* 1 (June 1907): 3.

26. *Progressive Woman* 3 (November 1909): 12 and 3 (December 1909): 12.

27. *The Worker*, December 20, 1903, and January 24, 1904; *Socialist Woman* 2 (October 1908): 16; and Buhle, *Women and American Socialism, 1870–1920*, pp. 34 and 111.

28. *The Worker*, November 29, 1903, March 15, 1905, November 4, 1905, November 6, 1906, December 15, 1906, January 12, 1907, January 26, 1907, June 1, 1907, and September 2, 1907; *The Arena* 30 (July 1903): 100; *Progressive Woman* 3 (December 1909): 14; and *New York Call*, September 25, 1911. Antoinette Konikow was a physician who strongly advocated birth control and sexual freedom, lectured often on the topics of suffrage and sex hygiene, and later became an active member of the Communist Party and a founder of the Trotskyite Socialist Workers Party. See, for example, Buhle, *Women and American Socialism, 1870–1920*, pp. 126, 176–78, 233, and 270–72; and *Socialist Woman* 2 (June 1908): 3–4.

29. *Socialist Woman* 1 (November 1907): 6; *Progressive Woman* 4 (July 1910): 13; *The Worker*, February 21, 1907, February 23, 1907, and November 30, 1907; *New York Call*, March 17, 1909, November 21, 1909, and May 26, 1911; and *Little Socialist Magazine for Boys and Girls* 3 (January 1910): 13. Frank Hubschmitt, a strong supporter of a more active role for women in Party affairs, was elected secretary of the New Jersey State Committee on Socialist Schools in 1910 and recording secretary of the State Committee of the Party in 1911.

30. *Socialist Woman* 1 (February 1908): 12, 1 (March 1908): 12, and 1 (July 1908): 10; and letter from Leland Hilligoss, St. Louis Public Library, to author, dated August 27, 1981.

31. *Socialist Woman* 1 (May 1908): 12, 2 (July 1908): 1, and 2 (August 1908): 2; *Progressive Woman* 3 (December 1909): 14; *New York Call*, June 11, 1908; *Little Socialist Magazine for Boys and Girls* 3 (May 1910): 13; Peggy Dennis, *The Autobiography of an American Communist: A Personal View of a Political Life, 1924–1975* (Westport, Conn.: Lawrence Hill, 1977), p. 20; and letter from Peggy Dennis, Berkeley, Calif., to author, dated February 4, 1982. Ethel Whitehead succeeded Josephine Cole as president of the Woman's Socialist Union of California in 1908. She also published poems and playlets, some of which were used in the Socialist Sunday schools (see Chapter Six).

32. *Young Socialists' Magazine* 12 (October 1918), p. 17.

33. *New York Call*, March 6, 1909, March 24, 1909, March 31, 1909, April 10, 1909, November 21, 1909, November 30, 1909, December 14, 1909, December 18, 1909, and February 22, 1910; and *Coming Nation*, December 10, 1910. See also Henry Bedford, *Socialism and the Workers in Massachusetts, 1886–1912* (Amherst: University of Massachusetts Press, 1966).

34. *The Worker*, October 20, 1901, and September 14, 1901; *New York Call*, January 16, 1909, June 21, 1909, June 24, 1915, February 20, 1916, September 3, 1919, and September 28, 1919; *Progressive Woman* 2 (April 1909): 14; *Young Socialists' Magazine* 4 (July 1911): 11, 5 (February 1912): 11, 11 (June 1917): 11, 12 (March 1918): 9, 13 (February 1919): 2, and 13 (April 1919): 17; *Milwaukee Leader*, June 27, 1918; "Rochester Socialist Sunday School Scrapbooks, vol. 2," in the Shedd Papers; Avrich, *The Modern School Movement*, p. 66; *Cleveland Citizen*, February 21, 1914, December 12, 1914, July 3, 1915, May 6, 1916, and September 16, 1916; and Oakley C. Johnson, *The Day Is Coming: Life and Work of Charles E. Ruthenberg, 1882–1927* (New York: International, 1957), pp. 46–47 and 84. Frederick Krafft was active in socialist politics throughout this period and in 1919 was elected as one of eight members of the National Executive Committee of the Party.

35. *New York Call*, September 24, 1909, September 27, 1909, October 8, 1909, January 25, 1910, October 2, 1910, November 27, 1910, December 6, 1910, May 2, 1912, and December 16, 1916; *Socialist Woman* 2 (September 1909): 9; *Progressive Woman* 3 (October 1909): 14; *Little Socialist Magazine for Boys and Girls* 3 (March 1910): 9; and *Young Socialists' Magazine* 4 (August 1911): 11, and 5 (December 1912): 13. Edward Perkins Clarke was already a prominent Party member by 1909, when he was considered for the position of executive secretary of the Rand School of Social Science (that eventually went to Algernon Lee). Clarke later served as State Secretary of the Party in Connecticut. See *New York Call*, January 25, 1910, and March 1, 1911; and

Frederic Cornell, "A History of the Rand School of Social Science—1906 to 1956," Ph.D. dissertation, Columbia University, 1976, p. 47.

36. *National Socialist,* April 27, 1912, May 25, 1912, June 8, 1912, and July 6, 1912; *New York Call,* December 3, 1914, January 16, 1916, and March 5, 1916; and letter from Julia Parks of Washington, D.C. to "Mrs. [Ella Reeve?] Bloor," dated August 6, 1913, a copy of which is contained in a folder of miscellaneous materials, the Shedd Papers.

37. *New York Call,* April 27, 1911, May 20, 1911, May 27, 1911, September 10, 1911, April 20, 1912, April 30, 1912, October 9, 1912, February 11, 1914, November 22, 1914, November 19, 1916, January 14, 1917, and November 9, 1919; and *Young Socialists' Magazine* 4 (September 1911): 15.

38. *Socialist Woman* 2 (November 1908): 16; *New York Call,* October 7, 1910, January 21, 1911, July 24, 1911, and October 21, 1911; and *International Socialist Review* 12 (May 1912): 794.

39. *The Worker,* October 5, 1907; *New Age,* February 16, 1918, February 23, 1918, March 2, 1918, March 16, 1918, April 6, 1918, April 20, 1918, May 18, 1918, and June 8, 1918; *New York Call,* August 8, 1919, and March 15, 1920; *Young Socialists' Magazine* 13 (March 1919): 19; and telephone interview with Ernest Kleine, Jr., Williamsville, N.Y., July 14, 1981.

40. *American Socialist,* January 2, 1915.

41. *New York Call,* April 18, 1913, August 30, 1914, May 9, 1915, January 2, 1916, June 25, 1916, January 17, 1917, and May 4, 1918; and letters from Kendrick Shedd of Rochester to Brockton SSS, dated June 17, 1914, from Thomas Heath Flood of Brockton to Kendrick Shedd, n.d., from Axel Berggren of Jamestown to Kendrick Shedd, dated March 15, 1915, from Kendrick Shedd to Axel Berggren, dated March 17, 1915, from Gladys Dobson of Jamestown to Bertha Vossler, dated February 14, 1916, and from Bertha Vossler to Gladys Dobson, dated February 29, 1916, in "Rochester Socialist Sunday School Scrapbooks, vols. 2 and 4," the Shedd Papers. Although Jamestown was a small town, it was populated by a significant number of Swedish-born immigrants (about one-third of the population). They took a more positive view of state management and labor collectivism than was typically the case among immigrants, which probably translated into support for a Socialist Sunday School. See Peter B. Bulkley, "Townsendism as an Eastern and Urban Phenomenon: Chautauqua County, New York, as a Case Study," *New York History* 55 (April 1974): 185–86.

42. *New York Call,* February 20, 1916, October 15, 1916, January 7, 1917, January 14, 1917, and September 14, 1917; *Young Socialists' Magazine* 13 (January 1919): 16 and 13 (April 1919): 17–18; *Wisconsin Comrade* 2 (July 1915): 3; and letter from Amelia P. Perlmutter of Syracuse to Rochester SSS, dated November 20, 1916, in "Rochester Socialist Sunday School Scrapbooks, vol. 4," the Shedd Papers. Bulkley's point about Swedish immigrants in Jamestown, N.Y. (see note 41) may have applied to Rockford as well.

43. *New York Call,* July 11, 1915; *Young Socialists' Magazine* 12 (September 1918): 2 and 12 (December 1918): 2; and letters from Martin Weber of Pittsburgh to Kendrick Shedd, dated April 11, 1915, and from T. J. Mead of Pittsburgh to Isadore Glickman of Rochester, dated October 29, 1916, in "Rochester Socialist Sunday School Scrapbooks, vol. 4," the Shedd Papers.

44. *Milwaukee Leader,* June 25, 1915, June 30, 1915, November 9, 1915, December 21, 1915, January 19, 1916, and August 7, 1917; *Wisconsin Comrade* 2 (July 1915): 3, 2 (October 1915): 4, and 2 (January 1916): 2–3; and *Young Socialists' Magazine* 12 (December 1918): 20 and 13 (February 1919): 2.

45. *Young Socialists' Magazine* 13 (January 1919): 16, 13 (February 1919): 2, 13 (July 1919): 12 and 15, 13 (September 1919): 1, and 13 (January 1920): 8; and *Eye Opener,* May 25, 1918.

46. *Young Socialists' Magazine* 12 (July 1918): 16, 12 (September 1918): 2, 12 (October 1918): 17, 13 (April 1919): 17, 13 (August–September 1919): 14, 13 (October 1919): 17, and 13 (January 1920): 8; and *New York Call,* November 6, 1918.

47. *Young Socialists' Magazine* 13 (June 1919): 11.

48. *Young Socialists' Magazine* 13 (March 1919): 17, 13 (April 1919): 18, and 13 (January 1920): 8; and *New York Call,* July 5, 1919, July 22, 1919, and July 29, 1919.

Chapter Three

1. For example, see William J. Reese, *Power and the Promise of School Reform: Grass-Roots Movements during the Progressive Era* (Boston: Routledge and Kegan Paul, 1986); Sally M. Miller, *Victor Berger and the Promise of Constructive Socialism, 1910–1920* (Westport, Conn.: Greenwood, 1973); Melvin Dubofsky, "Success and Failure of Socialism in New York City, 1900–1918: A Case Study," *Labor History* 9 (Fall 1968): 361–75; John Dutko, "Socialism in Rochester, 1900–1917," M.A. thesis, University of Rochester, 1953; and Frederick I. Olson, "The Milwaukee Socialists, 1897–1941," Ph.D. dissertation, Harvard University, 1952.

2. Joseph Freeman, *An American Testament: A Narrative of Rebels and Romantics* (New York: Farrar and Rinehart, 1936), p. 291; and Arthur Gorenstein, "A Portrait of Ethnic Politics—the Socialists and the 1908 and 1910 Congressional Elections on the East Side," *American Jewish Historical Quarterly* 50 (March 1961): 202.

3. Jeffrey S. Gurock, *When Harlem Was Jewish, 1870–1930* (New York: Columbia University Press, 1979), pp. 60–64; and Samuel Niger, *In a Struggle for a New Education: The Arbeiter Ring Schools, Their Origins, Development, Growth, and Current Events (1919–1939)* (New York: Arbeiter Ring Education Committee, 1940), pp. 41–43, translated for the author by Raphael Finkel.

4. *New York Tribune,* August 18, 1905; *The Worker,* January 26, 1907, February 2, 1907, and February 9, 1907; and *New York Call,* February 26, 1911.

5. *New York Call,* February 26, 1911; and *New York Times,* February 3, 1907.

6. *New York Call,* February 15, 1908; *New York Times,* May 22, 1932; and Aileen S. Kraditor, *The Radical Persuasion, 1890–1917: Aspects of the Intellectual History and the Historiography of Three American Radical Organizations* (Baton Rouge: Louisiana State University Press, 1981), p. 121.

7. *The Worker,* January 24, 1904; *Milwaukee Leader,* June 6, 1919; *New York Times,* August 16, 1960; Solon DeLeon, ed., *American Labor Who's Who*

(New York: Hanford, 1925); "National Convention Proceedings, 1901–1962," *Socialist Party of America Papers*, microfilm edition (Glen Rock, N.J.: Microfilming Corporation of America, 1975), reel 76; John William Leonard, ed. *Woman's Who's Who in America, 1914–1915* (New York: American Commonwealth, 1914), pp. 534–35; Mari Jo Buhle, *Women and American Socialism, 1870–1920* (Urbana: University of Illinois Press, 1981), p. 190; and Frederic Cornell, "A History of the Rand School of Social Science—1906 to 1956," Ph.D. dissertation, Columbia University, 1976, p. 54.

  8. Buhle, *Women and American Socialism, 1870–1920*, pp. 126, 176–78, 190, and 233.

  9. *The Worker*, October 5, 1907, October 19, 1907, October 26, 1907, December 19, 1907, and March 21, 1907; *New York Call*, June 4, 1908, June 5, 1908, June 8, 1908, June 13, 1908, January 23, 1909, March 6, 1909, May 1, 1909, November 5, 1909, December 12, 1909, and May 7, 1912; and *New York Times*, August 2, 1908.

  10. *Progressive Woman* 2 (March 1909): 15; Kraditor, *The Radical Persuasion, 1890–1917*, pp. 190–91; and *New York Socialist*, July 18, 1908.

  11. *New York Call*, December 30, 1908, January 14, 1909, October 8, 1909, October 10, 1909, October 17, 1909, October 2, 1909, November 7, 1909, and June 7, 1910; and *Young Socialists' Magazine* 5 (November 1912): 10 and 5 (December 1912): 12.

  12. *New York Call*, December 5, 1909, December 8, 1909, December 16, 1909, September 3, 1910, November 26, 1910, December 7, 1910, February 2, 1911, and February 26, 1911; *Progressive Woman* 3 (May 1910): 14; *Young Socialists' Magazine* 5 (December 1912): 12; and telephone interview with Gertrude Weil Klein, New York City, July 21, 1981.

  13. *New York Call*, September 18, 1909, December 30, 1909, January 4, 1910, January 5, 1910, September 18, 1913, March 8, 1914, September 25, 1914, April 16, 1916, November 15, 1916, November 16, 1916, December 25, 1916, January 26, 1917, March 15, 1917, and September 4, 1918. August Claessens's expulsion from the New York State Assembly is described in Thomas E. Vadney, "The Politics of Repression, a Case Study of the Red Scare in New York," *New York History* 49 (January 1968): 56–75.

  14. *New York Call*, May 11, 1910, May 13, 1910, and May 29, 1910.

  15. *New York Call*, September 4, 1910, October 5, 1910, October 17, 1910, and October 30, 1910; and William Mailly, "Undermining New York for Socialism," *Coming Nation*, October 8, 1910.

  16. *New York Call*, November 6, 1910, April 12, 1911, June 25, 1911, and December 22, 1912; *Coming Nation*, June 17, 1911; and *Young Socialists' Magazine* 4 (July 1911): 11, 4 (August 1911): 11, and 5 (December 1912): 12. For more on Lucien Sanial, see DeLeon, ed., *American Labor Who's Who*; and Oakley C. Johnson, *Marxism in United States History before the Russian Revolution (1876–1917)* (New York: Humanities, 1974), p. 115.

  17. *New York Call*, April 29, 1911, May 1, 1911, May 6, 1911, May 7, 1911, May 9, 1911, and May 14, 1911; and Frances M. Gill, "The Children's May Day," *Young Socialists' Magazine* 4 (June 1911): 7+.

  18. *New York Call*, October 27, 1912, November 4, 1912, November 29, 1912, and December 5, 1912; and *Young Socialists' Magazine* 5 (November 1912): 10.

19. *New York Call*, December 5, 1912; and *Young Socialists' Magazine* 5 (December 1912): 12.

20. Born in Russia in 1877, Abraham Shiplacoff came to the United States in 1891. He labored twelve hours a day as a sewing machine operator in a sweatshop for seven years but managed to study at night and eventually became a teacher at P.S. 84 in Brooklyn. After several years of teaching, he took a position as a clerk in the United States Bureau of Customs and became heavily involved in labor union and socialist activities. In 1915, Shiplacoff became the first socialist elected to the New York State Assembly and was reelected the following year. When he died in 1934 at the age of fifty-six, more than a thousand people attended his funeral and Mayor LaGuardia sent a message of condolence to his widow. *New York Call*, November 28, 1918, and September 3, 1919; *New York Times*, February 8, 1934, and February 9, 1934; and DeLeon, ed., *American Labor's Who's Who*.

21. *New York Call*, March 21, 1913, April 14, 1913, April 15, 1913, April 20, 1913, April 27, 1913, April 28, 1913, April 29, 1913, May 2, 1913, May 6, 1913, May 9, 1913, May 19, 1913, May 25, 1913, and May 31, 1913.

22. *New York Call*, January 8, 1914, February 1, 1914, February 16, 1914, March 8, 1914, May 3, 1914, and May 2, 1915; and *New York Times*, February 16, 1914.

23. *New York Call*, May 2, 1915.

24. *New York Call*, November 8, 1914, January 4, 1915, March 26, 1916, April 23, 1916, October 28, 1916, November 25, 1916, January 29, 1917, and November 17, 1917.

25. *New York Call*, January 30, 1916, February 9, 1916, November 17, 1916, and December 1, 1917.

26. Letter from M. Bagno of the Bronx to Bertha Vossler of Rochester, dated December 21, 1915, in "Rochester Socialist Sunday School Scrapbooks, vol. 4," in the Kendrick Philander Shedd Papers, located at the University of Rochester, Rush Rhees Library, Rare Books Department, Special Collections, Rochester, N.Y. (henceforth in this chapter referred to as the Shedd Papers); and *New York Call*, January 10, 1915, January 23, 1915, November 14, 1915, January 31, 1916, February 9, 1916, February 15, 1916, April 8, 1916, May 3, 1916, May 19, 1916, October 17, 1916, March 8, 1917, May 8, 1917, and May 12, 1917.

27. *New York Call*, May 21, 1917, July 18, 1917, July 23, 1917, August 5, 1917, August 26, 1917, and April 15, 1918.

28. *New York Call*, November 17, 1917, November 18, 1917, January 13, 1918, Janaury 14, 1918, April 23, 1918, May 7, 1918, September 19, 1918, November 29, 1918, and November 30, 1918.

29. *New York Call*, September 19, 1918, October 6, 1918, October 12, 1918, and October 28, 1918. Charles Solomon was reelected in 1920 and then, like Claessens, refused his seat.

30. *New York Call*, June 4, 1918.

31. *Young Socialists' Magazine* 12 (June 1918): 11.

32. *New York Call*, December 28, 1918, January 17, 1919, February 11, 1919, and February 12, 1919.

33. *New York Call*, June 11, 1919, July 5, 1919, July 22, 1919, and July 29, 1919; *Young Socialists' Magazine* 13 (June 1919): 3; and Bertram D. Wolfe,

A Life in Two Centuries (New York: Stein and Day, 1981), p. 190. In September, the Brooklyn Young People's Socialist League voted not to join the newly organized Communist Party but to leave the Socialist Party, in a shortlived attempt to be wholly "independent." *New York Call,* September 4, 1919, and September 18, 1919.

34. *New York Call,* July 27, 1918.

35. For instance, see *New York Call,* January 19, 1919; and *New York Times,* April 5, 1919, and April 12, 1919. See also Julian F. Jaffe, *Crusade Against Radicalism: New York during the Red Scare, 1914–1924* (Port Washington, N.Y.: Kennikat, 1972). Abraham Shiplacoff, for example, was indicted in the fall of 1918 for violating the Espionage Act in a speech in the Bronx. This was during the same time that he was becoming involved again in the work of the Brownsville SSS. Although the charges were later dropped, these and other events of the period clearly distracted him from his work with the Sunday school.

36. *New York Call,* January 19, 1919, February 9, 1919, February 10, 1919, March 20, 1919, April 15, 1919, May 28, 1919, May 29, 1919, June 11, 1919, December 11, 1919, February 18, 1920, and February 26, 1920; *Young Socialists' Magazine* 13 (February 1920): 7; and Robert K. Murray, *Red Scare: A Study in National Hysteria, 1919–1920* (New York: McGraw-Hill, 1955), p. 171.

37. The Brownsville and Williamsburg schools continued meeting throughout the 1920s. When the Socialist Party experienced a resurgence in the late 1920s and early 1930s, several more Sunday schools were organized in New York City. About ten schools in all were in operation at the peak of this later movement, although (except for the Brownsville school) with a considerably smaller enrollment (an average of about fifty per school). There is no indication that the schools were meeting after 1936, when the radical movement experienced another serious split. *American Labor Year Book, 1923–1924* (New York: Rand School of Social Science, 1924), pp. 140–41; *Socialist World* 6 (April 1925): 3–5 and 6 (May 1925): 12; *American Appeal,* December 11, 1926; *New Leader,* June 16, 1928, November 23, 1928, December 8, 1928, May 4, 1929, November 23, 1929, December 5, 1931, and January 20, 1934; telephone interview with Samuel Friedman, New York City, July 6, 1981; letter from Viola and Lou Yavner of New York City to author, dated December 15, 1981; telephone interview with Fred Shulman, Bloomfield, N.J., March 3, 1984; and interview with Fred Shulman, Bloomfield, N.J., June 26, 1987.

38. Dutko, "Socialism in Rochester, 1900–1917," pp. 16, 105, and 115; *Socialist Woman* 2 (December 1908): 15; *New York Call,* March 7, 1910; and "Rochester Socialist Sunday School Scrapbooks, vol. 1," the Shedd Papers.

39. "From The History of the Rochester Socialist Sunday School" and "Our Various 'Homes,'" in a folder of miscellaneous materials, the Shedd Papers; and *Progressive Woman* 4 (November 1910): 10.

40. *New York Call,* June 22, 1911; and "From the History of the Rochester Socialist Sunday School" and "Our Various 'Homes'" in a folder of miscellaneous materials, and letters from Fred Warren of Girard, Kans. to Kendrick Shedd, dated January 19, 1911, and February 2, 1911, and from Eugene Debs of Terre Haute, Ind. to Kendrick Shedd, dated April 1, 1911, in "Rochester Socialist Sunday School Scrapbooks, vol. 1," the Shedd Pa-

pers. The presence of a "Christmas" tree was criticized by several members of the local radical community. In subsequent years, a "Yule-tree" and then a "Yule-wheel" was used. (See also Chapter Six.)

41. *New York Call,* September 14, 1911, March 10, 1912, and April 7, 1912; and "Our Various 'Homes'" in a folder of miscellaneous materials, and "Rochester Socialist Sunday School Scrapbooks, vol. 1," the Shedd Papers.

42. *New York Call,* August 17, 1913; and "From the History of the Rochester Socialist Sunday School" and "Our Various 'Homes'" in a folder of miscellaneous materials, and "Rochester Socialist Sunday School Scrapbooks, vols. 1 and 3," the Shedd Papers.

43. "Rochester Socialist Sunday School Scrapbooks, vols. 1 and 3," and letter from Kendrick Shedd to "Comrade Kreusi" of Schenectady, dated January 14, 1914, in "Rochester Socialist Sunday School Scrapbooks, vol. 2," the Shedd Papers.

44. "Rochester Socialist Sunday School Scrapbooks, vol. 3," the Shedd Papers. For example, Shedd wrote the following ditty to "My Dear Crickets" (instead of "critics"): "The Local has a type-machine,/We seldom get to see it;/When it's away, it can't be seen;/And when it's here—well, we aren't allowed to use the d——— thing!"

45. "Rochester Socialist Sunday School Scrapbooks, vols. 3 and 4," the Shedd Papers.

46. "Rochester Socialist Sunday School Scrapbooks, vol. 4," the Shedd Papers.

47. Maurice Isserman, "Inheritance Lost: Socialism in Rochester, 1917–1919," *Rochester History* 39 (October 1977): 1–24; and Dutko, "Socialism in Rochester, 1900–1917."

48. Letters from Isadore Tischler to Rochester SSS, dated September 29, 1916, and November 8, 1916, in "Rochester Socialist Sunday School Scrapbooks, vol. 4," and diary entry, March 28, 1915, in "Experiences in Milwaukee" folder, the Shedd Papers; *Young Socialists' Magazine* 9 (September 1915): 12; *New Leader,* February 9, 1929; Dutko, "Socialism in Rochester, 1900–1917," pp. 189–90; telephone interviews with Bertha Tischler, Rochester, N.Y., July 16, 1980, and July 16, 1981; and interview with Lloyd Somers, Rochester, N.Y., July 8, 1980.

49. *National Cyclopaedia of American Biography,* vol. 43 (New York: James T. White, 1961), pp. 313–14; miscellaneous materials in various folders and boxes, the Shedd Papers; and *Rochester Times-Union,* December 5, 1953, a copy of which was given to me by Lloyd Somers. I am very grateful to Lloyd Somers, a former student of Shedd's at the University of Rochester, for sharing some of these materials with me.

50. Arthur J. May, *A History of the University of Rochester, 1850–1962* (Rochester, N.Y.: University of Rochester Press, 1977), pp. 141–42; and letter from Edith Allen Haglund, *Rochester Review* (Spring 1977), p. 1.

51. Dutko, "Socialism in Rochester, 1900–1917," pp. 147–49; and May, *A History of the University of Rochester, 1850–1962,* p. 142.

52. Interview with Lloyd Somers; and May, *A History of the University of Rochester, 1850–1962,* p. 142.

53. Upheaval in Shedd's personal life also may have influenced his actions. During this same period of time, he had to commit his wife to a

state hospital because of ill health. This in turn necessitated having his two daughters and son live with relatives.

The following account of Shedd's difficulties is based on *New York Call*, February 11, 1911; Dutko, "Socialism in Rochester, 1900–1917," pp. 151–80; May, *A History of the University of Rochester, 1850–1962*, pp. 142–44; and various materials given to the author at interview with Lloyd Somers, including copies of letters from Joshua Bernhardt to Lloyd Somers, dated February 10, 1963, from Louis Gottlieb to Lloyd Somers, dated January 20, 1975, and from Lloyd Somers to Edith Allen Haglund, dated March 13, 1977.

54. Kendrick Shedd, "Why Professor Kendrick Shedd Was 'Fired' from Rochester University," *Young Socialists' Magazine* 8 (April 1915): 5–6.

55. Isadore Tischler suggested that, as a language professor, Shedd was particularly interested in the definition of words. Capitalism to him meant "self-centered individualism," while socialism represented "societism or humanitism." Tischler's comments are contained in Dutko, "Socialism in Rochester, 1900–1917," p. 161.

56. Letters from Winnie E. Branstetter of Chicago to Kendrick Shedd, dated December 4, 1913, and January 30, 1914, in "Rochester Socialist Sunday School Scrapbooks, vol. 1," from Neil Touhey of New York City to Kendrick Shedd, dated January 2, 1915, in "Rochester Socialist Sunday School Scrapbooks, vol. 3," and from Kendrick Shedd to Thomas Heath Flood of Brockton, n.d., in "Rochester Socialist Sunday School Scrapbooks, vol. 2," the Shedd Papers; *New York Call*, November 12, 1911, April 18, 1913, and August 5, 1913; *American Socialist*, March 27, 1915; *Young Socialists' Magazine* 8 (February 1915): 8; Blake McKelvey, *Rochester—the Quest for Quality, 1890–1925* (Cambridge, Mass.: Harvard University Press, 1956), p. 280; and *National Cyclopaedia of American Biography*, vol. 43, p. 313.

57. "Experiences in Milwaukee" folder, the Shedd Papers; *Milwaukee Leader*, October 3, 1916; and letter from Laurence E. Shedd of Leesburg, Fla. to author, dated August 9, 1980. Shedd had the opportunity to return to New York State when he was offered a position as principal of a four-teacher public school in Forestport, N.Y. Later, still in New York State, he had brief stints as principal of Romulus High School, physical science teacher at Geneva High School, and principal and science teacher at Naples High School. He also worked as a life insurance agent and a private tutor until his retirement in 1940 at the age of 74. He died on December 3, 1953. One local obituary made prominent mention of his role in "a controversy which rocked . . . [Rochester] in 1911." Miscellaneous materials in various boxes and folders, the Shedd Papers; *National Cyclopaedia of American Biography*, vol. 43, p. 313; letter from William Vierhile of Naples Historical Society to author, containing an obituary notice from a local newspaper, dated March 23, 1981; and letters from Lloyd Somers of Rochester to author, dated September 17, 1980, and November 2, 1981.

58. Edward Friebert, Autobiography (unpublished manuscript, 1945), p. 271 of handwritten copy; letter from Bertha Vossler to Lloyd Somers, dated November 12, 1969, in a folder of miscellaneous materials, the Shedd Papers; and telephone interview with Joseph Ulrich, West Webster, N.Y., July 13, 1981.

59. Letters from Gladys Shedd Sterling, Newport News, Va. to author, dated September 25, 1980, and Laurence E. Shedd to author, dated

August 9, 1980. It was no doubt more than a little frustrating for Shedd to be a public school principal and teacher after having been a dynamic university professor and critic of the ideological slant of the public schools. In 1920, Theodore Debs wrote to Shedd: "You being in a High School is like putting an eagle in a bird-cage." Letter from Theodore Debs to Kendrick Shedd, dated January 13, 1920, in a folder of miscellaneous materials, the Shedd Papers.

60. Folder of miscellaneous materials, the Shedd Papers. During the last several decades of his life, Shedd received numerous cards and letters from former university students and associates (political and otherwise). They wrote admiringly about Shedd's inspired teaching, infectious optimism, boundless energy, sense of humor, warmth of character, and progressive social views.

61. *Milwaukee Leader*, December 24, 1914, January 9, 1915, January 19, 1915, January 22, 1915, February 24, 1915, and February 26, 1915. Oscar Ameringer was born in Germany in 1870 and immigrated to the United States in 1886. He worked first as a cabinet maker and joined the Knights of Labor. Later, he was a musician and a prominent socialist lecturer, journalist, and political candidate. He was described as "one of the funniest men in or out of socialism." Leslie Cross, "The *Milwaukee Leader*, an Unusual Newspaper," *Historical Messenger* 17 (December 1961): 13; and Solon DeLeon, ed., *American Labor Who's Who*. See also Ameringer's *If You Don't Weaken: The Autobiography of Oscar Ameringer* (New York: Henry Holt, 1940).

62. *Milwaukee Leader*, March 17, 1915, March 19, 1915, and March 29, 1915; and diary entry, March 28, 1915, in "Experiences in Milwaukee" folder, the Shedd Papers.

63. Diary entries, March 28, 1915, March 29, 1915, April 2, 1915, April 4, 1915, and April 11, 1915, in "Experiences in Milwaukee" folder, the Shedd Papers; and *Milwaukee Leader*, April 5, 1915, and April 12, 1915.

64. Diary entries, April 13, 1915, and June 6, 1915, "Experiences in Milwaukee" folder, the Shedd Papers; *Milwaukee Leader*, March 30, 1915, April 7, 1915, and April 13, 1915; *Wisconsin Comrade* 2 (April 1915): 2; and *New York Call*, April 11, 1915.

65. *Milwaukee Leader*, April 26, 1915, May 3, 1915, May 10, 1915, May 17, 1915, May 18, 1915, May 20, 1915, and May 25, 1915; and diary entries April 23, 1915, April 25, 1915, and May 2, 1915, May 9, 1915, May 30, 1915, and June 13, 1915, in "Experiences in Milwaukee" folder, the Shedd Papers.

66. *Milwaukee Leader*, May 21, 1915, May 24, 1915, June 1, 1915, June 9, 1915, June 10, 1915, June 25, 1915, June 26, 1915, June 29, 1915, July 1, 1915, July 2, 1915, July 6, 1915, and July 19, 1915; and diary entries, May 23, 1915, May 30, 1915, June 13, 1915, and June 27, 1915, in "Experiences in Milwaukee" folder, the Shedd Papers.

67. *Milwaukee Leader*, September 20, 1915, September 24, 1915, October 23, 1915, October 25, 1915, November 2, 1915, November 8, 1915, November 15, 1915, November 22, 1915, February 5, 1916, March 16, 1916, April 3, 1916, and May 29, 1916; and interview with Othelia Hampel Haberkorn, Milwaukee, Wis., May 14, 1981.

68. *Milwaukee Leader*, October 3, 1916, October 9, 1916, October 14, 1916, October 17, 1916, October 20, 1916, October 26, 1916, October 30,

1916, November 10, 1916, November 11, 1916, November 21, 1916, and December 15, 1916; and interview with Othelia Hampel Haberkorn. Edmund T. Melms has been described as "the person most responsible for the emphasis on organization" in the Milwaukee socialist community at this time. He sought the participation of every Party member, stressing branch meetings, paying dues, holding picnics and parties, and so on. No doubt he saw SSS work as a component of this effort. He may also have adopted a more traditional educational perspective than that held by Shedd and perhaps illustrated what could happen when well-intentioned Party officials who had little background in the teaching of children became involved in SSS work. For more on Melms, see *Milwaukee Leader*, November 2, 1922; Edward S. Kerstein, *Milwaukee's All-American Mayor: Portrait of Daniel Webster Hoan* (Englewood Cliffs, N.J.: Prentice-Hall, 1966), p. 77; Michael Jay Soref, "'Family Capitalism and Sewer Socialism' in Milwaukee, 1850–1910," M.A. thesis, University of Wisconsin–Madison, 1973, p. 225; and DeLeon, ed., *American Labor Who's Who*.

69. *Milwaukee Leader*, December 4, 1916, December 11, 1916, December 26, 1916, and December 28, 1916.

70. *Milwaukee Leader*, January 3, 1917, January 10, 1917, February 10, 1917, February 16, 1917, February 17, 1917, February 26, 1917, April 17, 1917, April 18, 1917, and May 3, 1917.

71. *Milwaukee Leader*, August 31, 1917, September 12, 1917, September 21, 1917, September 25, 1917, October 1, 1917, October 2, 1917, and October 12, 1917.

72. *Milwaukee Leader*, September 21, 1917, and May 22, 1918; *Intercollegiate Socialist* 4 (February–March 1916): 19; *New York Times*, December 3, 1972; *Who Was Who in America*, vol. 6 (Chicago: Marquis Who's Who, 1976), p. 17; Miller, *Victor Berger and the Promise of Constructive Socialism, 1910–1920*, pp. 176 and 211; and DeLeon, ed., *American Labor Who's Who*.

73. *Milwaukee Leader*, December 5, 1917, December 17, 1917, January 2, 1918, February 4, 1918, March 4, 1918, March 27, 1918, April 29, 1918, May 6, 1918, May 31, 1918, June 4, 1918, June 6, 1918, and July 1, 1918.

74. *Milwaukee Leader*, October 12, 1918, November 13, 1918, November 19, 1918, November 26, 1918, November 27, 1918, December 21, 1918, December 27, 1918, January 4, 1919, March 5, 1919, May 4, 1919, May 9, 1919, June 9, 1919, June 10, 1919, June 11, 1919, June 23, 1919, June 25, 1919, July 2, 1919, July 18, 1919, July 30, 1919, and August 4, 1919.

75. *Milwaukee Leader*, November 18, 1918, November 24, 1918, January 5, 1920, and January 8, 1920; and *New York Call*, May 16, 1919.

76. *Milwaukee Leader*, November 10, 1919, February 16, 1920, February 28, 1920, March 1, 1920, March 19, 1920, and May 5, 1920.

77. *Milwaukee Leader*, September 22, 1920, October 16, 1920, October 29, 1920, November 1, 1920, November 15, 1920, November 17, 1920, December 5, 1920, December 17, 1920, April 16, 1921, April 30, 1921, May 30, 1921, and August 22, 1921.

78. *Milwaukee Leader*, September 14, 1921, September 19, 1921, September 22, 1921, and September 26, 1921; and interviews with Joseph Friebert and Edward Friebert, Jr., Milwaukee, Wis., October 2, 1981.

79. Carl Haessler later became a staff correspondent and then managing editor of the Federated Press in Chicago until it folded in 1956. He also did publicity and editorial work for the United Auto Workers, helped to organize the American Newspaper Guild, lectured at Commonwealth College in Mena, Ark., and edited the American Federation of Labor's Detroit-based *Union Engineer*. In 1972, a *New York Times* obituary described Haessler as "a labor newsman and old-time socialist whose writings encouraged sit-down strikers in the worker turbulence of the 1930s." Of course, in a lifetime as full as his, the obituary contained no mention of his involvement in the International SSS. *Milwaukee Leader*, January 7, 1922, January 25, 1922, and April 4, 1922; *New York Times*, December 3, 1972; Raymond and Charlotte Koch, *Educational Commune: The Story of Commonwealth College* (New York: Schoken, 1972), p. 134; DeLeon, ed., *American Labor's Who's Who*; and *Who Was Who in America*, vol. 6, p. 174.

80. *Milwaukee Leader*, December 10, 1921, December 12, 1921, and April 5, 1922; Cross, "The *Milwaukee Leader*, an Unusual Newspaper," p. 15; "Wisconsin File (1911–1961)," in *Socialist Party of America Papers*, reel 112; and interviews with Joseph Friebert and Edward Friebert, Jr.

81. *Milwaukee Leader*, October 17, 1922, November 20, 1922, December 22, 1922, December 29, 1922, February 1, 1923, February 12, 1923, May 10, 1923, July 12, 1923, and July 23, 1923; and interview with Othelia Hampel Haberkorn.

82. *Milwaukee Leader*, June 27, 1923, October 11, 1923, October 13, 1923, December 6, 1923, December 8, 1923, December 26, 1923, and December 28, 1923; and Friebert, Autobiography, pp. 278–79.

Chapter Four

1. Jessie Wallace Hughan, *American Socialism of the Present Day* (New York: John Lane, 1911), p. 205.

2. *Milwaukee Leader*, January 9, 1915; *New York Call*, January 10, 1916; and Kendrick Shedd, "The Power of Early Impressions," *Young Socialists' Magazine* 8 (February 1915): 3.

3. *Milwaukee Leader*, January 9, 1915; and *New York Call*, January 8, 1911.

4. William Kruse, "Socialist Education for Children," *Young Socialists' Magazine* 11 (March 1917): 9.

5. *The Worker*, January 26, 1907.

6. *New York Call*, October 7, 1910.

7. "The Public Schools," *Young Socialists' Magazine* 6 (December 1913): 12.

8. *New York Call*, October 2, 1910, and July 26, 1914.

9. Telephone interview with Eleanore Levenson, New York City, July 9, 1981; *New York Call*, September 25, 1917; and *The Worker*, January 26, 1907.

10. Interview with Jennie Yavner Goldman, Putnam Valley, N.Y., July 4, 1981. In the Party locals, it was not unusual for the top leadership to be native-born while a majority of the rank and file were immigrants. Amer-

icanizing immigrant workers at the same time as they were being radicalized was viewed as helping to create greater solidarity among the working class, absent of ethnic divisions. See, for example, Walter Galenson, "Why the American Labor Movement Is Not Socialist," *American Review* 1 (Winter 1961): 44.

11. Letter from Kendrick Shedd to Bertha Vossler, dated July 7, 1911, "Rochester Socialist Sunday School Scrapbooks, vol. 1," in the Kendrick Philander Shedd Papers, located at the University of Rochester, Rush Rhees Library, Rare Books Department, Special Collections, Rochester, N.Y. (henceforth in this chapter referred to as the Shedd Papers); and *New York Call*, April 14, 1913, February 8, 1914, and May 3, 1914.

12. *New York Call*, June 23, 1911, January 10, 1915, July 11, 1915, and July 25, 1915.

13. Mary C. Livingston, "Socialist Sunday Schools," *Progressive Woman* 3 (November 1909): 12; *The Worker*, July 13, 1902; and *Socialist Woman* 1 (November 1907): 9.

14. *Young Socialists' Magazine* 12 (October 1918): 17.

15. Interviews with Joseph Friebert and Edward Friebert, Jr., Milwaukee, Wis., October 2, 1981; and telephone interview with Martin Ladewig, Milwaukee, Wis., October 2, 1981.

16. *Progressive Woman* 3 (December 1909): 14; and *Young Socialists' Magazine* 4 (September 1911): 15.

17. Oakley C. Johnson, *The Day Is Coming: Life and Work of Charles E. Ruthenberg, 1882–1927* (New York: International Publishing, 1957), p. 47.

18. "Rochester Socialist Sunday School Scrapbooks, vol. 3," the Shedd Papers.

19. Joseph Freeman, *An American Testament: A Narrative of Rebels and Romantics* (New York: Farrar and Rinehart, 1936), p. 280.

20. "National Convention Proceedings, 1901–1962," *Socialist Party of American Papers*, microfilm edition (Glen Rock, N.J.: Microfilming Corporation of America, 1975), reel 76.

21. *Milwaukee Leader*, June 29, 1915.

22. *The Worker*, April 27, 1907, May 18, 1907, and June 22, 1907.

23. *Party Builder*, May 31, 1913. See also "Work through the Public Schools Is Best," *Party Builder*, July 26, 1913.

24. *New York Call*, September 24, 1912; diary entry, April 13, 1915, in "Experiences in Milwaukee" folder, the Shedd Papers; Edward Friebert, autobiography (unpublished manuscript, 1945), pp. 274–75 of handwritten copy; and interview with Othelia Hampel Haberkorn, Milwaukee, Wis., May 14, 1981.

25. Quoted in John Spargo and George Louis Arner, *Elements of Socialism* (New York: Macmillan, 1912), p. 301.

26. Eden and Cedar Paul, *Proletcult (Proletarian Culture)* (New York: Thomas Seltzer, 1921), p. 81.

27. *Socialist World*, August 15, 1920. At the time, David Berenberg was teaching a related course at the Rand School (see Chapter Five).

28. *New York Call*, January 8, 1911, October 31, 1915, and January 16, 1916.

29. Kendrick Shedd, "Making Young Rebels," *Young Socialists' Magazine* (July 1915): 10; and *New York Call*, April 4, 1915, May 2, 1915, May 23, 1915, and June 6, 1915.

30. Folder of miscellaneous materials, the Shedd Papers; and *Cleveland Citizen*, September 4, 1915. See also J. Robert Constantine, ed., *Letters of Eugene V. Debs*, vol. 1 *(1874–1912)* (Urbana: University of Illinois Press, 1990), pp. 463–64, and *Letters of Eugene V. Debs*, vol. 2 *(1913–1919)* (Urbana: University of Illinois Press, 1990), pp. 173–75.

31. *New Age*, March 19, 1918.

32. Telephone interview with Nora Linn, Martha's Vineyard, Mass., June 25, 1981; and telephone interview with Fred Shulman, Bloomfield, N.J., March 3, 1984.

33. Of course, as young children and teenagers at the time, SSS participants interviewed for this study may not have been aware of (or do not remember) the difficulties faced by the schools because of opposition from outsiders. In addition, most of those interviewed attended schools in Milwaukee and New York City, where there were relatively strong radical movements. Their experiences may not be representative of what schools in other locations had to contend with.

34. *The Worker*, April 17, 1904.

35. David Goldstein and Martha Moore Avery, *Socialism: The Nation of Fatherless Children* (Boston: Thomas J. Flynn, 1911, 2nd ed.), pp. 229–37, and *Bolshevism: Its Cure* (Boston: Boston School of Political Economy, 1919), pp. 247–53. See also *The People*, December 16, 1900; *Milwaukee Leader*, January 3, 1920; and Edward T. James, Janet Wilson James, and Paul S. Boyer, eds., *Notable American Women, 1607–1950: A Biographical Dictionary*, vol. 1 (Cambridge, Mass.: Belknap, 1971), pp. 69–70.

36. *National Civic Federation Review*, 5 (September 25, 1920): 15; and Martha Moore Avery, "Socialist Sunday Schools," *National Civic Federation Review* 3 (May 1908): 11.

37. " 'Red' Sunday-Schools and Child Socialists," *American Review of Reviews*, 38 (July 1908): 112–13; and *New York Times*, February 3, 1907, August 2, 1908, and March 27, 1910.

38. *Living Age*, January 13, 1912; John R. Meader, "The Menace of Radical Education," *Common Cause* 1 (January 1912): 21–28; and Leslie Irving, "Teaching the Young Idea 'How to Shoot,' " *Common Cause* 1 (April 1912): 80–81.

39. *New York Times*, March 21, 1910; *Young Socialists' Magazine* 4 (July 1911): 11; *Coming Nation*, June 17, 1911; *New York Call*, June 25, 1911, and December 22, 1912; and Bertha H. Mailly, "The Socialist Schools of Greater New York," *Little Socialist Magazine for Boys and Girls* 4 (May 1911): 6. According to the *Times* report, John Wesley Hill's talk did not go unchallenged. When he finished speaking, a well-dressed young man rose from the audience, identified himself as a student for the Universalist ministry but also a socialist for two years, and remarked that he thought that the Socialist Sunday schools were "doing a lot of good."

40. *The Worker*, April 17, 1904.

41. *National Socialist*, April 27, 1912; *Socialist Woman* 2 (September 1909): 9; and *Young Socialists' Magazine* 4 (July 1911): 11.

42. *New York Call,* October 27, 1914, October 9, 1915, October 14, 1917, December 1, 1918, December 21, 1918, and December 24, 1918; *Young Socialists' Magazine* 6 (December 1913): 14; and *International Socialist Review* 12 (May 1912): 794.

43. *New York Call,* January 29, 1917, September 25, 1917, October 26, 1917, October 28, 1917, October 30, 1917, November 1, 1917, and March 7, 1918; telephone interview with Nora Linn; and Martin Weber, "The Pittsburgh Socialist Sunday School," *Young Socialists' Magazine* 12 (June 1918): 11.

44. *New York Call,* November 19, 1914, and September 18, 1919; and *Young Socialists' Magazine* 12 (June 1918): 11, and 13 (April 1919): 17.

45. See, for example, *New York Call,* September 8, 1909, and January 15, 1917; letter from Julia Parks to "Mrs. [Ella Reeve?] Bloor," dated August 6, 1913, a copy of which is contained in a folder of miscellaneous materials, the Shedd Papers; William F. Kruse, "How to Organize, Maintain and Conduct the 'S.S.S.'" (Chicago: Socialist Party Young People's Department, n.d. [1918?]), a copy of which is included in the *Socialist Party of America Papers,* reel 137; and *Young Socialists' Magazine* 4 (June 1911): 7.

46. *New York Call,* February 3, 1910, July 4, 1915, January 25, 1916, September 15, 1918, September 17, 1918, February 15, 1919, and February 23, 1919; *Young Socialists' Magazine* 13 (April 1919): 18; *Socialist Woman* 2 (September 1909): 9; and *Progressive Woman* 3 (October 1909): 14.

47. *Wisconsin Comrade* 2 (October 1915): 3.

48. Friebert, Autobiography, p. 274.

49. *New York Call,* February 26, 1920.

50. *New York Call,* December 6, 1913.

51. Letters from M. A. Rothmund to Kendrick Shedd, dated April 21, 1913, and from Kendrick Shedd to "Nell [Martindale?]," dated March 17, 1915, in "Rochester Socialist Sunday School Scrapbooks, vols. 1 and 4," and "Rochester Socialist Sunday School Scrapbooks, vol. 3," the Shedd Papers.

52. *New York Call,* December 17, 1911.

53. *New York Call,* December 6, 1913; and *Eye Opener,* May 25, 1918.

54. *New York Call,* February 26, 1920; and telephone interview with Gertrude Weil Klein, New York City, July 21, 1981. The director of the school was her father.

55. *Eye Opener,* May 25, 1918.

56. *Socialist Woman* 1 (March 1908): 12; *New York Call,* May 3, 1911; *American Socialist,* August 26, 1916; *American Labor Year Book, 1916* (New York: Rand School of Social Science, 1916), p. 154; and *Young Socialists' Magazine* 13 (April 1919): 17.

57. "Baltimore S.S.S. Discontinued," *Young Socialists' Magazine* 13 (March 1919): 18. A copy of Edward Perkins Clarke's letter to the *New York Call* is contained in "Rochester Socialist Sunday School Scrapbooks, vol. 3," the Shedd Papers.

58. Unfortunately, this songbook has not been located, leaving unknown the ways in which it differed from other songbooks already in use by the schools (see Chapter Six).

59. *Socialist Woman* 1 (March 1908): 12; *New York Call,* October 31, 1915; and *Milwaukee Leader,* November 13, 1918.

60. *Young Socialists' Magazine* 12 (September 1918): 2; "Our First Convention," *Young Socialists' Magazine* 13 (June 1919): 11; "Socialist Schools of Science," *Young Socialists' Magazine* 13 (August–September 1919): 14; and Kruse, "How to Organize, Conduct and Maintain the 'S.S.S.,'" *Socialist Party of America Papers*.

61. *New York Call*, February 2, 1912, and April 18, 1915.

62. Interview with Othelia Hampel Haberkorn; *Young Socialists' Magazine* 13 (January 1920): 8; and *New York Call*, June 21, 1909, March 26, 1911, January 24, 1915, and January 8, 1920.

63. *Milwaukee Leader*, December 16, 1916; Friebert, Autobiography, p. 276; and *New York Call*, July 5, 1914, and July 12, 1914.

64. Kruse, "How to Organize, Maintain and Conduct the 'S.S.S.,'" *Socialist Party of America Papers*; Bertha H. Mailly, *How to Organize Socialist Schools* (New York: Rand School of Social Science, n.d. [1911?]), a copy of which is contained in "Rochester Socialist Sunday School Scrapbooks, vol. 1," the Shedd Papers. See also Woman's National Committee of the Socialist Party, *How to Organize Socialist Schools* (Chicago: Socialist Party's Woman's National Committee, n.d.), a copy of which is contained in "Miscellaneous Materials," Socialist Party of U.S. Materials, 1912 Folder, Tamiment Institute, Elmer Holmes Bobst Library, New York University, New York City, N.Y.

65. *New York Call*, April 7, 1912, April 14, 1912, and January 25, 1916; and "Rochester Socialist Sunday School Scrapbooks, vol. 1," the Shedd Papers.

66. Kruse, "How to Organize, Maintain and Conduct the 'S.S.S.,'" *Socialist Party of America Papers*; diary entry, April 7, 1915, "Experiences in Milwaukee" folder, the Shedd Papers; *New York Call*, April 11, 1915; and *American Socialist*, March 27, 1915.

67. *Young Socialists' Magazine* 12 (July 1918): 16.

68. Weber, "The Pittsburgh Socialist Sunday School"; *Young Socialists' Magazine* 12 (October 1918): 17; and *The Worker*, November 29, 1903.

69. Frank Wilt, "The Cleveland Socialist Sunday School," *Young Socialists' Magazine* 12 (March 1918): 9–10; Rasa A. Smith, "The Children's Socialist Lyceum," *Young Socialists' Magazine* 12 (October 1918): 17; and *New Age*, March 16, 1918.

70. *New York Call*, February 2, 1912.

71. "Rochester Socialist Sunday School Scrapbooks, vols. 1 and 3," the Shedd Papers; and *New York Call*, June 13, 1915.

72. Wilt, "The Cleveland Socialist Sunday School."

73. Interview with Joseph Friebert.

74. *New York Call*, March 31, 1909; *Wisconsin Comrade* 2 (January 1916): 2–3; *Socialist Woman* 1 (March 1908): 12, and 2 (November 1908): 16; *Milwaukee Leader*, April 16, 1919; and letter from M. Bagno of the Bronx to Bertha Vossler, dated December 21, 1915, in "Rochester Socialist Sunday School Scrapbooks, vol. 4," the Shedd Papers.

75. *New York Call*, November 20, 1909, December 9, 1909, and May 21, 1911; and *Young Socialists' Magazine* (October 1911): 7.

76. *New York Call*, February 20, 1912, and March 12, 1912.

77. *New York Call*, June 2, 1910, August 25, 1911, and May 3, 1912.

78. *The Worker*, March 14, 1908; *Progressive Woman* 2 (August 1909): 15; "National Convention Proceedings, *1901–1962*," *Socialist Party of America Papers*; and "1912 Folder," vertical file, Socialist Party of U.S. Materials.

79. "Rochester Socialist Sunday School Scrapbooks, vol. 4," the Shedd Papers.

80. Ibid.; diary entry, April 7, 1915, in "Experiences in Milwaukee" folder, the Shedd Papers; and *New York Call*, May 2, 1915.

81. *Milwaukee Leader*, August 8, 1916; *Appeal to Reason*, August 19, 1916; and *International Socialist Review* 17 (October 1916): 249.

82. *American Socialist*, August 26, 1916.

83. *Eye Opener*, November 3, 1917.

84. *Young Socialists' Magazine* 12 (June 1918): 11; and *Eye Opener*, November 3, 1917. Kruse also announced that school texts and songbooks could now be obtained from the Young People's Department, at a cost ranging from 10 cents to two dollars apiece. Kruse, "How to Organize, Maintain and Conduct the 'S.S.S.,'" *Socialist Party of America Papers*.

85. *Young Socialists' Magazine* 12 (September 1918): 2, and 12 (December 1918): 2.

86. Kruse, "How to Organize, Conduct and Maintain the 'S.S.S.,'" *Socialist Party of America Papers*; *Young Socialists' Magazine* 12 (December 1918): 2, 13 (February 1919): 2, 13 (March 1919): 18–19, and 13 (April 1919): 17; and *Milwaukee Leader*, November 26, 1918, and March 5, 1919.

87. *Young Socialists' Magazine* 13 (January 1920): 9.

Chapter Five

1. Grass-roots radical activists often were referred to as the "Jimmie Higginses" of the movement. The original essay on "Jimmie Higgins" was written at the turn of the century by Ben Hanford, the Party's 1904 vice-presidential candidate, and reprinted in countless radical newspapers and journals in subsequent years. The fictional character was lauded as the backbone of the Socialist movement—"What did he do? Everything."—and was presumably intended to be genderless. *The Worker*, May 1, 1903. See also James Weinstein, *The Decline of Socialism in America, 1912–1925* (New York: Vintage, 1969), p. 42; and James R. Green, "The 'Salesmen–Soldiers' of the 'Appeal' Army: A Profile of Rank-and-File Socialist Agitators," in *Socialism and the Cities*, ed. Bruce M. Stave (Port Washington, N.Y.: Kennikat, 1975). For a critical appraisal of these "true believers," see Aileen S. Kraditor, *"Jimmy Higgins": The Mental World of the American Rank-and-File Communist, 1930–1958* (New York: Greenwood, 1988).

2. *New York Call*, April 14, 1912; and Hilda Kean, *Challenging the State? The Socialist and Feminist Educational Experience, 1900–1930* (London: Falmer, 1990), p. 66.

3. Woman's National Committee of the Socialist Party, *How to Organize Socialist Schools* (Chicago: Socialist Party's Woman's National Committee, n.d.), a copy of which is contained in "Miscellaneous Materials," Socialist Party of U.S. Materials, 1912 Folder, Tamiment Institute, Elmer Holmes

Bobst Library, New York University, New York City, N.Y.; and Frank Wilt, "The Cleveland Socialist Sunday School," *Young Socialists' Magazine* 12 (March 1918): 9–10.

4. *New York Call,* February 2, 1912, and April 14, 1912.

5. *New York Call,* May 4, 1911, and May 7, 1911. See also Paul Luttinger, *The Burning Question (Rational Education of the Proletariat)* (New York: Rational Education League, 1913).

6. *New York Call,* February 2, 1912; and Mari Jo Buhle, *Women and American Socialism, 1870–1920* (Urbana: University of Illinois Press, 1981).

7. "National Convention Proceedings, 1901–1962," *Socialist Party of America Papers,* microfilm edition (Glen Rock, N.J.: Microfilming Corporation of America, 1975), reel 76.

8. *Socialist Woman* 1 (August 1907): 10.

9. *Socialist Woman* 2 (June 1908): 10.

10. "Rochester Young People's Socialist League Scrapbooks, vol. 1," in the Kendrick Philander Shedd Papers, located at the University of Rochester, Rush Rhees Library, Rare Books Department, Special Collections, Rochester, N.Y. (henceforth in this chapter referred to as the Shedd Papers); Kendrick Shedd, "The Yipsels in the Socialist Sunday Schools," *Young Socialists' Magazine* 9 (June 1915): 4–5; *American Socialist,* March 27, 1915; and *Eye Opener,* May 25, 1918.

11. *New York Call,* February 26, 1920.

12. *New York Call,* November 8, 1913, and April 26, 1919; and *Socialist Woman* 2 (June 1908): 10. Alexander Fichandler was a public school principal and involved in workers' education at the time. Two decades later, he assisted those involved in the reorganizing of Socialist Sunday schools in New York City. Interview with Edward Gottlieb, Putnam Valley, N.Y., July 4, 1981.

13. *New York Call,* July 11, 1915, and January 25, 1916. Shedd held teacher meetings in Rochester on Wednesday evenings, preceding YPSL meetings, and in Milwaukee on Saturday evenings, and provided typewritten outlines of the week's lessons to the teachers. "Rochester Socialist Sunday School Scrapbooks, vol. 3," and diary entry, June 13, 1915, "Experiences in Milwaukee" folder, the Shedd Papers.

14. *New York Call,* November 12, 1908, September 22, 1909, February 3, 1911, February 4, 1911, February 8, 1911, February 11, 1911, April 5, 1911, November 5, 1911, December 31, 1911, January 25, 1912, March 5, 1919, and April 9, 1919. Henrietta Rodman was one of the younger set of more intellectual-minded and less Victorian-oriented socialists, interested in such issues as sexual freedom and birth control and not just economic justice. In 1914 she was suspended from her teaching position in New York City because of her agitation on behalf of a pregnant teacher's right to teach. See Buhle, *Women and American Socialism, 1870–1920,* p. 258; and *New York Call,* November 1, 1914, November 12, 1914, November 13, 1914, and November 15, 1914.

15. *New York Call,* January 11, 1919, February 1, 1919, March 21, 1919, and November 16, 1920. The Rand School bulletin described David Berenberg's course as "a lecture and discussion course, dealing with the conduct of Socialist schools and study groups for children and young people, reviewing past successes and failures, and applying pedagogical principles to

the planning of courses, selection of teachers, and methods of teaching."
Rand School of Social Science Bulletin, 1920–1921, p. 26.

16. *Rand School of Social Science Bulletin, 1920–1921*, pp. 2 and 5; and telephone interview with Fred Shulman, Bloomfield, N.J., March 3, 1984.

17. *New York Call*, February 25, 1914, March 4, 1914, April 18, 1914, April 25, 1914, and May 16, 1914; *The Worker*, January 24, 1904; *Socialist Woman* 2 (September 1909): 9; and *Milwaukee Leader*, March 20, 1917.

18. Located in a folder of miscellaneous materials, the Shedd Papers.

19. Interviews with Joseph Friebert and Edward Friebert, Jr., Milwaukee, Wis., October 2, 1981.

20. Telephone interview with Martin Ladewig, Milwaukee, Wis., October 2, 1981; interview with Jennie Yavner Goldman, Putnam Valley, N.Y., July 4, 1981; and *New York Call*, February 6, 1910, and December 9, 1920.

21. Telephone interview with Eleanore Levenson, New York City, July 9, 1981; interview with Jennie Yavner Goldman; interviews with Joseph Friebert and Edward Friebert, Jr.; *Young Socialists' Magazine* 13 (April 1919): 18; and *New York Call*, November 19, 1916.

22. Telephone interview with Alex Paalu, Milwaukee, Wis., October 11, 1980; interview with Ida Kaufman, Madison, N.J., June 26, 1981; telephone interview with Nora Linn, Martha's Vineyard, Mass., June 25, 1981; letter from Nora Linn, Bronx, N.Y., to author, dated October 6, 1980; letter from Peggy Dennis, Berkeley, Calif., to author, dated February 4, 1982; interviews with Joseph Friebert and Edward Friebert, Jr.; and interview with Jennie Yavner Goldman.

23. Telephone interview with Anthony Duoba, Rochester, N.Y., July 20, 1981; and telephone interview with Gertrude Weil Klein, New York City, July 21, 1981.

24. Telephone interview with Anthony Duoba; and telephone interview with Gertrude Weil Klein.

25. *New York Call*, April 24, 1910.

26. Letter from Peggy Dennis to author, dated February 4, 1982.

27. *Milwaukee Leader*, March 9, 1918, and March 12, 1918; *Milwaukee Sentinel*, September 25, 1981; and interview with Joseph Friebert.

Chapter Six

1. "Rochester Socialist Sunday School Scrapbooks, vol. 3," in the Kendrick Philander Shedd Papers, located at the University of Rochester, Rush Rhees Library, Rare Books Department, Special Collections, Rochester, N.Y. (henceforth in this chapter referred to as the Shedd Papers); and *New York Call*, January 25, 1916. Unless otherwise indicated, all of Shedd's lesson materials can be found in the "Rochester Socialist Sunday School Scrapbooks, vols. 1–4," the Shedd Papers.

2. *New York Call*, January 25, 1916.

3. Myles Horton is quoted in Brenda Bell, John Gaventa, and John Peters, eds., *We Make the Road by Walking: Conversations on Education and Social Change* (Philadelphia: Temple University Press, 1990), p. 147. The lesson on "Work" was witnessed by J. Mahlon Barnes, a former national secre-

tary of the Party. Subsequently, Barnes wrote to Shedd about how much he enjoyed his visit to the school and that he "was most agreeably surprised with the presentation·and the apparent understanding of fundamentals shown by the pupils." Barnes also wrote to a Party official in Rochester to praise Shedd and his work, and to suggest that Shedd's "field of labor . . . be widely increased." Letters from J. Mahlon Barnes of Philadelphia to Kendrick Shedd, dated November 24, 1912, and from J. Mahlon Barnes to George Weber, n.d., in "Rochester Socialist Sunday School Scrapbooks, vol. 1," the Shedd Papers.

 4. Quoted in Betty Yorburg, "People in Protest: Three Generations of American Socialists," Ph.D. dissertation, New School of Social Research, 1968, p. 62.

 5. Letters from Emma Silien of Rochester to Kendrick Shedd, dated November 17, 1914, and from Kendrick Shedd to Emma Silien, dated November 19, 1914, in "Rochester Socialist Sunday School Scrapbooks, vol. 3," the Shedd Papers.

 6. *Milwaukee Leader*, January 14, 1916, and September 29, 1917; *New York Call*, January 25, 1916; "Socialist Sunday Schools," in *Socialist Party of America Papers*, microfilm edition (Glen Rock, N.J.: Microfilm Corporation of America, 1975), reel 81; and Walter Thomas Mills, *The Struggle for Existence* (Chicago: International School of Social Economy, 1904). Mills was a popular socialist lecturer and educator throughout the 1900–1920 period. His most noteworthy written contribution to the radical movement was *The Struggle for Existence*, which was reprinted several times and allegedly sold half a million copies. See James R. Green, *Grass-Roots Socialism: Radical Movements in the Southwest, 1895–1943* (Baton Rouge: Louisiana State University Press, 1978), pp. 41–42 and 157.

 7. *Milwaukee Leader*, December 1, 1917, December 3, 1917, December 26, 1917, and December 31, 1917.

 8. *Milwaukee Leader*, May 3, 1919, May 10, 1919, May 17, 1919, and May 24, 1919.

 9. *Milwaukee Leader*, December 8, 1920, and June 1, 1921. It is possible to conclude from the change to a serialized story that the school's pedagogy became more teacher-directed and lecture-oriented. However, it may instead have been the case that class activities essentially remained the same but that there was simply a lack of time to provide detailed lesson outlines for publication. Or perhaps the newspaper only wanted to publish the essential content that was to be taught and not the ways in which it was to be presented.

 10. *Milwaukee Leader*, October 6, 1921.

 11. Bertha Matthews Fraser, *Outlines of Lessons for Socialist Schools for Children* (New York: Children's Socialist Schools Committee of Local Kings County, 1910), a copy of which can be found in the Radical Pamphlets Literature Collection, reel 27, located at the Tamiment Institute, Elmer Holmes Bobst Library, New York University, New York City, N.Y.; *New York Call*, September 24, 1910; and Woman's National Committee of the Socialist Party, *How to Organize Socialist Schools* (Chicago: Socialist Party's Woman's National Committee, n.d.), a copy of which is contained in "Miscellaneous Materials," 1912 Folder, Socialist Party of U.S. Materials, located at the Tam-

iment Institute, Elmer Holmes Bobst Library, New York University, New York City, N.Y. See also *International Socialist Review* 10 (April 1910): 946.

12. *New York Call*, August 1, 1910, August 8, 1910, August 15, 1910, August 22, 1910, August 29, 1910, and September 12, 1910; *New Age*, June 1, 1918, and June 8, 1918; *Milwaukee Leader*, March 1, 1919, and February 18, 1920; and *Young Socialists' Magazine* 13 (April 1919): 11. A typewritten copy of Edith Breithut's lessons, apparently brought back to Milwaukee from New York City by Edna Peters when she was a full-time student at the Rand School, can be found in the Social Democratic Party Collection, Box 2 File 9, located at the Milwaukee County Historical Society, Manuscripts Division, Milwaukee, Wis.

13. David S. Greenberg, *Socialist Sunday School Curriculum* (New York: Socialist Schools Publishing Association, 1913). Greenberg studied at Teachers College of Columbia University. In 1917, he authored a six-part series in the *New York Call* on "School's Place in a Democracy." *New York Call*, February 3, 1911, November 19, 1917, November 20, 1917, November 21, 1917, November 22, 1917, November 23, 1917, and November 24, 1917. See also *Unity of Labor*, 1 (April 1911): 5–7; and, for a review of a book he wrote, *New York Times*, July 13, 1913.

14. *Young Socialists' Magazine* 4 (October 1911): 7–8.

15. As briefly mentioned in the previous chapter, in 1920 the Rand School announced that it had been commissioned by the Party to prepare "a textbook for Socialist children's schools." The *Milwaukee Leader* publicized the same news. It was reported at the Party's National Executive Committee meeting in March 1921 that David Berenberg had begun preparing the textbook, with Bertha Mailly urging that it be published as soon as possible, perhaps with financial help from the Workmen's Circle. A former student and later principal at the Brownsville SSS worked on the book with Berenberg and recalls that about one hundred pages were written. But the manuscript was never completed, and he lost his copy of what had been compiled. One could argue, of course, that, by 1921, it was an ill-timed effort anyway. *Rand School of Social Science Bulletin, 1920–1921*, p. 2; *Milwaukee Leader*, December 13, 1919; *Socialist World*, March 15, 1921; and interview with Fred Shulman, Bloomfield, N.J., June 26, 1987.

16. *Who Was Who in America*, vol. 5 (Chicago: Marquis Who's Who, 1973), p. 191; *American Women*, vol. 3 (Los Angeles: American Publications, 1939), p. 240; *New York Times*, May 15, 1944; *Young Socialists' Magazine* 12 (March 1918): 9, 12 (June 1918): 11, 12 (September 1918): 2, and 13 (March 1919): 19; *New York Call*, January 7, 1909; *Milwaukee Leader*, January 23, 1917, and January 24, 1919; "School Class Rooms" folder, Social Democratic Party Collection, Box 2 File 6; letter from M. Bagno of the Bronx to Rochester SSS, dated December 21, 1915, in "Rochester Socialist Sunday School Scrapbooks, vol. 4," the Shedd Papers; Woman's National Committee of the Socialist Party, "How to Organize Socialist Schools," Socialist Party of U.S. Materials; and telephone interview with Fred Shulman, Bloomfield, N.J., March 3, 1984. All of Katherine Dopp's books were published by the Chicago-based Rand McNally and Company. The other three books in the "Industrial and Social History" series are *The Early Sea People: First Steps in the Conquest of the Waters* (1912); *The Early Herdsmen: First Steps in Taming the*

Grass-Eating Animals (1923); and *The Early Farmers: First Steps in the Cultivation of Plants* (1929). At least later in life, Dopp identified herself as a Republican.

17. William F. Kruse, "How to Teach History in the Primary Grades," *Young Socialists' Magazine* 13 (January 1920): 7.

18. Katherine E. Dopp, *The Tree-Dwellers: The Age of Fear* (Chicago: Rand McNally, 1903), p. 159.

19. Dopp's *The Tree-Dwellers* did not go unnoticed in the scientific and educational communities. For example, see the letters in *Science* 19 (April 1, 1904): 550–51, 19 (May 6, 1904): 737–38, and 20 (July 1, 1904): 20–23; and *American Journal of Sociology* 9 (March 1904): 724–26. The review published in the *American Journal of Sociology* criticized the book's somewhat deductive nature but still hailed it as a pioneering work that "is firmly rooted in the present, however far it may reach into the past."

20. Nicholas Klein, *The Socialist Primer* (Girard, Kan.: Appeal to Reason, 1908); and Samuel Yellen, "A Socialist Boyhood," *American Mercury* 21 (October 1930): 200. See also *New York Call*, January 9, 1909, and March 6, 1909. During the first two decades, Klein was a prominent socialist organizer and journalist, and then a labor lawyer. Although he stayed active in Cincinnati politics, he later became less enamored with the radical movement. Evidently, *The Socialist Primer* became a source of considerable embarrassment for him. The local library kept its copy of the book locked in a bank vault for safekeeping to protect it from being destroyed by Klein, who did not want its existence known. Letters from Jane E. Wager, Public Library of Cincinnati and Hamilton County, to author, dated March 18, 1981, and October 6, 1981; letter from Yeatman Anderson III, Public Library of Cincinnati and Hamilton County, to author, dated November 3, 1981; Barnett M. Brickner, "The Jewish Community of Cincinnati—Historical and Descriptive, 1817–1933," Ph.D. dissertation, University of Cincinnati, 1933, p. 331; and *New York Times*, October 23, 1951.

21. For example, see *New York Call*, October 17, 1908; "Rochester Socialist Sunday School Scrapbooks, vol. 1," the Shedd Papers; and materials from Ernest Kleine, Jr., Williamsville, N.Y., sent with letter to author, dated September 1, 1980. *The Socialist Primer* was the subject of several attacks in the mainstream press and in speeches like the one by Reverend John Wesley Hill (cited in Chapter Four). See *New York Times*, March 21, 1910, and March 27, 1910; Ada C. Sweet, "Socialists Active in the American Educational Field," *National Civic Federation Review* 3 (March 1909): 20; and *Living Age*, January 13, 1912.

22. John Spargo, *Socialist Readings For Children* (New York: Woman's National Progressive League, 1909).

23. *Party Builder*, October 4, 1913; *New York Call*, January 9, 1909; *Progressive Woman* 3 (October 1909): 14, and 3 (December 1909): 6; *Eye Opener*, May 25, 1918; and *Milwaukee Leader*, November 24, 1916.

24. Caroline Nelson, *Nature Talks on Economics* (Chicago: Charles H. Kerr, 1912). Nelson was a veteran militant who was involved in educational work and birth control agitation, and particularly concerned with the failure of the radical movement to attract the masses of immigrant women. See Mari Jo Buhle, *Women and American Socialism, 1870–1920* (Urbana: University of Illinois Press, 1981), pp. 276–80.

25. *Appeal to Reason,* April 6, 1912.

26. Emilie Poulsson, *Finger Plays for Nursery and Kindergarten* (Boston: Lothrop, 1893). A new, unabridged edition of Poulsson's *Finger Plays* was issued as recently as 1971 by Dover Publications. The publishers describe Poulsson's volume as having gone through "edition after edition before the turn of the century, remaining so popular that it was re-copyrighted by the author in 1921."

27. Interview with Jennie Yavner Goldman, Putnam Valley N.Y., July 4, 1981; Upton Sinclair, ed., *The Cry for Justice: An Anthology of the Literature of Social Protest* (Philadelphia: John Winston, 1915), pp. 59–62; and *Young Socialists' Magazine* 5 (August 1912): 1. There is evidence that a socialist "Mother Goose" collection was written by Henry M. Tichenor, a public speaker and editor, and published in a thirty-two-page pamphlet. It has not been located, however, so it is unclear whether or not this was the same collection used by the New York City Socialist Sunday schools. See Oakley C. Johnson, *Marxism in United States History before the Russian Revolution (1876–1917)* (New York: Humanities, 1974), pp. 142–43.

28. *Socialist Woman* 4 (July 1910): 3. Schools in places like Los Angeles, Passaic, Cleveland, Rochester, and New York City reported using the magazine. See *Little Socialist Magazine for Boys and Girls* 3 (May 1910): 10, and 4 (February 1911): 11; *Young Socialists' Magazine* 4 (July 1911): 11, and 6 (January 1913): 12; and "Rochester Socialist Sunday School Scrapbooks, vol. 1," the Shedd Papers. In addition, at least one Ferrer Modern School in Manhattan used it. See Florence M. Tager, "A Radical Approach to Education: Anarchist Schooling—The Modern School of New York and Stelton," Ph.D. dissertation, Ohio State University, 1979, pp. 215–16.

29. *Young Socialists' Magazine* 13 (July 1919): 9–10.

30. For example, from May 1910 to October 1910 alone, the radical youth periodical printed short sections from Paine's *Common Sense,* Bellamy's *Looking Backward,* Sinclair's *The Jungle,* London's *Call of the Wild,* and Gorky's *The Sky. Little Socialist Magazine for Boys and Girls* 3 (May 1910): 4, 3 (June 1910): 9, 3 (July 1910): 11, 3 (August 1910): 11, and 3 (October 1910): 9.

31. *Little Socialist Magazine for Boys and Girls* 3 (May 1910): 13.

32. *Little Socialist Magazine for Boys and Girls* 3 (January 1910): 5–6, 3 (February 1910): 5, 3 (May 1910): 5, 3 (September 1910): 5, and 4 (March 1911): 7. Frederick Krafft's lesson on Washington was cited in a published attack on the Socialist Sunday schools, which claimed that the schools were producing "a prolific crop of degenerate citizens." David Goldstein and Martha Moore Avery, *Socialism: The Nation of Fatherless Children* (Boston: Thomas J. Flynn, 1911, 2nd ed.), pp. 230–31.

33. For these and other examples, see *Young Socialists' Magazine* 4 (October 1911): 2, 6 (February 1913): 8, 7 (July 1914): 6, 8 (February 1915): 3, 8 (March 1915): 7, 9 (September 1915): 7, 10 (May 1916): 12, 11 (January 1917): 7, 11 (April 1917): 8, and 11 (May 1917): 13.

34. For these and other examples, see *Little Socialist Magazine for Boys and Girls* 2 (December 1909): 9, 3 (January 1910): 8, 3 (February 1910): 8, 3 (March 1910): 8, 3 (May 1910): 8, 3 (June 1910): 8, 3 (October 1910): 8, 4 (January 1911): 10, and 4 (March 1911): 8; and *Young Socialists' Magazine* 4

(July 1911): 8, 4 (September 1911): 8, 5 (April 1912): 10, and 7 (February 1914): 8.

35. "Rochester Socialist Sunday School Scrapbooks, vol. 4" and folder of miscellaneous materials, the Shedd Papers; and *New York Call*, April 11, 1915.

36. *Milwaukee Leader*, December 29, 1917.

37. *New York Call*, May 2, 1914, and April 11, 1915.

38. *Milwaukee Leader*, October 26, 1916.

39. *New York Call*, April 4, 1915; *Young Socialists' Magazine* 9 (July 1915): 9; and "Rochester Socialist Sunday School Scrapbooks, vol. 3," the Shedd Papers. Shedd soon realized that grading the exam papers was problematic. First, the children varied in age and in experience. He suggested, "We should take such handicaps into consideration and rate accordingly." Second, some of the children came from immigrant homes where English was not the native tongue. Their writing tended not to be on the same level as the other children. Third, Shedd recognized that some of the answers, if judged exactly by what the youngsters wrote, could be marked very low. But, he felt, "one should read between the lines and give credit for what the children evidently meant to say." Finally, he suggested that more should be expected of those children who obviously possessed greater academic ability and educational experience. That is, in Shedd's mind, a kind of "noblesse oblige" was to be followed.

40. "Rochester Socialist Sunday School Scrapbooks, vol. 1," the Shedd Papers; and *New York Call*, April 4, 1915.

41. *The Worker*, July 20, 1907; *Socialist Woman* 1 (August 1907): 10; Martha Moore Avery, "Socialist Sunday Schools," *National Civic Federation Review* 3 (May 1908): 11; and Sweet, "Socialists Active in the American Educational Field," p. 19.

42. *New York Call*, May 9, 1915.

43. Harvey P. Moyer, ed., *Songs of Socialism* (Chicago: The Co-operative, 1905); Charles H. Kerr, ed., *Socialist Songs with Music* (Chicago: Charles H. Kerr, 1908); Kendrick P. Shedd, "Foreward," in his edited collection, *Some Songs for Socialist Singers* (Rochester, N.Y.: Rochester Socialist Sunday School, 1913, 2nd ed.); "Rochester Socialist Sunday School Scrapbooks, vol. 1," the Shedd Papers; *New York Call*, April 14, 1912; Josephine R. Cole, ed., *Socialist Songs, Dialogues and Recitations* (Chicago: Charles H. Kerr, 1906); *Socialist Sunday School Song Book* (Brooklyn, N.Y.: Brownsville Socialist Sunday School, 192?); *Some Socialist Songs* (Buffalo, N.Y.: Schools of Social Science, 1919); and William F. Kruse, "How to Organize, Conduct and Maintain the 'S.S.S.'" (Chicago: Socialist Party Young People's Department, n.d. [1918?]), a copy of which is included in the *Socialist Party of America Papers*, reel 137. The "International Socialist Sunday School Song Cards" are contained in the "Red Falcons of America" folder, Social Democratic Party Collection, Box 3 File 11.

44. Interview with Othelia Hampel Haberkorn, Milwaukee, Wis., May 4, 1981; miscellaneous materials sent with letter from Ernest Kleine, Jr. to author; and "Rochester Socialist Sunday School Scrapbooks, vol. 2," the Shedd Papers.

45. Moyer, ed., *Songs of Socialism*. Samuel Yellen describes "My Money Lies over the Ocean" as a popular song at socialist children's pa-

rades in New York City during these years, in "A Socialist Boyhood," p. 201.

46. "International Socialist Sunday School Song Cards," in the "Red Falcons of America" folder, Social Democratic Party Collection; and interview with Othelia Hampel Haberkorn.

47. Carol Poore, "German-American Socialist Workers' Theatre, 1877–1900," in *Theatre for Working-Class Audiences in the United States, 1830–1980*, ed. Bruce A. McConachie and Daniel Friedman (Westport, Conn.: Greenwood, 1985), pp. 61–68; and Raphael Samuel, "Theatre and Socialism in Britain (1880–1935)," in *Theatres of the Left, 1880–1935: Workers' Theatre Movements in Britain and America*, ed. Raphael Samuel, Ewan MacColl, and Stuart Cosgrove (London: Routledge and Kegan Paul, 1985), p. 13. Emma Goldman is quoted in Tager, "A Radical Approach to Education," p. 75.

48. Interview with Jennie Yavner Goldman; telephone interview with Nora Linn, Martha's Vineyard, Mass., June 25, 1981; and interview with Othelia Hampel Haberkorn.

49. "Rochester Socialist Sunday School Scrapbooks, vol. 1," the Shedd Papers; *Milwaukee Leader*, April 26, 1916, and April 12, 1923; interview with Othelia Hampel Haberkorn; and International Socialist Sunday School Dramatic Scripts Collection, located at the Golda Meir Library, University of Wisconsin–Milwaukee, Milwaukee, Wis.

50. "Henry Dubb" was the main character in a series of cartoons originated by Ryan Walker. He represented workers who are foolishly taken in by capitalist propaganda. Walker, known chiefly for his drawings in the *Appeal to Reason* and the *New York Call*, drew the illustrations for Nicholas Klein's *The Socialist Primer* and has been referred to as "the father of American labor cartoonists." Johnson, *Marxism in United States History before the Russian Revolution (1876–1917)*, pp. 116, 144–45, and 168.

51. *New York Call*, November 24, 1915; *Young Socialists' Magazine* 12 (February 1918): 11ff; and International Socialist Sunday School Dramatic Scripts Collection.

52. *Young Socialists' Magazine* 12 (March 1918): 15; 12 (April 1918): 11; 12 (May 1918): 16ff; 12 (June 1918): 15–16; 12 (July 1918): 17–18; 12 (August 1918): 12–13; 12 (September 1918): 18–19; and 13 (October 1919): 17; and *Little Socialist Magazine for Boys and Girls* 3 (May 1910): 10. Ethel Whitehead wrote other plays that were performed by SSS children. For example, her "Columbia's Garden" was produced by the Cleveland SSS in 1911 and by one of the Schools of Social Science in Buffalo in 1913. Another play, "The Way of Happiness," was performed by the Borough Park SSS in Brooklyn in 1912 and the Children's Socialist Lyceum of Los Angeles in 1919. The scripts of her other plays have not been located. *Young Socialists' Magazine* 4 (July 1911): 11; *New Justice*, May 15, 1919; *New York Call*, May 7, 1912; and miscellaneous materials sent with letter from Ernest Kleine, Jr. to author.

53. Jack Zipes, *The Trials and Tribulations of Little Red Riding Hood: Versions of the Tale in Sociocultural Context* (South Hadley, Mass.: Bergin and Garvey, 1983).

54. *Milwaukee Leader*, April 16, 1919, May 9, 1919, May 12, 1919, May 20, 1919, June 2, 1919, June 9, 1919, June 10, 1919, June 12, 1919, June 14, 1919, and June 17, 1919.

55. *Milwaukee Leader*, May 20, 1920, May 22, 1920, May 26, 1920, May 28, 1920, May 29, 1920, and May 31, 1920. Clearly, in this play Carl Haessler had current affairs in mind. For instance, the judge, Kennesaw Mountain Lynchem, is obviously modeled after Judge Kenesaw Mountain Landis. Before becoming baseball commissioner in 1920, Landis presided over the trials of Industrial Workers of the World members (including William Haywood), Socialist activists like Victor Berger and William Kruse, and other radicals. He was known as a superpatriot who handed out maximum prison sentences (although many of the convictions were later overturned by the Supreme Court). For example, see J. Robert Constantine, ed., *Letters of Eugene V. Debs*, vol. 2 *(1913–1919)* (Urbana: University of Illinois Press, 1990), pp. 337–38, 404, and 461.

56. "Rochester Socialist Sunday School Scrapbooks, vols. 1 and 2," and letter from Bertha Vossler of Rochester to Kendrick Shedd, dated November 6, 1915, in a folder of miscellaneous materials, the Shedd Papers. In the fall of 1915, a portrait of Kendrick Shedd, who had left for Milwaukee during the previous spring, was added to the show.

57. *New York Call*, December 17, 1911.

58. "Rochester Socialist Sunday School Scrapbooks, vol. 1," the Shedd Papers; and *New York Call*, December 22, 1912.

59. *New York Call*, March 10, 1912; and "Rochester Socialist Sunday School Scrapbooks, vol. 1," the Shedd Papers.

60. *Young Socialists' Magazine* 12 (August 1918): 17. Similarly, in Los Angeles, "familiar 'Tag' and 'Tug-of-war' were given a 'worker versus boss' interpretation." See Peggy Dennis, "The Twenties," *Cultural Correspondence* 6–7 (Spring 1978): 84.

61. *Little Socialist Magazine for Boys and Girls* 3 (May 1910): 13.

62. *Young Socialists' Magazine* 6 (February 1913): 13.

Chapter Seven

1. For example, see Paul Avrich, *The Modern School Movement: Anarchism and Education in the United States* (Princeton, N.J.: Princeton University Press, 1980).

2. Bertha H. Mailly, "The Socialist Schools of Greater New York," *Little Socialist Magazine for Boys and Girls* 4 (May 1911): 6.

3. Ellen Key, *The Century of the Child* (New York: G. P. Putnam's Sons, 1909), pp. 123–24; and *Milwaukee Leader*, June 28, 1915.

4. No information about "Nesor" has been located. Jeanette Pearl was a writer and secretary of the Socialist Party of New York County. In 1919, she joined New York City's Left-Wing Committee and then the Communist Labor Party. During the next decade she wrote regularly for the *Daily Worker*, often about women's issues. She was married to Louis Fraina, a well-known left-wing journalist who was one of the founders of the Communist Party. J. Robert Constantine, ed., *Letters of Eugene V. Debs*, vol. 2 *(1913–1919)* (Urbana: University of Illinois Press, 1990), pp. 462–63.

5. *New York Call*, October 12, 1911.

6. *New York Call*, October 29, 1911.

7. *New York Call,* November 12, 1911.

8. *New York Call,* December 16, 1911.

9. See, for example, Herbert M. Kliebard, *The Struggle for the American Curriculum, 1893–1958* (Boston: Routledge and Kegan Paul, 1986); and Lawrence A. Cremin, *The Transformation of the School: Progressivism in American Education, 1876–1966* (New York: Random House, 1961).

10. Charlotte Perkins Gilman, *Concerning Children* (Boston: Small, Maynard, 1900), p. 115; and May Reinhardt Schocken, "Our Sunday Schools," *Young Socialists' Magazine* 11 (December 1917): 8–9.

11. *Progressive Woman* 3 (December 1909): 14; and *Young Socialists' Magazine* 4 (September 1911): 15.

12. *Party Builder,* July 26, 1913.

13. "Rochester Socialist Sunday School Scrapbooks, vols. 2 and 3," in the Kendrick Philander Shedd Papers, located at the University of Rochester, Rush Rhees Library, Rare Books Department, Special Collections, Rochester, N.Y. Henceforth in this chapter, this collection is referred to as the Shedd Papers.

14. *Eye Opener,* November 3, 1917; and William F. Kruse, "Socialist Education for Children," *Young Socialists' Magazine* 11 (March 1917): 9–10.

15. *Young Socialists' Magazine* 12 (March 1918): 10; and *New Age,* February 23, 1918, March 16, 1918, and April 13, 1918.

16. James M. Reilly, "To Work with Young People," *Young Socialists' Magazine* 6 (June 1913): 2. During the 1930s, a less optimistic time for socialists, New York City SSS activists sought "to give these young people, with all their distractions, to give them a yen for Socialism. . . . And if it gives them a yen for Socialism then it's worthwhile, even if you don't teach them anything specific." Telephone interview with Samuel H. Friedman, New York City, July 6, 1981.

17. *New York Call,* September 28, 1919.

18. *New York Call,* March 21, 1913.

19. Interview with Joseph Friebert and Edward Friebert, Jr., Milwaukee, Wis., October 2, 1981.

20. Edward Willard Stevens, Jr., "The Political Education of Children in the Rochester Public Schools, 1899–1917: A Historical Perspective on Social Control in Public Education," Ph.D. dissertation, University of Rochester, 1971, pp. 105–93.

21. Bertha H. Mailly, "The Socialist Schools of Greater New York," p. 6.

22. *New York Call,* June 20, 1915; and Kruse, "Socialist Education for Children," p. 9.

23. Carol Poore, "German-American Socialist Workers' Theatre, 1877–1900," in *Theatre for Working-Class Audiences in the United States, 1830–1980,* ed. Bruce A. McConachie and Daniel Friedman (Westport, Conn.: Greenwood, 1985), p. 67.

24. Michael W. Apple, *Ideology and Curriculum* (London: Routledge and Kegan Paul, 1979), p. 9.

25. *The Worker,* January 24, 1904. Raymond Williams makes a similar point when he alludes to our everyday indebtedness to workers for the

simple fact that the lights in our rooms work. Raymond Williams, *The Long Revolution* (Harmondsworth, Eng.: Pelican, 1965), pp. 324–25.

26. Oscar Ameringer, *If You Don't Weaken: The Autobiography of Oscar Ameringer* (New York: Greenwood, 1969), p. xi. Ameringer's comments, originally published in 1940, are similar to Gramsci's notion of individuality being "the hub" of an "ensemble" of social relations, past and present. Gramsci commented: "It is necessary to elaborate a doctrine in which these relations are seen as active and in movement, establishing quite clearly that the source of this activity is the consciousness of the individual man who knows, wishes, admires, creates (in so far as he does know, wish, admire, create, etc.) and conceives of himself not as isolated but rich in the possibilities offered him by other men and by the society of things of which he cannot help having a certain knowledge." Antonio Gramsci, *Selections from the Prison Notebooks*, ed. and trans. by Quintin Hoare and Geoffrey Nowell Smith (New York: International Publishers, 1971), pp. 352–54.

27. Interview with Joseph Friebert and Edward Friebert, Jr.

28. Quoted in *New York Socialist*, July 25, 1908.

29. "Rochester Socialist Sunday School Scrapbooks, vol. 4," the Shedd Papers.

30. Barry Wood, "American History Revisited: What They Didn't Tell Us," *Edcentric* 3 (May/June 1971): 3–7. See also Howard Zinn, "Objections to Objectivity," *Z Magazine* (October 1989): 58–62.

31. *New York Call*, March 21, 1913; Bertha H. Mailly, "Socialist Schools," *Unity of Labor* 1 (April 1911?): 10–11; and Kevin Reilly, "Notes on Revising a Radical World History Textbook," *Radical History Review* 39 (September 1987): 128.

32. Letter from Rachel Adler of Deerfield Beach, Fla., to author, dated September 15, 1980. Also, telephone interview with Eleanore Levenson, New York City, July 9, 1981; and interview with Jennie Yavner Goldman, Putnam Valley, N.Y., July 4, 1981.

33. Edward Friebert, Autobiography (unpublished manuscript, 1945), pp. 272–73 of handwritten copy.

34. *New York Call*, December 6, 1918.

35. Eliot Wigginton, *Sometimes a Shining Moment: The Foxfire Experience* (Garden City, N.Y.: Anchor, 1985), p. 308.

36. "Rochester Socialist Sunday School Scrapbooks, vol. 2," the Shedd Papers.

37. Quoted in Stephen Yeo, "A New Life: The Religion of Socialism in Britain, 1883–1896," *History Workshop Journal* 4 (Autumn 1977): 6.

38. For example, see George S. Counts, *Dare the School Build a New Social Order?* (Carbondale: Southern Illinois University Press, 1978 [originally published in 1932]); and Herbert Kohl, "Can the Schools Build a New Social Order?" *Journal of Education* 62 (Summer 1980): 57–66.

39. Henry A. Giroux, *Schooling and the Struggle for Public Life: Critical Pedagogy in the Modern Age* (Minneapolis: University of Minnesota Press, 1988), p. 93.

40. *New York Call*, May 8, 1910.

41. Raymond and Charlotte Koch, *Educational Commune: The Story of Commonwealth College* (New York: Schocken, 1972), pp. 58 and 65.

Conclusion

1. Jean Anyon, "Ideology and United States History Textbooks," *Harvard Educational Review* 49 (August 1979): 361–86.

2. Allen Luke, "Making Dick and Jane: Historical Genesis of the Modern Basal Reader," *Teachers College Record* 89 (Fall 1987): 109 and 111.

3. Christine E. Sleeter and Carl A. Grant, "Race, Class, Gender, and Disability in Current Textbooks," in *The Politics of the Textbook,* ed. Michael W. Apple and Linda K. Christian-Smith (New York: Routledge, Chapman and Hall, 1991), p. 98.

4. Interview with Jennie Yavner Goldman, Putnam Valley, N.Y., July 4, 1981.

5. Michael Moore, "'Roger' and I, off to Hollywood and Home to Flint," *New York Times,* July 15, 1990.

6. This is not to suggest that there has been no space for critical perspectives in our public discourse. For example, see Catherine R. Stimpson, "Multiculturalism: A Big Word at the Presses," *New York Times Book Review,* September 22, 1991.

7. Paulo Freire, *Pedagogy of the Oppressed* (New York: Seabury, 1970); and, for example, Henry A. Giroux, *Theory and Resistance in Education: A Pedagogy for the Opposition* (South Hadley, Mass.: Bergin and Garvey, 1983).

8. Interview with Linda Gordon, in *Visions of History,* ed. Henry Abelove et al. (New York: Pantheon, 1984), p. 80; and Michael Omi and Howard Winant, *Racial Formation in the United States: From the 1960s to the 1980s* (New York: Routledge and Kegan Paul, 1966), pp. 2–3 and 6.

9. See, for example, Michael W. Apple and Kenneth Teitelbaum, "Education and Inequality," in *Democracy Upside Down: Public Opinion and Cultural Hegemony in America,* ed. Calvin F. Exoo (New York: Praeger, 1987), pp. 141–65; and Michael W. Apple, ed., *Cultural and Economic Reproduction in Education: Essays on Class, Ideology and the State* (London: Routledge and Kegan Paul, 1982).

10. Marty Rosenbluth, "Are Your Kids Being Taught What the Boss Wants Them to Think?" *Solidarity* 27 (February 1–15, 1984): 11.

11. Sheila Harty, *Hucksters in the Classroom: A Review of Industry Propaganda in Schools* (Washington, D.C.: Center for Study of Responsive Law, 1979).

12. Herbert M. Kliebard and Barry M. Franklin, "The Course of the Course of Study: History of Curriculum," in *Historical Inquiry in Education,* ed. John Hardin Best (Washington, D.C.: American Educational Research Association, 1983), p. 153. Similarly, as Fred Inglis suggests in *The Management of Ignorance: A Political Theory of the Curriculum* (Oxford, Eng.: Basil Blackwell, 1985), "To become aware of the limits of your imagination is to move them" (p. 117).

13. Henry A. Giroux, *Schooling and the Struggle for Public Life: Critical Pedagogy in the Modern Age* (Minneapolis: University of Minnesota Press, 1988), p. 100.

14. Richard Johnson, "'Really Useful Knowledge': Radical Education and Working-Class Culture, 1790–1848," in *Working-Class Culture: Studies in History and Theory,* ed. John Clarke, Chas Critcher, and Richard Johnson

(London: Hutchinson, 1979), pp. 75–102. See also Stanley Aronowitz and Henry A. Giroux, *Education Under Siege: The Conservative, Liberal and Radical Debate Over Schooling* (South Hadley, Mass.: Bergin and Garvey, 1985), pp. 157–58.

15. Harry Braverman, *Labor and Monopoly Capital: The Degradation of Work in the Twentieth Century* (New York: Monthly Review, 1974).

16. Maxine Greene, *The Dialectic of Freedom* (New York: Teachers College Press, 1988), p. 127.

17. Cameron McCarthy and Michael W. Apple, "Race, Class and Gender in American Educational Research: Toward a Nonsynchronous Parallelist Position," in *Class, Race, and Gender in American Education*, ed. Lois Weis (Albany: State University of New York Press, 1988), pp. 9–39.

18. Inglis, *The Management of Ignorance*, p. 126.

19. Quoted in Michael W. Apple, *Ideology and Curriculum* (London: Routledge and Kegan Paul, 1979), p. 156.

20. Samuel Bowles, "Events in Eastern Europe Could Revitalize Leftist Scholarship," *Chronicle of Higher Education*, April 4, 1990.

21. Joseph Featherstone, "Foreword," in Herbert Kohl, *Growing Minds: On Becoming a Teacher* (New York: Harper and Row, 1984), p. xvi.

22. Marcus G. Raskin, *The Common Good: Its Politics, Policies and Philosophy* (New York: Routledge and Kegan Paul, 1986), p. 6. We are not without examples in this regard, of course. For instance, Robert E. Peterson, "Teaching How to Read the World and Change It: Critical Pedagogy in the Intermediate Grades," in *Literacy as Praxis: Culture, Language, and Pedagogy*, ed. Catherine E. Walsh (Norwood, N.J.: Ablex, 1991), pp. 156–82; Ira Shor, ed., *Freire for the Classroom: A Sourcebook for Liberatory Teaching* (Portsmouth, N.H.: Heinemann, 1987); Nancy Schniedewind and Ellen Davidson, *Open Minds to Equality: A Sourcebook of Learning Activities to Promote Race, Sex, Class, and Age Equity* (Englewood Cliffs, N.J.: Prentice-Hall, 1983); and journals and newspapers such as *Democracy and Education* (affiliated with the Institute for Democracy and Education and *Rethinking Schools*.

23. Howard Zinn, *A People's History of the United States* (New York: Harper and Row, 1980), pp. 10–11.

Index